PRAISE FOR *THE TRIUNE GOD*

Beginning with doxology, rooted in Scripture, and centered on the missions of the Son and the Spirit, this book is a lucid, rich, lively, and timely reframing of Trinitarian theology, with highly fruitful implications for dogmatics and exegesis.

Suzanne McDonald, Professor of Systematic and Historical Theology, Western Theological Seminary, Holland, MI

In contemporary theology, the doctrine of the Trinity is the subject of intense discussion and debate. Meanwhile, the "theological interpretation of Scripture" has reemerged in recent years. In this erudite, articulate, and delightful book, Fred Sanders makes very important contributions to both fields. Here a leading scholar of the doctrine offers helpful insights that will repay careful study. Even better, he leads us to a more profound doxology. I highly recommend this volume.

Thomas H. McCall, Professor of Biblical and Systematic Theology, Trinity Evangelical Divinity School, Deerfield, IL

Evangelical theologians are at the forefront of a new Trinitarian revival, one rooted in Scripture and common classical Christian tradition—and Fred Sanders is a key voice in that revival. He offers a clearly written and succinct Trinitarian theology that is greatly to be welcomed.

Lewis Ayres, Head of Department and Professor of Catholic and Historical Theology, Durham University

NEW STUDIES IN DOGMATICS

THE TRIUNE GOD

NEW STUDIES IN DOGMATICS

THE TRIUNE GOD

FRED SANDERS

MICHAEL ALLEN AND SCOTT R. SWAIN,
GENERAL EDITORS

ZONDERVAN

The Triune God
Copyright © 2016 by Fred Sanders

This title is also available as a Zondervan ebook.

Requests for information should be addressed to:
Zondervan, 3900 *Sparks Dr. SE, Grand Rapids, Michigan 49546*

Library of Congress Cataloging-in-Publication Data

Names: Sanders, Fred (Fred R.), author.
Title: The triune God / Fred Sanders ; Michael Allen and Scott R. Swain, general editors.
Description: Grand Rapids, MI : Zondervan, [2016] | Series: New studies in dogmatics |
     Includes bibliographical references and indexes.
Identifiers: LCCN 2016031606 | ISBN 9780310491491 (softcover)
Subjects: LCSH: Trinity. | God (Christianity)
Classification: LCC BT111.3 .S28 2017 | DDC 231/.044—dc23 LC record available at https://
     lccn.loc.gov/2016031606

Cover design: *Micah Kandros*
Interior design: *Kait Lamphere*

Printed in the United States of America

HB 01.27.2025

To Phoebe—
I commend her to you, for she has been a
helper of many, and of me also.

CONTENTS

DETAILED CONTENTS

SERIES PREFACE

New Studies in Dogmatics follows in the tradition of G. C. Berkouwer's classic series, Studies in Dogmatics, in seeking to offer concise, focused treatments of major topics in dogmatic theology that fill the gap between introductory theology textbooks and advanced theological monographs. Dogmatic theology, as understood by editors and contributors to the series, is a conceptual representation of scriptural teaching about God and all things in relation to God. The source of dogmatics is Holy Scripture; its scope is the summing up of all things in Jesus Christ; its setting is the communion of the saints; and its end is the conversion, consolation, and instruction of creaturely wayfarers in the knowledge and love of the triune God until that knowledge and love is consummated in the beatific vision.

The series wagers that the way forward in constructive theology lies in a program of renewal through retrieval. This wager follows upon the judgment that much modern theology exhibits "a stubborn tendency to grow not higher but to the side," to borrow Alexander Solzhenitsyn's words from another context. Though modern theology continues to grow in a number of areas of technical expertise and interdisciplinary facility (especially in both the exegetical and historical domains), this growth too often displays a sideways drift rather than an upward progression in relation to theology's subject matter, scope, and source, and in fulfilling theology's end. We believe the path toward theological renewal in such a situation lies in drawing more deeply upon the resources of Holy Scripture in conversation with the church's most trusted teachers (ancient, medieval, and modern) who have sought to fathom Christ's unsearchable riches. In keeping with this belief, authors from a broad evangelical constituency will seek in this series to retrieve the riches of Scripture and tradition for constructive dogmatics. The purpose of retrieval is neither simple repetition of past theologians nor repristination of an earlier phase in church history; Christianity, at any rate, has no golden age east of Eden and short of the kingdom of God. Properly understood, retrieval is an inclusive and enlarging venture, a matter of tapping into a vital root and, in some cases, of relearning a lost grammar of theological discourse, all for the sake of equipping the church in its contemporary vocation to think and speak faithfully and fruitfully about God and God's works.

While the specific emphases of individual volumes will vary, each volume will display (1) awareness of the "state of the question" pertaining to the doctrine under discussion; (2) attention to the patterns of biblical reasoning (exegetical, biblical-theological, etc.) from which the doctrine emerges; (3) engagement with relevant ecclesiastical statements of the doctrine (creedal, conciliar, confessional), as well as with leading theologians of the church; and (4) appreciation of the doctrine's location within the larger system of theology, as well as of its contribution to Christian piety and practice.

Our prayer is that by drawing upon the best resources of the past and with an awareness of both perennial and proximate challenges to Christian thought and practice in the present, New Studies in Dogmatics will contribute to a flourishing theological culture in the church today. Soli Deo Gloria.

Michael Allen and Scott R. Swain

ACKNOWLEDGMENTS

Many people and many circumstances helped me write this book. Part of the work was done during a sabbatical semester from my teaching position in the Torrey Honors Institute at Biola University. Just as our shared teaching labor in Torrey Honors equipped me to read better and write better, time away from the classroom enabled me to pull the project together. I'm especially grateful to Paul Spears and Greg Peters for administrating and scheduling around me. Rob Price carried burdens for me, not just for one mile, but for the second mile also.

Some of my sabbatical time was spent at Tyndale House in Cambridge, where I enjoyed the bracing experience of justifying my systematic-theological existence to sympathetic biblical scholars. The vibrant theological community at Biola University (I speak without irony; come and see) helped guide my thinking in many ways, especially the friends who read portions of the manuscript and offered critical appreciation.

When I found it uncommonly difficult to complete the manuscript, my dear editors intervened perfectly. Katya, Scott, and Mike have been great to work with.

Distributed across chapters 6–8 are a number of paragraphs from my article "Trinitarian Theology's Exegetical Basis: A Dogmatic Survey," published in *Midwestern Journal of Theology* 8.2/9.1 (Spring 2010): 78–90. They are used here with permission.

My daughter, Phoebe, has known for years that "the next real book" I wrote would be dedicated to her, and here it is at last. She has been a joy and an encouragement to me, even on that day when she wrote four times as many words as I did.

INTRODUCTION: THE ARGUMENT OF THIS BOOK

The goal of this book is to secure our knowledge of the triune God by rightly ordering the theological language with which we praise the triune God. Its central contention is that the manner of the Trinity's revelation dictates the shape of the doctrine; it draws its dogmatic conclusions about how the doctrine should be handled on the basis of the way the Trinity was revealed. For this reason, *The Triune God* recommends some dogmatic principles for Trinitarian exegesis and offers systematic help for reconstructing the plausibility structures of biblical Trinitarianism. Since the book's structure is intentionally unconventional, it is worth describing that structure in advance.

The first chapter begins with praise in order to invite a doxological attunement of the theological mind, issuing this summons: *sursum corda*! To contemplate the Trinity is to lift up your heart and to "set your mind on the things above."[1] No author can enforce such spiritual injunctions on a reader, but the history of writing treatises on the Trinity includes not only the tradition of invoking the Trinity, but of doing so in a way that enlists the reader's strict and holy attention for what is essentially a spiritual exercise. Examples could be drawn from the early pages of

---

1. Colossians 3:2 NASB. The richness of the root *phroneō* in "τὰ ἄνω φρονεῖτε" accounts for the range of translations that have been offered for this exhortation, from "set your affections" to "think on." John Davenant said that it "embraces two acts; the act of the mind or of the understanding reflecting about any thing; and the act of the will and affections approving and loving any thing" (*An Exposition of the Epistle of St. Paul to the Colossians* [London: Hamilton, Adams, 1832], 7). Is it plausible, and could it be exegetically responsible, to take the Trinity as the ultimate referent of τὰ ἄνω to which the apostle turns our minds? Only if the risen Christ's sitting at the right hand of God (the proximate referent) and our inclusion in it ("your life is hidden") can be construed, on the basis of the total witness of Scripture, as salvation-historical accomplishments that make known God's eternal character as Father, Son, and Holy Spirit. The burden of this book is to show how this is so.

nearly any theological work on the Trinity written from Irenaeus in the second century to John Owen in the seventeenth. But the prayer of Hilary of Poitiers at the conclusion of book 1 of *On the Trinity* is especially apt:

> Therefore we wait for you to set in motion these timid first steps of our undertaking, to confirm it so that it may make progress, and to call us into fellowship with the Spirit who guided the prophets and apostles, so that we may apprehend their words in no other sense than that in which they spoke them, and explain the proper meanings of the words according to the realities they signify. For we shall be speaking of what they preached in mystery . . .
>
> Grant us, therefore, precision of words, light of understanding, honorable speech, and true faith. Enable us to believe that which we also speak, so that we may confess you, one God our Father, and one Lord Jesus Christ as taught by the prophets and apostles; and now against the contradictions of the heretics, proclaim you as God (yet not solitary), and Him as God (not falsely).[2]

But the subjective tuning of the theologian's intellect is not the only reason to begin with praise. Trinitarian theology, I argue, is essentially a doxological movement of thought that gives glory to the Father, Son, and Holy Spirit by beginning with confession of the work of God in salvation history and then reasoning back to its antecedent principles in God.

The second chapter sets the doctrine of the Trinity within a biblical theology of mystery, as that which "was kept secret for long ages but has now been disclosed" (Rom 16:25–26). The mode of revelation is crucial: God has made his triunity known through salvific actions joined inwardly to explanatory words. The "explanatory words" part of that formula has been unpopular in late modern theology, but it was as crucial to the original formulation of the doctrine as it is of abiding importance today. Without it, Trinitarian exegesis has become detached from divine revelation and has often floated free, vulnerable to prevailing winds of doctrine.

With verbal revelation restored as a constituent of Trinitarian revelation, chapter 3 considers the missions of the Son and Spirit as revelatory

---

2. Hilary of Poitiers, *On the Trinity* 1:38, my translation.

or communicative missions. These two sendings have made present among us a communication that overflows from the eternal conversation of the triune life. Taking seriously the fact that this revelation is the only source of our knowledge of the Trinity requires the demotion of experience and tradition to a lesser status. Each of them is considered as a possible foundation for the doctrine of the Trinity, and found wanting. Experience and tradition cannot even serve the more modest task of opening a means of access to the doctrine of the Trinity by themselves, because in both cases they are placeholders for appeals to revelation. Each, however, brings considerable benefits to Trinitarian theology when handled ministerially rather than magisterially—as servants, not masters. In what may be an unexpected move for a book that has already commended verbal inspiration and *sola Scriptura*, this chapter also takes care to set the biblical witness within a wider conceptual horizon, subordinating it to a more direct form of revelation.

That more direct form of revelation is the subject of chapter 4: Incarnation and Pentecost. Properly speaking, it is the visible missions of the Son and the Holy Spirit that constitute the actual revelation of God's triunity. This chapter engages in an extended dogmatic description of the missions of the Son and the Holy Spirit, tracing the way these missions make known the eternal processions that are the life of the living God. These missions must be kept central in all our thinking about the Trinity. Failure to guard their biblical centrality with sufficient jealousy has been the root cause of much disorder and distraction in Trinitarian theology, cumbering the exegetical pathway and rendering Scripture opaque to Trinitarianism. Failure to recognize that they are manifestations of eternal processions has kept much modern Trinitarianism abstract and brittle. Recognizing the clarity and centrality of the triune missions is what makes the present study a constructive statement of Trinitarian theology that is shaped at every point by the mode of the revelation of the Trinity. The fundamental question posed in any theological interpretation of the missions of the Son and the Spirit is the question of what God has revealed about himself in them. The classic answer is eternal, internal processions.

Chapter 5 gives more direct attention to the divine processions, those internal actions of God that mark the divine life as triune. Based strictly on the incarnation and Pentecost, Trinitarian theology gives an account of the one God as three persons. This is the God of the gospel, the one who has made himself known when the Father sent the Son and the Holy Spirit. The exposition in this chapter also proceeds by addressing the most important theological terms that have proven useful for establishing good order in Trinitarian theology (processions, internal actions, persons), which relativizes the more recent habit of talking in terms of the economic Trinity and the immanent Trinity.

Chapter 6 connects these theological judgments to the task of exegesis. The church has always known that the doctrine of the Trinity is profoundly biblical and yet not straightforwardly taught in the Bible. The obliqueness of Trinitarianism's exegetical foundation is both a blessing and a burden for Christian doctrine. In addition, the last few centuries have seen major changes in biblical interpretation, requiring that some traditional arguments be dropped, some new ones be acquired, and the entire approach to biblical Trinitarianism be put on a more secure footing.

Chapter 7 then turns to the attestation of the salvation-historical missions in their irreplaceably primary theological witness: the New Testament. The New Testament is indirect in its statements about the Trinity precisely because the actual revelation has already taken place in the personal advent of the Son and the Spirit, an extratextual event on which the New Testament documents are reflecting. I do not undertake a complete survey of New Testament Trinitarianism, but I do attend to the main lines of the Gospels and Epistles.

Only after attending to the coming of the Son and the Spirit, and then reading the New Testament reflections on them, do we turn to the Old Testament in chapter 8. Trinitarian interpretation of the Old Testament is an exercise in rereading, applying to the earlier part of a text what is learned from the later part. In the time period documented by the Old Testament, God was triune but was not actively revealing that triunity to his covenant people. Whatever adumbrations may be found in the text, no revelations are to be sought there, if we take both words literally: shadowing versus unveiling. For this reason, it is best not to press the Old Testament to make it yield Trinitarian revelation. The text of the Old Testament and the trajectory of its events do generate a host of unusual phenomena that need to be accounted for. They are best accounted for by Trinitarian theology as it throws a light backward from the New Testament to the Old. I commend the ancient practice of identifying divine speakers in the oracles of the old covenant (prosoponic exegesis), but consider and reject the tradition of identifying distinct Trinitarian presences in the Old Testament (christophanies).

The sequence of these chapters indicates the crucial order to be observed in our knowledge of the Trinity: revelation in the missions, attestation in the New Testament, adumbration in the Old Testament. Chapter 9 concludes the book with a series of summary theses on the revelation of the Trinity and its implications for a well-ordered doctrine of the Trinity and the overall shape of a theological system.

Readers may note that the history of doctrine receives little direct attention in this outline, especially relative to the amount of space devoted to hermeneutical concerns, biblical interpretation, and dogmatic description. Even if a more voluminous interaction with the history of doctrine might have strengthened the argument at many points, I hope its absence does not count as a weakness. At least I can offer the assurance that the mode of argument is intentional. By design, the biblical exposition and the doctrinal extrapolations drawn from it constitute the bulk of the volume and dictate its framework. The history of the doctrine of the Trinity is enchantingly rich, so much so that it can easily loom too large in a general treatment of Trinitarian theology, sometimes throwing off the balance. Too many books on the Trinity rush over the biblical discussion in a few pages (with sincere apologies) on the way to more extended discussions of historical development. If this book gives extensive discussion to scriptural issues and rushes by the history of doctrine (with sincere apologies), it does so in the hope of giving the impression that Trinitarianism is a gift of revelation before it is an achievement of the church. The alternative approach, while not illegitimate, risks giving the impression that the Bible delivers a relatively meager serving of raw materials that cannot be Trinitarian until they are cooked up into something hearty by theologians, who of course add a dash or two of their own spices. In spite of the absence of large-scale reporting on the history of doctrine, there is considerable interaction with major voices from the history of doctrine dispersed throughout the book, and I have frequently indicated where my arguments are indebted to and informed by the great tradition of Trinitarianism. A healthy deference to doctrinal tradition is indispensable to serious theology, and this book (appropriately for a volume in the New Studies in Dogmatics series) is an exercise in retrieval. But the way to retrieve the insights of the church fathers is not to pay more attention to them than to Scripture. It often seems that while patristic books about the Trinity were mostly about the Bible, even the best modern books about the Trinity are mostly about the church fathers. As long as it can be done without amnesia or ingratitude, the most patristic way to proceed is, after all, to study Scripture.

CHAPTER 1

ATTUNEMENT: *GLORIA PATRI*

Glory to the Father, and to the Son, and to the Holy Ghost! As it was in the beginning, is now, and ever shall be, world without end.

The glory of God is from everlasting to everlasting, but while the praise of the Trinity will have no end, it had a beginning.

There was never a time when God was not glorious as Father, as Son, and as Holy Spirit. But there was a time when that singular glory (singular because, to gloss the Athanasian Creed, there are not three glorious, but one[1]) had not yet disclosed itself so as to invite creatures to its praise. To join in the ancient Christian prayer called the *Gloria Patri*, directing praise to Father, Son, and Holy Spirit, is to come into alignment here in the world "as it is now" with triune glory "as it was in the beginning." All theology ought to be doxology, but Trinitarian theology in particular is essentially a matter of praising God. This doxological response is the praise of a glory (ἔπαινον δόξης, Eph 1:6, 12, 14) that always was, and whose epiphany in time entails its antecedent depth in eternity. Those whom God has blessed with every spiritual blessing in Christ are summoned to join that praise: "Blessed be God the Father, who has blessed us in the Beloved and sealed us with the Holy Spirit of promise" (Eph 1:3–14, condensed).

---

1. Or, in Cappadocian idiom, "One is the dominion and authority over us; we do not send up glories to God, but glory" (Basil of Caesarea, *On the Holy Spirit* [Crestwood, NY: St. Vladimir's Seminary Press, 2001], 72).

TURNING THE MIND TO DOXOLOGY

Theology too can be attuned to this praise of glory when it pursues its "proper calling," which John Webster has identified as "the praise of God by crafting concepts to turn the mind to the divine splendor."[2] Trinitarian theology, when conducted rightly, deploys a venerable and copious set of conceptual tools for precisely that task of mind-turning (μετάνοια), because, having heard the word of the one who said "and now, Father, glorify me in your own presence with the glory that I had with you before the world existed" (John 17:5), it breaks forth in praise that has the character of verbal-conceptual profusion. It names him as only-begotten and the filially proceeding and declares that his prevenient glory is shared with the Father and the Holy Spirit undividedly, consubstantially, and perichoretically, as three persons subsisting in relation. These are just the most historically prominent of the concepts crafted to assist the mind in turning to the glory of the Trinity. Each of them, and the entire corpus of them, directs us to the scriptural witness as the triune God's self-testimony. Trinitarian theology is an intellectual *Gloria Patri*, a reasonable service (λογικὴν λατρείαν, Rom 12:1), an ascription of one glory to three persons then, now, and always. "The doctrine of the Trinity is a doxology using the means of thought," writes Helmut Thielicke, concluding that for this reason the *Gloria Patri* "is both formally and materially the most fitting form of the Trinitarian confession."[3]

The great step forward taken in the Christian doctrine about the triune God is the retrospective recognition that what God manifested to us in Christ is ultimate divine reality, meaning that (in Barth's words) "He is the Son or Word of God for us because He is so antecedently in Himself."[4] Athanasius, considering the revelation of God in Christ and the Spirit, drew the necessary conclusion about the antecedent being of God: "There is one Glory of the Holy Triad . . . For if the doctrine of God is now perfect in a Triad, and this is the true and only religion, and this is the good and the truth, it must have been always so, unless

---

2. John Webster, "Life in and of Himself," in *God and the Works of God*, vol. 1 of *God Without Measure: Working Papers in Christian Theology* (New York: Bloomsbury T&T Clark, 2015), 27. Webster goes on to warn that "deeply important as they are, concepts are only serviceable as the handmaids of spiritual apprehension."

3. Helmut Thielicke, *The Evangelical Faith*, vol. 2 (Grand Rapids: Eerdmans, 1977), 174.

4. See Karl Barth, *Church Dogmatics*, ed. G. W. Bromiley and T. F. Torrance (Edinburgh: T&T Clark, 1957–1975), I/1, 416 (hereafter *CD*).

the good and the truth be something that came after, and the doctrine of God is completed by additions."[5]

With the confession that the Son and the Holy Spirit are from the Father and that "it must have been always so," the doctrine of the Trinity arises like praise from the horizon of salvation history. This insight that the Son and the Holy Spirit are not mere surface phenomena of God's ways with the world is the insight that must be articulated in order to set the history of salvation in the right context. "The economy of grace in all of its dynamism drives one to say something about its source, its very condition of possibility," writes Christopher R. J. Holmes.[6] The Son and the Holy Spirit are sent by the Father because they are, together and in person, the source of salvation, and the divine condition of its possibility. Trinitarian praise points back to that triune source. This is the matrix of Trinitarian theology: wonder, love, and praise that God has done for us and our salvation something that manifests and enacts what he is in himself.

THE STRUCTURE OF PRAISE

Some such movement further up, further in, and further back is the implicit goal of all biblical praise. In the form of simple gratitude, praise may terminate provisionally on proximate blessings,[7] but is always on a trajectory past the gifts, toward the giver. When the source of the divine giver's largesse is his own inner plenitude, biblical praise is restless until it finds fulfillment in the spiritual gesture indicating that eternal depth. All theology, not just that which takes place in the subregion of the doctrine of the Trinity, is marked by its doxological provenance and orientation. This is true not merely in the sense of Herman Bavinck's admonition that "theology is about God and should reflect a doxological tone that glorifies him,"[8] but in a more constitutive sense as well. Theology is

---

5. Athanasius, *Against the Arians*, in *A Select Library of Nicene and Post-Nicene Fathers of the Christian Church* (hereafter NPNF), 2nd ser., vol. 4, ed. A. Robertson (Grand Rapids, Eerdmans, 1978), 1:18.

6. Christopher R. J. Holmes, "The Aseity of God as a Material Evangelical Concern," *Journal of Reformed Theology* 8 (2014): 62. He goes on: "without the 'backward reference' little recourse is available for resisting the immanentizing tendencies of contemporary theology and for doing descriptive justice to the biblically attested completeness of God's inner life."

7. See Claus Westermann's *Blessing in the Bible and the Life of the Church* (Philadelphia: Fortress, 1978) for helpful analysis of the blessing concept in various biblical traditions. Westermann may overdraw the distinction between creational blessing and salvation-historical deliverance, but he provides ample material for a canonical synthesis.

8. Herman Bavinck, *Prolegomena*, vol. 1 of *Reformed Dogmatics* (Grand Rapids: Baker Academic, 2003), 61.

not itself if it is not also praise. Because theological statements have their point of departure in the local and the limited, but their intended point of arrival in the Transcendent One, their very mode of referentiality is doxological in structure. As Wolfhart Pannenberg has noted, "They express adoration of God on the basis of his works. All biblical speech about God, to the extent that its intention is to designate something beyond a particular deed, namely, God himself and what he is from eternity to eternity, is rooted in adoration and is in this sense doxological."[9]

Praise penetrates into the very structure of every theological statement as such. Theology is faith seeking understanding because it is praise seeking underpinning.

The biblical witness itself gives rise to the impulse to admire God's works not only in themselves but with respect to God's eternal being. The book of Psalms, the textual heart of biblical praise, marks its key structural points with the repeated formula that consummates praise by directing attention to God's eternity: "Blessed be the LORD, the God of Israel, from everlasting to everlasting!"[10] The same movement of thought animates Hebrews 13:8, which looks from what God has done once and for all in Christ to the conclusions that must be drawn about its eternal significance: "Jesus Christ is the same yesterday and today and forever."

This formal phenomenon (biblical doxology seeking its source) finds its comprehensive material fulfillment in the doctrine of the Trinity, which is the summarizing formula for praising God on the basis of the entire economy of salvation. Trinitarian theology describes the connection between the economy of salvation and the eternal God who is its author and perfecter, its *arche* and *telos*.[11]

Trinitarian theology is the fulfillment of praise in three ways. First, because of its comprehensive scope: as a doctrine of God that

---

9. Wolfhart Pannenberg, "Analogy and Doxology," in *Basic Questions in Theology* (London: SCM, 1970), 215. By relating doxology constructively to analogy, Pannenberg avoids the common errors of denying referential force to doxological statements, substituting praise for doctrine, or contrasting doxology and description. For an example of the latter errors, see Dietrich Ritschl, *The Logic of Theology: A Brief Account of the Relationship Between Basic Concepts in Theology* (Philadelphia: Fortress, 1987), who thought he could solve numerous problems by ruling out "deductions from the doxological statements of the immanent doctrine of the Trinity in the form of the derivation of descriptive statements from ascriptive statements" (142).

10. The full statement "Blessed be the LORD, the God of Israel, from everlasting to everlasting" occurs at the juncture between books 1 and 2 of the canonical Psalter (Ps 41:13), as well as between books 3 and 4 (Ps 106:48). Besides these prominent transitional points, the phrase "from everlasting to everlasting" also occurs in Psalms 90:2 (where it refers to God's being) and 103:17 (where it refers to his lovingkindness).

11. For ἀρχὴ and τέλος, see Revelation 21:6, but also Hebrews 12:2 (ἀρχηγὸν καὶ τελειωτὴν), where the proximate referent is Jesus' relationship to our faith.

comprehends within its territory Christology, pneumatology, and soteriology, it is a field-encompassing field.[12] But secondly, Trinitarian theology is the fulfillment of praise because the missions of the Son and the Spirit are the fulfillment of salvation, and Trinitarian theology responds intellectually to those missions and their meanings. With its response to the Father through the Son and the Holy Spirit, Christian confession of the triune God radicalizes and completes the movement of biblical praise; it speaks from the resources of the Son and the Spirit that it has received and internalized. "New Testament δοξάζειν no longer has the δόξα of God as its object, but as its inner principle," as Hans Urs von Balthasar puts it.[13] Thirdly and finally, Trinitarian theology is the fulfillment of biblical praise because it thanks God for an event so great that its praise has nowhere to terminate but in eternal relations within God. The sending of the Son and the Spirit is an event so significant that Trinitarian theology traces its antecedent all the way back to the eternal, internal processions that are nothing less than the livingness of the living God. Trinitarian theology is the material fulfillment of the form of biblical praise because of the comprehensiveness of its scope, the fullness of the salvation it responds to, and the ultimacy of its antecedent reference.

TRINITARIAN THEOLOGY AS *GLORIA PATRI*

We begin this book on the Trinity with a call to worship by quoting the ancient doxological formula named (from its opening words) the *Gloria Patri* or (from its brevity in contrast to longer formulas) the "lesser doxology." It is "the earliest example of an ancient Christian prayer which is still in everyday use."[14] Nobody knows when or where it originated, but it is not hard to discern how the need for it arose. Praise seeks out the ultimate horizon of blessing, and the liturgical genre called doxology

---

12. For illuminating remarks and responsible conditions for viewing Trinitarianism as a framework or "field theory" for Christian doctrine, see Christoph Schwöbel, "Trinitätslehre als Rahmentheorie des christlichen Glaubens," in *Gott in Beziehung: Studien zur Dogmatik* (Tübingen: Mohr Siebeck, 2002), 24–51.

13. Hans Urs von Balthasar, *Glory of the Lord*, vol. 7 (San Francisco: Ignatius, 1983), 398–99. This remark is at the climax of a long discussion of Ephesians 1:3–14 titled "Glorification as Assimilation and Return of the Gift." Balthasar is paraphrasing the expression "that we might be to the praise of his glory."

14. Herbert Thurston, "Notes on Familiar Prayers" (May 1918); cited in Nicholas Ayo, *Gloria Patri: History and Theology of the Lesser Doxology* (Notre Dame, IN: University of Notre Dame Press, 2007), 27.

accordingly developed as "not merely benediction, but a praise into infinity."[15] Uniquely among the liturgical possibilities, doxologies make the leap to theology proper. Gilles Emery, after noting the inner relation between doxologies and Trinitarian doctrine, writes that "doxologies do not regard an action of God, as do other liturgical forms of expression, but rather they are focused directly on the glory of God and his sanctity. They do not express a wish, but rather they declare the reality of God."[16] Reaching out toward a comprehensive ascription of praise, the liturgical mind of the early church joined two triads around the numinous word *glory*. Combining the three persons named in Matthew 28:19 (Father, Son, and Holy Spirit) with the three tenses of Hebrews 13:8 (yesterday, today, and forever) yields the declarative formula: glory to three persons in three tenses.

The *Gloria Patri* is not Holy Scripture, but humble commentary— very early commentary that uses modest means to reach a remarkable end. It articulates an early Christian insight into and a summary judg- ment about all of Scripture. It shows that Christians began to praise the triune God very early; in fact it may be no exaggeration to say there has been human praise of the Trinity as long as there have been Christians. Robert Wilken notes that "before there was a 'doctrine' of the Trinity, Christian prayers invoked the Holy Trinity."[17] And if Leonard Hodgson puts the point too drastically when he says that "Christianity began as a Trinitarian religion with a unitarian theology,"[18] he at least gives us a dramatic indication of the priority of praise as a response to God's self-revelation, and the confident position from which early theologians set out to achieve greater conceptual articulation and creedal fluency. Trinitarian theology was always praise seeking understanding, feeling for its foundation in the personal God.

---

15. Eric Werner, "The Doxology in Synagogue and Church: A Liturgico-Musical Study," *Hebrew Union College Annual* 19 (1945–1946): 278. Werner argues that the *Gloria Patri* is an early Christian transformation of the Jewish Kedushah prayer, itself a combination of Isaiah 6:3 and Ezekiel 3:12. Though Werner's methods are speculative and his conjectures have not been verified, he does succeed in demonstrating how deeply embedded these later doxologies are in biblical speech and thought-forms.

16. Gilles Emery, *The Trinity: An Introduction to Catholic Doctrine on the Triune God* (Washington, DC: Catholic University of America Press), 6.

17. Robert L. Wilken, *The Spirit of Early Christian Thought: Seeking the Face of God* (New Haven, CT: Yale University Press, 2003), 31.

18. Leonard Hodgson, *The Doctrine of the Trinity: Croall Lectures 1942–1943* (New York: Scribner's Sons, 1944), 103. Hodgson needs to put the point so agonistically in order to set up his view that "the question at issue in the age of the Fathers was whether the religion should transform the theology or the theology stifle the religion."

Without tracing the whole history of the *Gloria Patri*'s use in the Christian church, we can see something of the way it typifies Trinitarian theology by noting three key moments in its development. The first key moment is in the third century, when Origen taught that prayers should begin and end with some such glorification, and that it should be markedly Trinitarian: "It is right, as one began with ascription of glory, to bring one's prayers to an end in ascription of glory, singing and glorifying the Father of all through Jesus Christ in the Holy Spirit—to whom be glory unto eternity."[19] Because he does not present this as a novel idea that needs to be supported by arguments, we may assume he was "merely registering the contemporary and traditional practice of the Church."[20] Here we can see the spiritual instinct of Christian prayer reaching out toward the glorification of God and toward the explicit formulation of Trinitarianism at the same time. Trinitarian theology as *Gloria Patri* is a doctrine about God, spoken in the presence of God, to the end of praising God.

The second key moment has already occurred by sometime late in the fourth century, when we begin to hear that there is a tradition in place of reciting the lesser doxology after every psalm. John Cassian is the most important historical witness to this practice,[21] reporting that he observed the practice among the desert fathers of Egypt but had not heard it elsewhere. Medieval legend attached it to Jerome as author and Pope Damasus as authoritative sponsor, but this ascription has long been discredited as based on spurious letters supposed to have been exchanged between the two.[22] By the sixth century, its connection to the psalms was firmly established in the West; psalms would rarely be used liturgically without the appended *Gloria Patri*. Accompanied by this Trinitarian commentary, the Hebrew Psalter would go on thriving in the life of the Christian churches, and the doctrine of the Trinity, as *Gloria Patri*, would be configured as an exegetical signal pointing back to the ancient texts.

The success of this association brings us to the third key moment, when medieval commentators followed the cue to treat the *Gloria Patri*

---

19. Origen, *On Prayer*, Patrologia Graeca 11, col. 557.

20. Ayo, *Gloria Patri*, 43.

21. Ibid., 28 (citing John Cassian's *Institutes of the Coenobia* II:8).

22. As late as the nineteenth century, the story was still circulated by sources such as Adolphe Didron's *Christian Iconography: The History of Christian Art in the Middle Ages*, vol. 2 (1851; repr., New York: Ungar, 1965), 29, but the 1913 *Catholic Encyclopedia* already knows better. See *The Catholic Encyclopedia*, vol. 5 (New York: Appleton, 1913), under the entry "Doxology."

as a comprehensive summary of the canonical glorification of God. As Holy Scripture, the psalms are already perfect praise, verbally inspired by the God who bears witness to himself in manifold ways. When the *Gloria Patri* is added as new covenant commentary, the psalms are lifted into dialogue with the New Testament: prophets and apostles praise the triune God antiphonally across the two Testaments of Christian Scripture, joined by the church of later ages. With this move, Trinitarian theology as *Gloria Patri* comes into its own.

For example, the Carolingian theologian Gerhoch of Reichersberg's extensive commentary on the Psalms concludes its treatment of each psalm not only with the *Gloria Patri* but with a creative elaboration of it. Gerhoch praises serially the persons of the Trinity, finding in each psalm's language the appropriate terms for the Father, the Son, and the Holy Spirit. The famous Twenty-Third Psalm concludes thus: "And therefore: Glory be to the Father, Who anoints our head with oil; and to the Son, the Shepherd of His people; and to the Holy Ghost, Who provides for us that inebriating chalice which is so excellent. As it was in the beginning, is now, and ever shall be: world without end. Amen."[23] There is a world of reflection in assigning the Father the role of anointer in this psalm. In doing so, Gerhoch is analyzing the phenomenology of anointing in a way redolent of Irenaeus, who said that "in the name of Christ is implied, He that anoints, He that is anointed, and the unction itself with which He is anointed. And it is the Father who anoints, but the Son who is anointed by the Spirit, who is the unction, as the Word declares by Isaiah, 'The Spirit of the Lord is upon me, because He hath anointed me,'—pointing out both the anointing Father, the anointed Son, and the unction, which is the Spirit."[24]

By identifying the Father as the one who anoints, Gerhoch is also implying that the psalm should be read as a statement fulfilled in Christ, the son of David, who is finally and fully anointed. While identifying the Son as the Shepherd of his people is a more obvious move (canonical resonances abound),[25] identifying the Spirit as the giver of the "inebri-

---

23. Gerhoch's Psalms commentary is not available in English. Excerpts from it appear throughout J. M. Neale and R. F. Littledale, *A Commentary on the Psalms: from Primitive and Mediaeval Writers* (London: Masters, 1869).

24. Irenaeus, *Against Heresies* 3:18.3.

25. John 10's "I am the good shepherd" is the most obvious; for its importance in Johannine thought at large, see Karoline M. Lewis, *Rereading the "Shepherd Discourse": Restoring the Integrity of John 9:39–10:21* (New York: Lang, 2008). Less obvious is how it has Ezekiel 34 and related texts in the background. For this, see Gary Manning, *Echoes of a Prophet: The Use of Ezekiel in the*

ating chalice" is more elliptical. It makes more sense as a comment on the Latin—*calix meus inebrians*—than on the familiar English ("my cup runneth over") or the original Hebrew. But as an allusion to the cup of the Lord's Supper, and to the Spirit as the agent who subjectively applies the benefits of redemption that run full to excess, it has some purchase. Gerhoch follows the tradition of setting the *Gloria Patri* as a seal on the total text of Scripture, and the result is an insight into the triune nature of the God who has always been the Trinity ("antecedently in himself") but has not always been in the business of revealing that triunity. In the fullness of time the Father sent the Son and the Holy Spirit (the Anointer sent the Shepherd and the Chalice-Giver in person). Gerhoch's *Gloria Patri* on each psalm plays the same role that Trinitarian theology as a whole seeks to play: ceding respect to the words of the Old Testament revelation and their location at a particular point in the unfolding of redemptive and revelatory history, it seals that witness with the climactic revelation of God's identity.[26]

SEEKING THE FACE OF GOD

How is the *Gloria Patri* a model of Trinitarian theology? In many ways. It is a modest act of praise, taking its rise immediately from Scripture and answering to God's self-revelation in an appropriate form. It speaks back to God as praise what it hears from him in revelation, stirred up by God's works but seeking their source in his eternal being and character.[27] Its doxological nature refuses to rest in what God does, but with relentless biblical personalism seeks the very face of God. Trinitarian theology as *Gloria Patri* follows the spiritual impulse voiced by the Puritan Jeremiah Burroughs in his treatise on true contentment. He asks himself, "Suppose you have the peace of God. Will not that quiet you?" "No," he replies, "I must have the God of peace; as the peace of God, so the God of peace; that is, I must enjoy that God that gives me the peace; I must have the Cause as well as the effect; I must

---

Gospel of John and in Literature of the Second Temple Period (London: T&T Clark, 2004). Psalm 80 is a remarkable expansion of the Levitical blessing in terms of the Lord as a shepherd. See also Matthew's shepherd Christology and its Old Testament basis in Joel Willitts, *Matthew's Messianic Shepherd-King: In Search of "The Lost Sheep of the House of Israel"* (Berlin: de Gruyter, 2007).

26. For more on Gerhoch, see chapter 8.

27. Trinitarian theology carried out as *Gloria Patri* also has a retrospective quality that contrasts sharply with the futuristic orientation of certain modern Trinitarianisms with a tendency to Hegelianize.

see from whence my peace comes and enjoy the Fountain of my peace, as well as the stream of my peace.[28]

That commitment to seek the fountain behind the stream and the giver behind the gift can also be expressed in biblical idiom as seeking the face of God behind the works of God. It was with deep insight that Augustine took "seeking the face of God" as the motif of his book *On the Trinity*. Edmund Hill identifies "the theme-setting text for the whole work" as Psalm 105:3–4: "Let their hearts rejoice who seek the Lord; seek the Lord and be strengthened; seek his face always."[29] Augustine launches his quest into Trinitarian theology with this passage (I.2,5), returns to it at a critical juncture (IX.1,1), and concludes with it (XV.2,2).[30] All of Augustine's conceptual moves and hermeneutical negotiations throughout that demanding volume of Trinitarian theology are in service of that spiritual quest, answering the divine summons to seek the face of God.

Anyone who knows something of the history of the doctrine of the Trinity knows how the quest that begins so simply becomes complex soon enough, for Augustine as for all Trinitarian theology. Historical revelation demands close attention; theology requires precision of thought and expression; distinctions must be drawn and implications accepted. The *Gloria Patri* itself necessarily unfolds into complexity as soon as we ask about the "and" that joins Father to Son to Spirit. Though the formula itself, following the phrasing of Matthew 28, "places all three divine persons on a level of equality separated only by coordinating conjunctions,"[31] it does so on the basis of the Father's working all things by the Son and in the Spirit in the economy of salvation. That is, the co-doxology ascribes coeternity and coequality to the three and so turns the mind to the immanent Trinity. But as the doxological commentary on salvation-historical actions, it presupposes the events of salvation history, primarily the incarnation of the Son and the outpouring of the Holy Spirit: from the Father, through the Son, in the Holy Spirit. Both levels of discourse are possible; which level is most apt? Or could

---

28. Jeremiah Burroughs, *The Rare Jewel of Christian Contentment* (London: Bentley, 1651), 19. I have changed some commas to semicolons for clarity.

29. Saint Augustine, *The Trinity*, part 1, vol. 5 of *The Works of Saint Augustine*, ed. John E. Rotelle, trans. Edmund Hill (Brooklyn, NY: New City Press, 1991), 91 n. 11; see 1.1.5, 68. In all citations referring to Augustine's *Trinity*, I will be quoting from this edition and using its page numbers.

30. Ibid., 21.

31. Ayo, *Gloria Patri*, 26.

the doxology be rephrased using prepositions that indicate neither the immanent equality nor the economic actions, but the eternal relations of origin among the persons? Or would it be better to say: to the Father, through the Son, by the Holy Spirit, because in the doxology we are not describing the downward motion of God's grace toward us, but the upward motion of our praise returning to God?

An entire doctrine of God lurks in the littlest words, in the conjunctions and prepositions of Trinitarian statements. Basil of Caesarea knew that "none of the words used to describe God should be passed over without exact examination," and that "therefore to scrutinize syllables is not a superfluous task."[32] But he also knew there was such a thing as "quibbling over prepositions"[33] in a way that deflected the pious mind from its goal in seeking the face of God.[34] In spite of the danger, Basil gave close attention to those smallest parts of speech because they mark relations, and the doctrine of the Trinity stands or falls with the right understanding of the relations in God. Trinitarian theology ought to be conducted in such a way that it maintains high standards of right speaking while enacting and enabling the movement of seeking God's face.

---

32. Basil, *On the Holy Spirit*, 15, 16.

33. Ibid., 19.

34. For an account of how Basil wrote in opposition to heresy, but also in correction of Gregory of Nazianzus's more restrictive hermeneutics of the doxology, see Christopher A. Beeley, *Gregory of Nazianzus on the Trinity and the Knowledge of God: In Your Light We Shall See Light* (New York: Oxford University Press, 2013), 297.

CHAPTER 2

REVELATION OF THE TRIUNE GOD

God made it known that his unity was triunity precisely when the Father sent the Son and the Holy Spirit, in fulfillment of the promise of redemption. The Trinity is thus a mystery in the New Testament sense of the term: something always true, long concealed, and now revealed. God's identity is made known on the basis of the twofold central action in the economy, the self-interpreting missions of the Son and the Holy Spirit. So fundamental is this event for theology that it is the paradigm case of what revelation is, according to Christian doctrine: divine acts and words bound together by an inner unity.

If the Father, Son, and Holy Spirit had not made themselves personally known, we would not have attained knowledge that the one God is the triune God. A theology that operated without revelation might reason its way to abstract monotheism or to the polytheism of multiple divine agents working in the world, but triunity has to be carefully taught by God. John of Damascus speaks for the mainstream of Christian thought when he identifies divine self-revelation as the exclusive source of the confession of God's triunity. The opening lines of his theological compendium "On the Orthodox Faith" are a classic instance of the position. Stitching together a few key statements of Scripture and providing just enough commentary to signal his purpose, he asserts that revelation is both absolutely necessary and utterly exclusive:

No one hath seen God at any time; the Only-begotten Son, which is in the bosom of the Father, He hath declared Him (John 1:18). The Deity, therefore, is ineffable and incomprehensible. For no one knoweth the Father, save the Son, nor the Son, save the Father (Matt 11:27). And the Holy Spirit, too, so knows the things of God as the spirit of the man knows the things that are in him (1 Cor 2:11).

Moreover, after the first and blessed nature no one, not of men only, but even of supramundane powers, and the Cherubim, I say, and Seraphim themselves, has ever known God, save he to whom He revealed Himself.[1]

The initial Johannine statement restricts knowledge of God the Father to those who have heard the declaration of the Son, while the Matthean statement closes the loop by adding that knowledge of the Son is restricted to the Father. The juxtaposition of these passages shows the Father-Son circle of knowledge to be a closed one, but the Damascene adds a pneumatological statement from Paul to the effect that the Holy Spirit also participates in that inner-divine knowledge, to its very depths. "On the basis of Scripture," explains Charles Twombly, "knowledge of God as Trinity is itself declared to have a Trinitarian origin."[2] Twombly goes on: "Each hypostasis is able to reveal because each speaks, as it were, from the inside. And what each reveals, according to the passages cited, is one or more of the other hypostaseis, though not necessarily the one making the revelation."[3] Knowledge of the Trinity is inside knowledge, given by insiders. Even the highest of the angels are outsiders, the Damascene adds for emphasis.

REVELATION OF THE MYSTERY

But by revelation, the persons of the Trinity have truly made each other and therefore themselves known. How has this happened? The Father sent the Son and the Holy Spirit. These two were sent to bring salvation and knowledge of the Trinity, in fulfillment of the promises proclaimed beforehand. John of Damascus affirms this as well: God "has

---

1. Saint John of Damascus, "The Orthodox Faith," in *Saint John of Damascus: Writings,* trans. Frederic H. Chase Jr. (Washington, DC: Catholic University Press, 1958), 165.

2. Charles C. Twombly, *Perichoresis and Personhood: God, Christ, and Salvation in John of Damascus* (Eugene, OR: Pickwick, 2015), 13.

3. Ibid., 14–15.

given us knowledge of Himself in accordance with our capacity, at first through the Law and the Prophets and then afterwards through His only begotten Son, our Lord and God and Savior, Jesus Christ."[4] Though this knowledge is accommodated to "our capacity," it is nevertheless true knowledge of God. And though it is apocalyptically new when it arrives in the advent of the Son and Spirit of God, it nevertheless had a vast preparatory economy in "the Law and the Prophets." In fact, the preparatory economy is so necessary to the final disclosure of the Son and Spirit that it must be reckoned metonymically part of the revelation itself. As the fulfillment of a promise, the gospel is not just good news but faithful good news of one who keeps covenant. Because the gift of salvation came in two parts (promise and fulfillment), it includes within itself a structure of correspondence and internal consistency. Since the light of final revelation already cast a shadow back into the time before it, adumbration necessarily preceded revelation.

The doctrine of the Trinity is a revealed doctrine. It is in some ways less revealed than other doctrines, and in other ways more revealed. It is less revealed in this sense: it is not directly proposed in the words of Scripture and presented to us in a formulated state. Some doctrines are. Consider the vocabulary of the divine perfections, which seem to be verbal-propositional glosses on the divine name spoken in character by God himself: "The LORD, the LORD, a God merciful and gracious, slow to anger, and abounding in steadfast love and faithfulness." Characteristic divine actions that flow from these enumerated perfections then follow: "keeping steadfast love for thousands, forgiving iniquity and transgression and sin" (Ex 34:6–7). These are doctrines simply stated in Scripture in propositional form, and dogmatic reflection on them involves paraphrasing their claims conceptually, describing them in their relation to their narrative emplotment, and comparing them with other doctrines.

But the triunity of God is not made known in that way. It is not set forth in oracular idiom in the Old Testament ("Thus saith the Lord: I am Father and Son and Spirit"), nor is it made the subject of focused and deliberate teaching in the New Testament ("Now concerning the persons of God, I would not have you ignorant . . ."). The basic vocabulary of Trinitarian theology is not found on the surface of the text (person, nature, relation, threeness), and the conceptual elements of Trinitarianism are not gathered in one place and related to each other

4. Saint John of Damascus, "The Orthodox Faith," 166.

by Scripture itself. We nevertheless call it a revealed doctrine, and even a biblical doctrine, because, as the Westminster Confession of Faith reads, "the whole counsel of God . . . is either expressly set down in Scripture, or by good and necessary consequence may be deduced from Scripture."[5] The triunity of God is among those things "by good and necessary consequence deduced" from what is "expressly set down." To call it less revealed than other doctrines is simply to admit, with calm confidence and equanimity, that it is not verbally formulated for us, and that some assembly is required.

But the doctrine is also, in another and higher sense, more revealed than most doctrines. The root idea of revelation is not verbal announcement but the unveiling or disclosing of something that has been present, though concealed. In order to inform us that the Father has a Son and a Holy Spirit, the Father sent the Son and the Holy Spirit in person. The triunity of God was revealed when the persons of the Trinity became present among us in a new way, showing up in person and becoming the object of our human observation. The apostles testified that what they saw with their eyes and touched with their hands was "that which was from the beginning," because it "was with the Father and was made manifest" to them (1 John 1:1–3). Doctrines that are first announced verbally have the character of revealedness less directly; the doctrine of the Trinity has it more directly. There are profound reasons that the doctrine of the Trinity has this special status, but at this point it is sufficient to note this is an indicator that the doctrine of the Trinity is more than just another doctrine on the list of true things we have been taught by God about God. It is God's self-revelation by way of presence in a more direct, intense, and personal way.

In the fullness of time, God did not give us facts about himself, but gave us himself in the person of the Father who sent, the Son who was sent, and the Holy Spirit who was poured out. These events were accompanied by verbally inspired explanatory words; but the latter depend on the former. Doctrinal information and propositional knowledge can easily be derived from that eloquent, self-interpreting central happening of salvation history, that personal disclosure and saving presence of God with us. But because the revelation of the Trinity occurred in a special way, it requires special handling. Redemption and revelation are together

---

5. See Joel R. Beeke and Sinclair B. Ferguson, eds., *Reformed Confessions Harmonized: With an Annotated Bibliography of Reformed Doctrinal Writings* (Grand Rapids: Baker, 1999), 12.

the root of the doctrine of the Trinity, and while an awareness of this has characterized Christian theology in all ages, it has especially affected the way modern theologians have approached the doctrine.

Consider the Karls. Karl Barth took as his starting point for a modern rehabilitation of the doctrine of the Trinity the fact that "God reveals himself as Lord."[6] Karl Rahner, reacting to what seemed to him to be the neoscholastic reduction of the doctrine to a merely verbal mystery, insisted in *Mysterium Salutis* that "the Trinity is a mystery of salvation, otherwise it would never have been revealed."[7] Karl Henry[8] was considerably less troubled than Rahner by the idea of propositional revelation, and he handled this doctrine as fundamentally a matter in which God performed mighty acts in history and then "supernaturally communicated his revelation . . . in the express form of cognitive truths" such that "the inspired prophetic-apostolic proclamation reliably articulates these truths in sentences that are not internally contradictory."[9] Perhaps these are simply three examples of theologians who allowed their respective doctrines of revelation to determine in advance the shape their Trinitarianism would take. But in all three cases, there is evidence that these theologians worked out their doctrine of the Trinity (the more material concern) in a way that shaped their doctrine of revelation (the more formal or methodological concern). Whatever judgment we may render on these theologians and a number of other moderns, we can at least say that any particular doctrine of revelation will find itself entangled with a corresponding doctrine of the Trinity. Because the doctrine of God ought to have priority in theological knowledge, a well-ordered theological project will let the actual concrete doctrine of God determine the doctrine of revelation.

It is not quite enough to say that the doctrine of the Trinity is a revealed doctrine. That could situate the locus on the Trinity within the

---

6. Barth, *CD* I/1, 295. Barth even gave the impression that the doctrine could be derived analytically from this sentence, but he did not mean this and took pains to correct the impression (296). It was not the *idea* of God's self-revelation as Lord, but the *fact* of it that required the doctrine of the Trinity.

7. Karl Rahner, *The Trinity* (New York: Herder, 1997), 21. Rahner's book on the Trinity first appeared in English in 1970, but had originally been a section from the ambitious multi-volume *Mysterium Salutis* project in which a group of Catholic theologians collaborated to extend the dogmatic implications of Vatican II. Rahner's chapter treated the Trinity as the transcendental primal basis of salvation history: "Der dreifaltige Gott als transzendenter Urgrund der Heilsgeschichte," in *Mysterium Salutis* vol. 2, ed. Johannes Feiner and Magnus Löhrer (Einsiedeln: Benziger, 1967).

8. Okay . . . Carl. But you have to admit it makes for a memorable triad.

9. Carl F. H. Henry, *God, Revelation, and Authority*, vol. 3 (Waco, TX: Word, 1980), 456–57.

locus on revelation, constraining the doctrine of God by the doctrine of revelation. But the doctrine of revelation must already be dictated by a reality we can only define as Trinitarian in its material content (an account of salvation history as an economy of God's self-revelation in the Son and the Spirit[10]) before it can be generalized or formalized. The doctrine of the Trinity is the doctrine that norms and forms the doctrine of revelation itself. Barth wrote that "the doctrine of the Trinity is what basically distinguishes the Christian doctrine of God as Christian, and therefore what already distinguishes the Christian concept of revelation as Christian, in contrast to all other possible doctrines of God or concepts of revelation."[11] No doubt he had some particular (not to say, idiosyncratically Barthian) goals in mind when he announced this early in his *Church Dogmatics*. But the insight itself is unexceptionable, and not the property of any school. A doctrine of revelation uninformed by Trinitarian realities could not be the proper setting for the doctrine of the Trinity. Even if some remarks on the character of revelation may need to be offered before the details of Trinitarian theology, those remarks must be based already on the content of revelation. Such a doctrine of revelation, drawn from the actual content of revelation and using propositions borrowed from the doctrine of the Trinity and its mode of revelation, is offered here.

HIDDEN, BUT NOW REVEALED

The Trinity is often called a mystery, with good reason. It is a mystery for cognitive and epistemic reasons in the sense that it transcends our understanding. It "cannot be comprehended by reasoning, nor be perceived by senses, nor be expressed in words, nor be taught by experience, nor be explained by an example," as the Leiden Synopsis says.[12] But this cognitive mysteriousness is not the primary association we ought to make when we call the Trinity a mystery. Cognitive mysteriousness is an aspect of God's incomprehensibility, not his triunity.[13]

Instead, the most appropriate context for talking about the Trinity

---

10. For the best brief account of this, see Scott R. Swain, *Trinity, Revelation, and Reading: A Theological Introduction to the Bible and Its Interpretation* (London: T&T Clark, 2011), esp. 4–8.

11. Barth, *CD* I/1, 301.

12. Dolf te Velde, ed., *Synopsis Purioris Theologiae / Synopsis of a Purer Theology* (Leiden: Brill, 2015), 195.

13. Though I am recommending the Pauline *mysterion* as the primary association for the mystery of the Trinity, I am not denying the other associations. The thickest account in modern

as a mystery is the biblical theology of mystery, especially its New Testament sense. For the New Testament, a mystery is something that has always existed but has only been revealed by God more recently. Thus Paul proclaims "the revelation of the mystery that was kept secret for long ages but has now been disclosed" (Rom 16:25–26), and "the plan of the mystery hidden for ages in God . . . now . . . made known" (Eph 3:9–10). In most of the contexts where Paul uses the language of mystery, his immediate referent is the surprising turn that salvation history has taken as it incorporates the Gentiles. But because Paul considers this salvation-historical phenomenon as something planned long ago by the Father and carried out in the work of the Son and the Spirit, he is also speaking indirectly about the doctrine of God. It is characteristic of Paul's usage that he continues to call these things mysteries even after they have been disclosed. As if to mark perpetually the epochal shift from before the revelation to after the revelation, he does not treat it as something that was once a mystery but has now been rendered non-mystery. Instead he calls it a mystery that was hidden but is now revealed, a mystery that has gone from hidden mystery to revealed mystery. The historical structure of mysteriousness predominates, so the revealed truth retains the name of mystery.

Much changes if we keep at the front of our minds the biblical theology of mystery as what we mean by calling the Trinity a mystery. We no longer emphasize that the Trinity is cognitively impenetrable, or that it is a matter of the divine essence and therefore ineffable, or that it is inside knowledge withheld from outsiders. What we emphasize in calling the Trinity a mystery in the biblical sense is that it was previously concealed but has been revealed in the fullness of time. It is not so much a mystery of words or of the nature of salvation, but a mystery of progressive revelation. The *mysterium trinitatis* in fact signals precisely this connection between the Old Testament and the New Testament. The fact that the one God who spoke in many ways in times past has spoken in these final days in his Son (Heb 1:1–3) is the ground of the unity of the two Testaments. In this case, the proper business of theology is not so much seeking the Trinity in Scripture as recognizing that the two-Testament canon of Christian Scripture came into being in the first place to bear witness that the God of Israel spoke a conclusive word in his

---

times of the cognitive mysteriousness of the Trinity is Matthias Scheeben, *The Mysteries of Christianity* (New York: Crossroad, 2015), part 1, "The Mystery of the Holy Trinity," 23–196.

Son and the Holy Spirit. B. B. Warfield described the New Testament as "the documentation of the religion of the incarnate Son and of the outpoured Spirit, that is to say, of the religion of the Trinity."[14] We will be arguing throughout this book that the Trinity is a biblical doctrine. But it is not enough to say that the mystery of the Trinity is in the Bible unless we recognize that the thing we are calling the Bible is a set of texts that were written, redacted, and canonized to prepare for and report on the missions of the Son and the Spirit. To somebody about to comb through the texts to find elements of the doctrine, we have to say: the Trinity is in the Bible because the Bible is in the Trinity.[15]

Situating the doctrine of the Trinity within the biblical theology of mystery also requires a more concrete account of the two temporal poles of the biblical mystery. In particular, questions of continuity and discontinuity between Old and New Testaments take on more urgency. Is the mystery completely unknown before its revelation, or is it dimly known before a more complete revelation? In a recent study of the biblical theology of mystery, G. K. Beale and Benjamin Gladd have argued for the latter: partial revelation in the Old Testament followed by fuller revelation in the New.[16] In fact, they show that even within the limitations of its Old Testament provenance, the idea of mystery already includes within itself the notion of partial revelation followed by fuller revelation. The primary Old Testament background for the idea of mystery is the book of Daniel, where God tends to reveal eschatological realities in two stages. First comes a hidden form, such as the king having dreams whose content he either does not divulge or cannot comprehend. Next comes the interpretation of the dream. On both ends of the process, before and after its interpretation, the content of the dream is called a mystery: Daniel and his friends "seek mercy from the God of heaven concerning this mystery," and then "the mystery was revealed to Daniel" (Dan 2:18–19). In this case, God shows forth a future reality in a preliminary and symbolic phase, and then in a final and interpretive phase. This Old Testament usage of mystery sets the pattern for the New Testament usage, leading Beale and Gladd to define biblical mystery generally as "the revelation of God's partially hidden wisdom,

---

14. B. B. Warfield, "The Biblical Doctrine of the Trinity," in *Biblical and Theological Studies* (Philadelphia: Presbyterian and Reformed, 1952), 35.

15. See the conclusion of chapter 3, below.

16. G. K. Beale and Benjamin L. Gladd, *Hidden But Now Revealed: A Biblical Theology of Mystery* (Downers Grove, IL: IVP Academic, 2014).

particularly as it concerns events occurring in the 'latter days.'"[17] The emphasis is on the idea of something partially hidden, because even in Daniel itself "the revelation of mystery is not a totally new revelation but the full disclosure of something that was to a significant extent hidden."[18]

One implication of nudging the *mysterium trinitatis* back into alignment with mystery in the biblical sense is that Trinitarian theology will necessarily take the form of a certain kind of biblical theology (though admittedly one more comfortable with ontological claims than is conventional for projects under the banner of biblical theology), that is, an account of the unity of the Old and New Testaments.[19] What binds the two Testaments together as one canon? We are perhaps more accustomed to thinking of a soteriological impulse and a salvation-historical superstructure for construing Old and New Testaments as canonically one. But if the technical term "the economic Trinity" is worth continued use,[20] it could be of assistance for signaling a Trinitarianism whose center of attention is the *oikonomia* (Eph 1:10) but whose horizon includes the eternal being of God above history. Such a Trinitarianism would be able to contemplate soteriology and theology together very closely without losing one in the other. It could therefore recognize that while the Trinity was not yet clearly revealed in the time of the Old Testament, the reality of the Trinity is signaled in those texts precisely as much as the gospel itself is, "preached beforehand" because its results are "foreseen" by Scripture itself (see Gal 3:8). The Trinity is concealed-then-revealed across the span of Scripture exactly as the gospel is, because the Trinity and the gospel are comprehended in the same sweep of revelation and redemption.

The Christian doctrine of revelation was, historically, a by-product of the doctrine of the Trinity. The early church elaborated the doctrine

---

17. Ibid., 20.

18. Ibid., 30. It is notoriously difficult to state the continuity and discontinuity between the Testaments with sufficient balance. For a compelling account that preserves a note of greater novelty in the New Testament, see Sigurd Grindheim, "What the OT Prophets Did Not Know: The Mystery of the Church in Eph 3,2–13," *Biblica* 84 (2003): 531–53; for a very balanced overview, see D. A. Carson, "Mystery and Fulfillment: Toward a More Comprehensive Paradigm of Paul's Understanding of the Old and the New," in *The Paradoxes of Paul*, vol. 2 of *Justification and Variegated Nomism*, ed. D. A. Carson, Peter T. O'Brien, and Mark A. Seifrid (Tübingen: Mohr Siebeck, 2004), 298–412.

19. Contemporary Trinitarian theology will thrive in the context of a canonical approach that has fully digested the way Old and New Testaments interpenetrate. See Christopher R. Seitz, *The Character of Christian Scripture: The Significance of the Two-Testament Bible* (Grand Rapids: Baker Academic, 2011). Seitz has not spelled out all the implications for Trinitarianism, though see his interaction with relevant theological interpreters on pages 68–70.

20. See the end of chapter 5 for light on its dubious genealogy and for reasons to doubt its ongoing usefulness.

of the Trinity as just the kind of two-Testament theological conclusion we are considering, rendering a statement about the identity of God on the basis of the revealed mystery of Christ and the Spirit. Though their focal attention was on the identity of God in Christ, in their peripheral vision the church fathers saw numerous other doctrines coming into alignment. It is a strength and not a weakness that in this early period, Christology, pneumatology, soteriology, and the doctrine of God were all a relatively undifferentiated mass. Basil Studer has argued that historians of doctrine should shake off the bad habit of tracing each doctrine separately, because the "burning actuality" of early Christian confession makes it "better to speak of a single formulation of the question" in which "the eternal Trinity is in the end only revealed in the historical mystery of Easter."[21] Studer has in mind especially the unity of soteriology and the doctrine of God, or "how closely interrelated God and our salvation in Jesus Christ are."[22] But the same web of mutual implication holds also for the doctrine of creation (sharpened into *creatio ex nihilo* during the fourth century by the recognition that the Son's begetting is not an act of creation), ecclesiology (both in the church's constitution as the body of Christ in the work of the Spirit and in its internal struggle with heresies regarding both Trinitarian persons), and the shape of the canon (a gathering of the documents that bore witness to the Son and the Spirit). As the early church explicitly discussed the doctrine of the Trinity, the rest of its theology gelled around it more or less implicitly and took on the shape that would best serve a Trinitarian construal of the economy of salvation. The doctrine of revelation was a by-product of Trinitarian theology in the sense that the doctrine of the Trinity generated the kind of theology of revelation it needed.

AN INAPT DOCTRINE OF REVELATION

A fruitful way of understanding some of the difficulties of modern Trinitarian theology is to note how much the doctrine of the Trinity was influenced by a modern alteration in the doctrine of revelation. If a self-consciously Christian doctrine of revelation ought to be shaped by reflection on the missions of the Son and the Holy Spirit, then

---

21. Basil Studer, *Trinity and Incarnation: The Faith of the Early Church* (Collegeville, MN: Liturgical Press, 1994), 2.
22. Ibid., 1.

REVELATION OF THE TRIUNE GOD

any doctrine of revelation shaped by alien concerns fetched from other regions will be likely to distort Trinitarianism. In some theological projects, the doctrine of the Trinity became almost a casualty of the doctrine of revelation, while in most projects it was only wounded. We will examine the most influential case, that of Karl Rahner, in the next section. But Rahner is complex, and for the sake of a clear focus there is no better case study than Leonard Hodgson's 1944 book *The Doctrine of the Trinity*. Hodgson (1889–1969) is not generally considered a key figure in twentieth-century Trinitarianism, partly because his book appeared a few years prior to the postwar publishing boom in Trinitarian theology.[23] But he was a prestigious theologian in his time (he was Regius Professor of Divinity at Oxford from 1944 to 1958 and gave the Gifford Lectures from 1955 to 1957) and represents the midcentury academic establishment as well as anybody. His book on the Trinity is admirable for its methodological transparency, especially with regard to the doctrine of revelation.

Hodgson agrees with those who say "the dominant problem of contemporary religious thought is the problem of revelation," though reluctantly, since he considers the problem of revelation to be "part of the curse of Adam, a recurrent weed in the garden of thought."[24] Looking back to the nineteenth century, Hodgson says that Christian believers considered the statements of Scripture to be "statements of fact to be accepted as true because uttered by God." On this view, "divine revelation was given in the form of a collection of statements or propositions to be accepted and believed on the authority of the Giver. The Bible was this collection of divinely guaranteed propositions; it was the Word of God because it contained the words of God."[25] The whole intellectual trend of the century was to render that view impossible on critical grounds, both historical and scientific. Hodgson laments the "rather dreary period when the conclusions of criticism seemed so largely negative" and believers felt they were forced to choose between

---

23. He has not been completely ignored. Cornelius Plantinga Jr., in an unpublished but widely cited dissertation, identified Hodgson's importance for the development of social Trinitarianism (see "The Hodgson-Welch Debate and the Social Analogy of the Trinity," PhD dissertation, Princeton Theological Seminary, 1982). Hodgson proposed marriage to Dorothy Sayers in 1917; John Thurmer has pondered the possibility of Hodgson's influence on Sayers's 1941 book *Mind of the Maker*, or vice versa. See Thurmer's *A Detection of the Trinity* (Exeter: Paternoster, 1984), "Appendix: The Missing Link."

24. Leonard Hodgson, *The Doctrine of the Trinity: Croall Lectures 1942–1943* (New York: Scribner's Sons, 1944), 17.

25. Ibid., 18–19.

faith's edification and reason's clarification. "Those were days of mental agony for thinking Christians, days when reading the Bible seemed like walking among quicksands," he recalls. But according to Hodgson, that dark period is now past, and the educated Christian of 1944 stands on solid ground thanks to the honest intellectual work of the generations just past. Though modern believers cannot, like their ancestors, "take for granted the belief that the Bible was a collection of propositions expressing words of God," they are nevertheless in a position to "take for granted a post-critical approach to the Bible and make the first aim of our study the discernment of whatever God wills to reveal to us through its pages."[26]

The benefit of having made it through this "agonizing transition" from pre-critical to post-critical is

> a clearer apprehension than was given to any previous age that the revelation of God is not given in words but in deeds; that the reason why "the holy Scriptures contain sufficiently all Doctrine required of necessity for eternal salvation through faith in Jesus Christ" is because they bear witness to the activity in history of God our Creator, Redeemer and Sanctifier. This is not, indeed, a new idea. But in earlier ages it was entangled with the thought of the Bible as containing the divine revelation given in the form of propositions; it is only of recent years that we have been able to see it standing clear, so that we can more fully appreciate its significance.[27]

Having disentangled itself from the distracting notion of revelation in propositions, theology can focus more intently on the task of finding revelation transmitted in Scripture by more oblique means. What counts as the word of God for believers is "not a proposition or series of propositions prescribing what we are to believe or think."[28] Instead, God's word to us "is a series of divine acts to which the Bible bears

---

26. Ibid., 19. The structure of Hodgson's argument (in which a doctrine's traditional formulation faces a modern paradigm shift necessitating the task of creative new formulation) is rendered programmatic in all the essays in Peter Hodgson and Robert King, eds., *Christian Theology: An Introduction to Its Traditions and Tasks* (Minneapolis, Fortress, 1982). I do not think the two Hodgsons are related. A helpful analysis of this mode of theologizing can be found in Ian Markham, "Revisionism," in *The Oxford Handbook of Systematic Theology*, ed. John Webster, Kathryn Tanner, and Iain Torrance (New York: Oxford University Press, 2007), 610–16.

27. Hodgson, *Doctrine of the Trinity*, 19–20.

28. Ibid., 22.

witness. These acts give rise to propositions when they are reflected on by the mind as it seeks to grasp their significance."[29] Revelation, in other words, is not given in words: "The revelation of God is given in deeds; the doctrines of the faith are formulated by reflection on the significance of those deeds."[30]

So on Hodgson's account, the doctrine of the Trinity is the product of revelation because God is at work at two points: in the events themselves, and then in the illumination of the interpreters to understand the events. "The divine revelation is given in acts rather than in words, and is received by those whose eyes God opens to see the significance of what He does."[31] Those whose eyes are first opened are the biblical writers. So illumined, they generate propositions in order to pass along to future generations what they have seen and understood. Hodgson is vigilant to avoid any suggestion of divine action in generating those propositions; in fact, he repeatedly denies that God is the author of the propositions in which the illuminated writers pass along their interpretation of the events: "It is not these propositions as such which are the *revelatum*. They bear record to the *revelatum*, but as the ages go by they can only continue to mediate the revelation in so far as in each generation men's eyes are opened to see for themselves the significance of the revelatory acts of God to which they bear witness."[32]

Hodgson's judgment that revelation comes not through divinely authored propositions recorded in Scripture but through divine actions witnessed to in Scripture and then interpreted by theologians (the latter two moments constituting together the process of formulating doctrines by "reflection on the significance of those deeds") is not something he provides much evidence for, as it is not the point of his book. He takes this view of revelation to be the obvious conclusion for any educated observer who was paying attention during the nineteenth century.[33] Perhaps it was based on convictions shared widely enough to command agreement in academic theological culture in the middle of the twentieth

29. Ibid.
30. Ibid.
31. Ibid., 35.
32. Ibid.
33. For some historical background and considerable conceptual analysis of "propositional revelation," see Avery Dulles, *Models of Revelation* (Maryknoll, NY: Orbis Books, 1994), 36–53. Most critics of Hodgson's book did not directly address his view of revelation. Claude Welch was a prominent challenger of Hodgson's view of the derivation of the doctrine of the Trinity, but not, apparently, of his doctrine of revelation. See Hodgson's response to Welch in "The Doctrine of the Trinity: Some Further Thoughts," *Journal of Theological Studies* 5:1 (1954): 49–55.

century. William Temple's 1940 Gifford Lectures, for instance, argued that the same formal principle of revelation applied to the "uniform world process" as well as to Scripture: in both cases, "the principle of revelation is . . . the coincidence of event and appreciation."[34] From this consensus there were eloquent dissenters. Geerhardus Vos began his 1948 *Biblical Theology* with a warning that this sort of approach to revelation feinted toward greater objectivity (the mighty acts of God!) but struck home with doctrinal subjectivity: "A favorite form" of the move was "to confine revelation proper to the bare acts of self-disclosure performed by God, and then to derive the entire thought-content of the Bible from human reflection upon these acts. Such a theory, as a rule, is made a cover for involving the whole teaching of the Bible in the relativity of purely human reflection."[35]

But Hodgson's book is not primarily on the doctrine of revelation or Scripture. His focus is on the doctrine of the Trinity, which he develops solely on the basis of a theological interpretation of God's actions in Christ and the Spirit. He describes his project thus:

> The doctrine of the Trinity . . . is the product of rational reflection on those particular manifestations of the divine activity which centre in the birth, ministry, crucifixion, resurrection and ascension of Jesus Christ and the gift of the Holy Spirit to the Church . . . It could not have been discovered without the occurrence of those events, which drove human reason to see that they required a Trinitarian God for their cause.[36]

It is in many ways an admirable theological performance. Hodgson especially warms to his task when he traces the intentions of Jesus for his disciples, which were only completed when his own death and resurrection were brought home to the disciples through the outpouring of the Holy Spirit. When they received the Spirit, "our Lord's ambition for His disciples" was fulfilled, "His ambition that they should share in His

34. William Temple, *Nature, Man and God: Being the Gifford Lectures Delivered in the University of Glasgow* (London: Macmillan, 1940), 315. A few pages before this, Temple had expressed his rejection of propositional revelation in the formula, "There is no such thing as revealed truth. There are truths of revelation, that is to say propositions which express the results of correct thinking concerning revelation; but they are not themselves directly revealed" (312).

35. Geerhardus Vos, *Biblical Theology: Old and New Testaments* (Grand Rapids: Eerdmans, 1948), 12.

36. Hodgson, *Doctrine of the Trinity*, 25.

relationship to the Father and His outlook on the world, that for them, as for Him, life in the flesh should be the seeking, finding and doing of the Father's will in the guidance and power of the Spirit. This was to be the characteristic way of life for the Christian, and at Pentecost it began."[37] In short, Hodgson spells out robustly what he calls his central thesis: "The Doctrine of the Trinity represents the conception of God involved in the Christian life of adopted sonship in Christ."[38] Hodgson has a firm grasp of the fit between specifically Christian soteriology and the doctrine of God implied by it.

"IN SEARCH OF A NEW FOUNDATION" (WILES)

Yet something is missing, and its absence undercuts much that is laudable in Hodgson's accomplishment. Critical reviewers aware of being to Hodgson's theological right were quick to point out what he had omitted. Jesuit theologian E. J. Fortman noted that Hodgson "adopts the Liberal Protestant theory of revelation in 'acts,' largely derived from Ritschl and Rothe" and that "enthusiasm for this theory" seemed "to blind him to its inadequacy and contrary-to-factness. But it is hard to believe that he can long fail to perceive that if Christ was truly God, then His every statement about the Trinity was divine revelation given in the form of propositions, to be accepted and believed on the authority of the Giver."[39] But it was a critic who wrote from Hodgson's left, Maurice Wiles, who in a perceptive 1957 critique pointed out the fundamental problem.[40] Hodgson's book was well regarded enough by then that Wiles seems aware of being contrarian when he calls into question "whether the full implications of his approach to this subject have been recognized."

When Hodgson excludes propositional revelation from consideration, says Wiles, he dooms himself to reconstruct the doctrine of the Trinity without adequate materials. If we follow Hodgson's method, then, unlike the early church, "we are not starting with the assumption

---

37. Ibid., 48.
38. Ibid., 55–56.
39. E. J. Fortman, review of *The Doctrine of the Trinity: Croall Lectures 1942–1943*, in *Thought: Fordham University Quarterly* 20:1 (1945): 175–76. Fortman's overall judgment on the book is: "The analysis of the doctrine of Aquinas is defective. The treatment is 'liberal' in its spirit, rationalistic in its bent, empirical in its method. Orthodoxy suffers."
40. Maurice Wiles, "Some Reflections on the Origin of the Doctrine of the Trinity," *Journal of Theological Studies* 8:1 (1957): 92–106.

of a revealed Trinitarian doctrine of God" already established and then comparing it to "the manner of God's self-revealing activity in the world to see if it can appropriately be understood in a way which corresponds to the already known Trinitarian nature of God."[41] What we cannot take for granted, on Hodgson's view, is some sort of established doctrine which we can test for its correspondence to God's actions. "We are, on the contrary, seeking to look at the activity of God to see if it is of such unquestionably threefold character that we are forced . . . to postulate a threefold character in God himself."[42] God's activity, even his activity in salvation and in bringing about a consciousness of having been adopted, simply doesn't produce the kind of inevitable and unquestionable threefoldness that would be required for even a fairly thin account of Trinitarianism. The divine actions under consideration can nearly all be construed in multiple ways, yielding accounts of the divine agents that are twofold, threefold, fourfold, or morefold.

By way of illustration, Wiles contrasts pre-Nicene ways of talking about the Trinity with Nicene ways. Theologians of the first three centuries were notoriously inconsistent among themselves about whether certain activities were best attributed to the Son or to the Spirit: they agreed that the figure of wisdom in person was useful for talking about God's ways with the world, but which person was wisdom? Wisdom pneumatology and wisdom Christology vied with each other, seeming either interchangeable or equally viable. Coming to terms with the two poles of divine transcendence and immanence, early patristic thought frequently fell into a binitarian form. If these theologians nevertheless pushed through to make Trinitarian statements, it was more nearly in spite of their analysis of the history of salvation and of Christian experience than because of it. What accounts for this? Wiles says "the answer appears to be that the threefold form was a basic datum for Christian thought from the very beginning."[43] They had the threefold distinction before they began to interpret the actions.

While the pre-Nicene theologians tended to think of the three persons performing distinct actions, however much they might disagree about who did what, Nicene theologians were strongly motivated to resist heresy by seeing a correspondence between the undivided being

---

41. Ibid., 93.
42. Ibid.
43. Ibid., 99.

of the Trinity and the undivided work of the Trinity. "Time and again, in arguing for the identity of substance between the three persons of the Trinity, they base their case upon the identity of their operations."[44] But with this shift in patristic argumentation, what becomes of our ability to read Trinitarian distinctions off of salvation history? If the external works of the Trinity are undivided, they cannot be the basis of our knowledge of Trinitarian distinctions. Wiles rightly points out that for Athanasius, the answer is verbal, even textual: he is guided all the while by the baptismal command in Matthew 28.[45] And this holds true also for the Cappadocians, whose "belief in the three persons has the same basis as that of Athanasius, with an even greater emphasis upon the baptismal formula."[46] Wiles's conclusion is that "Dr. Hodgson's approach will not carry us the whole way to the fully articulated doctrine of the Trinity," because "the Cappadocian construction was built upon and logically requires the foundation belief that the threefold form of the Godhead is a datum of revelation given in clear propositional form."[47]

So Wiles's critique of Hodgson leads to the Bible—and a Bible that contains verbal-propositional revelation at that. It may even seem that Wiles was herding the argument toward that orthodox conclusion from the outset. But Wiles is not that kind of theologian.[48] He canvases three possible conclusions for his argument. The first option would be to accept divine revelation in the form of propositions. Of this option, he says that "one must simply say that it appears to conflict with the whole idea of the nature of revelation to which biblical criticism has led us,"[49]

---

44. Ibid., 101.

45. Athanasius, *Letters to Serapion concerning the Holy Spirit* 4:3–6 (cited in Wiles, "Some Reflections," 101).

46. Wiles, "Some Reflections," 102. See chapter 5 below for a study of Nazianzus's use of the baptismal command.

47. Ibid., 104. Wiles does not call into question here Hodgson's claims about divine action. An entirely different line of thought would follow for theologians who could not accept straightforward claims about God taking action in history, with an entirely different approach to Trinitarianism. One of the trailheads for that sort of theology is Langdon Gilkey's influential article "Cosmology, Ontology and the Travail of Biblical Language," *Journal of Religion* 41 (July 1961): 196–203. Perhaps by the time he gave the 1986 Bampton Lectures, Wiles was more clearly on this track. See the rejection of miracles in Maurice Wiles, *God's Action in the World* (London: SCM, 1986).

48. Wiles, having devoted more attention than Hodgson to patristics, easily recognized that the church fathers pervasively approached Scripture as a source of divine statements. Hodgson, who should have known better, permitted himself the optical illusion of attributing this view only to more recent orthodoxies. Hodgson wrote as if new "post-critical" approaches to Scripture solved a problem of recent centuries; Wiles rightly saw that the new doctrine of revelation went against the grain of the entire Christian tradition so far. He also endorsed the newer view and accepted the break with tradition. Wiles was thus in two senses more radical.

49. Wiles, "Some Reflections," 104.

since this is a conclusion Wiles is no more inclined to consider than is Hodgson. He quickly moves on.

A second option would be to trace a threefoldness in every act of God, such that the Trinity could be known by an intensive analysis of every divine act rather than by parceling out the divine actions among the persons serially. Wiles attributes something like this view to Karl Barth (he is thinking of Barth's elaboration of revelation as having a threefold "God reveals himself as Lord" structure, or needing a Trinitarian explanation) and finds it wanting: "The whole argument sounds suspiciously like a later rationalization to support a doctrine really based on [the first, verbal-propositional alternative] and now in search of a new foundation."[50] To pursue this line, one would at least need to alleviate suspicions by offering good reasons that a fundamentally new method would yield the original result, and also show that the old method was not secretly and unwarrantedly still doing some of the work under cover of the new. Lacking that, Wiles's suspicions seem warranted, and Hodgson's project is less a forward advance than an exercise in retreating and retrenching.

Wiles proposes a striking third alternative. Perhaps, after all, "our Trinity of revelation is an arbitrary analysis of the activity of God, which though of value in Christian thought and devotion is not of essential significance."[51] Whatever may be "of essential significance" to the Christian doctrine of God, this "arbitrary analysis" yielding a threefold pattern would not be. It would instead have the character of a helpful interpretive structure for the various phenomena of Christian spiritual experience. This option, notes Wiles, "is admittedly revolutionary, but no more so than the break-away from the idea of propositional revelation of which it appears to be the logical conclusion."[52] Wiles completes his thought project with a few gestures toward some possible non-triadic construals of God.[53] This seems to be the direction Wiles commends, though he does not himself take up the constructive project.

The crucial point in Wiles's critique is that "the break-away from the idea of propositional revelation" ought to be recognized as revolutionary,

---

50. Ibid., 105.
51. Ibid., 104.
52. Ibid., 105.
53. Wiles makes a wondrously feeble attempt to indicate a couple of places in the tradition where such reconfigurations might find precedent. His appeal to Hippolytus is merely peculiar; his appeal to Aquinas perverse. These buttresses actually weaken and clutter his case, which can stand or fall without them.

and that its displacement by a doctrine of divine action plus the illumination of the interpreters has a "logical conclusion" for the doctrine of the Trinity. That conclusion is the dissolution of the doctrine of eternal threeness in God. Wiles summarizes the implications of his argument thus:

> The "threeness" of the completed orthodox doctrine of the Trinity can logically be known only on the basis of a propositional revelation about the inner mysteries of the Godhead or through some other kind of specific authoritative revelation. If that basis be removed, then the necessity (though not necessarily the desirability or the value) of Trinitarian thought is removed.[54]

Hodgson's lovely analysis of the doctrine of the Trinity as a conceptual unfolding of the Christian experience of adoption (participation by the Spirit in sonship from the Father) may still be edifying, satisfying, and valuable, but what it can never be is necessary or sufficient reason for claiming there is a corresponding eternal threeness behind this divine act of salvation. On the one hand, the externally unified character of divine action suggests undifferentiated oneness in God; on the other hand, "no convincing reason can be given why, in view of the rich manifoldness of divine functions and activities, the number of the hypostases may not be increased indefinitely."[55] Historically speaking, the doctrine of the Trinity was formulated by theologians who believed they were working with some amount of propositional revelation that guided their interpretation of the events. Dogmatically speaking, the doctrine cannot get any purchase on the eternal being of God if all propositional revelation is deemed inadmissible for theological reflection or downgraded to human reflection on inspired insight. But Hodgson does not view his meditation on the Trinitarian form of adoptive sonship to be merely an edifying but optional exercise. In the absence of verbal revelation, Hodgson sets forth his work as another foundation for our knowledge of the eternal Trinity.[56]

---

54. Wiles, "Some Reflections," 106.

55. Ibid., citing D. M. Edwards, *Christianity and Philosophy* (Edinburgh: T&T Clark, 1932), 339, 354–55.

56. Hodgson's book has more problems than its denial of propositional revelation, though it is striking how many of its problems can be traced to this. For example, Hodgson admits he has "not the least idea of what is meant by either filiation or procession in respect of the divine Being," a fact we might expect to limit his exposition of adoption, as well

RAHNER'S VERSION

Leonard Hodgson's presuppositions about the nature of divine revelation have been shared widely in modern systematic theology. Even when they are not made explicit, the influence these presuppositions exert on Trinitarian theology tends toward similar ends. When Karl Rahner announced as his theological *Grundaxiom* that the economic Trinity is the immanent Trinity and vice versa, he had many reasons for doing so.[57] The reason we are concerned with is his rejection of the notion that divine revelation was verbal-propositional. Rahner had a more sophisticated philosophical outlook than Hodgson, elaborated with a Teutonic grandeur (in running dialogue with Martin Heidegger and Joseph Maréchal) that contrasts with Hodgson's Oxonian nonchalance ("we can take for granted a post-critical approach"). A simple retrenchment from words to historical events was not available to Rahner, for complex reasons.

Briefly, those reasons are as follows: Rahner's concept of revelation is based on an a priori human openness toward God as a condition of all possible experience. Human nature, according to Rahner, is structurally open to an infinite horizon that is the necessary condition of human acts of self-transcendence (such as knowledge and will). This unbounded background of human experience is present to everybody as a pre-apprehension (*Vorgriff*) of something ever greater. It is present but not hepatized, which means that people need not be aware of it. A person can perform acts of self-transcendent thinking and willing without conceiving of the transcendent reality that makes these acts possible. This transcendent reality is being–itself, which is a way of apprehending God. It is not passively available for humans to grasp; if a human is to grasp it, it must reveal itself. Divine self-communication actually happens when the transcendental crosses over and becomes categorical in human history and experience. The crossing over is both the actual history of the coming of the Son incarnate and the graced reception of salvation by a human subject (which takes place in the Holy Spirit).

as to hobble his account of the divine life. In his review, E. J. Fortman ventures that the disorder and weakness in Hodgson's Trinitarianism "seems to stem proximately from his neglect of the doctrine of processions, ultimately from his attempt to present the doctrine of the Trinity without some of its essential elements" (Fortman, review of *The Doctrine of the Trinity*, 176).

57. Fred Sanders, *The Image of the Immanent Trinity: Rahner's Rule and the Theological Interpretation of Scripture* (New York: Lang: 2005), 47–82.

Rahner's view is complex, and this explanation is greatly telescoped,[58] but we have said enough to see why Rahner cannot simply decamp from revelation in words to revelation in events, as Hodgson does. For Rahner, historical events, illuminated insights, and interpretive words are all instances of the transcendent itself becoming concretely apprehended, but they cannot be conceived of as interventions into the world by God. Rahner's constant nemesis was extrinsicism, a way of relating God and the created order merely externally. In the doctrine of providence, extrinsicism would suggest that for God to do a particular work in the world, he needed to suspend the laws of nature. In the doctrine of grace, extrinsicism would suggest that human nature could be considered a relatively complete thing in itself, with salvation as an extra blessing added on top of it. In the doctrine of revelation, extrinsicism would suggest the merely verbal transmission of information from a speaker to a hearer, transferring ideas without imparting the self. In general and on principle, Rahner is opposed to any notion of divine intervention from without, except the sort that are particularizations of the one great intervention in which God stands in relation to the world as its underlying cause.[59] Certain occurrences in human history and experience are "the becoming historical and . . . concrete of that 'intervention' in which God as the transcendental ground of the world has from the outset embedded Godself in the world as its self-communicating ground."[60] Rahner's approach has the advantage of clearing away from the field of theology any suggestion that God's works are a series of discrete episodes, each bearing its own meaning. Each divine act must mean everything, as a concretizing of the one transcendent relation. Grace is not the sum total of random acts of divine

---

58. Rahner's thought is a form of transcendental Thomism, that is, a theology inspired by Thomas Aquinas, with a Kantian and Heideggerian inflection. His foundational commitments are most on display in his *Hearer of the Word: Laying the Foundation for a Philosophy of Religion* (New York: Bloomsbury Academic, 1994); the nearest he came to a complete synthesis of his thought was *Foundations of Christian Faith: An Introduction to the Idea of Christianity* (New York: Crossroad, 1978).

59. This metaphysical allergy to intervention is something Rahner's thought shares with that of his contemporary Paul Tillich, who described verbal revelation, petitionary prayer, and miracles as "demonic" in conceptual structure. Tillich viewed all such historical concretions as a finite thing claiming finality (his definition of demonic). The demonic charge is pervasive in Tillich's writings; it is most fully elaborated in his *Systematic Theology*, vol. 1 (Chicago: University of Chicago Press, 1951), 216–17. Rahner's writing style was too circumspect to permit him such invective and radical posturing.

60. Rahner, *Foundations of Christian Faith*, 87, quoted in Dennis W. Jowers, *Karl Rahner's Trinitarian Axiom: The Economic Trinity Is the Immanent Trinity and Vice Versa* (Lewiston, NY: Mellen, 2006), 85–86.

kindness. Coming to awareness of God, however shocking the experience may be, is always a matter of making contact with the ultimate truth underlying one's own existence.[61]

If a certain concentration of the doctrines of grace and revelation counts as advantages of Rahner's project, nevertheless the attendant disadvantages for the doctrine of the Trinity are considerable. Though metaphysically thicker than Hodgson's, Rahner's view of revelation commits him to the same sort of task. He must read the reality of the Trinity off of the events of salvation history, eschewing any appeal to verbal-propositional revelation as the foundation of the doctrine. This is why Rahner treats the economy of salvation as the exclusive source of our knowledge of the Trinity and provides the epistemological reason for Rahner's Rule: "The economic Trinity is the immanent Trinity." By Rahner's lights, it must be. Rahner's seminal work, *The Trinity*, contributed much to the surge of attention the doctrine received in the late twentieth century. Few have noted the way Rahner's approach to the Trinity is constrained by his doctrine of revelation. Dennis Jowers's 2006 book, *Karl Rahner's Trinitarian Axiom*, was among the first to call into question "the propriety of making the economy of salvation Trinitarian theology's exclusive starting point."[62] Jowers argued contra Rahner that the doctrine of the Trinity requires "some basis other than, or at least some basis supplementary to, the divine acts that make up the economy of salvation" and went on to propose that "it seems both more plausible and more orthodox to trace human knowledge of the Trinity ultimately to a cognitive and at least mediately verbal revelation of God."[63] Rahner is utterly opposed to the sort of approach Jowers identifies as normative. Even if such verbal revelation were a possibility, according to Rahner, it would be inadequate for God's purposes because all it would deliver to human recipients is an external word about something mysterious; the resulting doctrine about the Trinity would be "unintelligible and insignificant." Rahner dreads this verbal extrinsicism, holding instead that "in order for human beings to know the Trinity itself . . . they must experience God's triune nature in some way in the depths of their

---

61. How Rahner correlates the twofold self-communication of God (in Christ and in the uncreated grace that is the Holy Spirit) with the course of salvation history and then with a psychological analogy is a very dense matter. See Catherine Mowry LaCugna's brief introduction to these issues in the Milestones in Catholic Theology reissue of Rahner's *The Trinity* (New York: Crossroad, 1997).

62. Jowers, *Karl Rahner's Trinitarian Axiom*, iv.

63. Ibid., vi.

own being; indeed, the Trinity must become, in some sense, an aspect of their being."[64]

Rahner is able to treat the words of Scripture as revelation only by viewing their "material contents" as "verbalized objectifications of the 'revelation' which is already present in the gratuitous radicalizing of human transcendentality in God's self-communication."[65] This enables Rahner to appeal to Scripture's statements pervasively enough that the reader may fail to notice how differently the words of Scripture function for his doctrine of the Trinity. Jowers points out:

> Rahner's view of the content of Christian revelation renders the doctrine of the Trinity, as traditionally understood, quite problematic. For in the traditional view, the acts of the Trinitarian persons *ad extra* are absolutely indistinguishable, so that neither creation nor grace engenders elements in human experience from which one can legitimately infer the existence of the immanent Trinity. In order for human beings to possess any certain knowledge at all about the tripersonality of God, the traditional view holds, God must reveal this tripersonality to them through a conceptual, and even verbal, revelation. In Rahner's nonmiraculous understanding of Christianity, however, the kind of divine intervention necessary for the conveyance of such a revelation simply does not occur.[66]

Rahner must reconstruct the doctrine of the Trinity, which the early church arrived at through its interpretation of divine actions plus its construal of inspired words, with only half the equipment the church fathers had at their disposal. With words ruled out in advance, he is left with actions (and actions of a peculiarly transcendental-but-concretized sort). Those actions, furthermore, are tasked with letting us distinguish the three persons of the Trinity at all, which pits Rahner's project against the pro-Nicene axiom that the external operations of the Trinity are undivided.

Rahner himself did not choose to attack that patristic dictum

---

64. Ibid., 86. "Part of their own being" may be a stark way of putting it, but Jowers is paraphrasing what Rahner has elaborated and nuanced throughout his corpus under the headings of obediential potency, the supernatural existential, and quasi-formal causality as the created termini of God's self-communication. The salient point is that the word of God does not come as an alien thing but comes to those whose existence is to hear it.

65. Cited in ibid., 12.

66. Ibid., 85.

directly,[67] nor did he draw all the conclusions that some interpreters drew from his project. For instance, though Rahner himself tended away from social Trinitarianism (even warning that the word *person* was no longer helpful, given its modern connotations), subsequent proponents of a social Trinity have often arrived at their views starting from Rahner's reading of the stripped economy. Similarly, while advocates of a thoroughly historicized ontology have flocked to Rahner's Trinitarianism (perhaps even more than to Hegel's), the whole point of Rahner's own ontology was to synthesize historicist elements with transcendental elements. But the enthusiastic reception of Rahner's *The Trinity* followed very closely Rahner's own sense of excitement about the possibilities it opened up for Trinitarianism, which seemed like practically a new research agenda for theology. His intense focus on the economy of salvation as the exclusive starting point for the doctrine of the Trinity was greeted as the key that unlocked a storehouse of salvation-historical theological possibilities. It is certainly possible to see the impulse of Rahner's drastically economic Trinitarianism as having led to a beneficial recentering of modern Trinitarian thought onto salvation history.[68] But Jowers's critique is correct: Rahner's Trinitarian method is so constrained by his understanding of revelation that it can only begin and end in a self-imposed revelatory poverty.[69] Having received the doctrine of the Trinity from the theological tradition, Rahner performs a creative act of dogmatic reverse engineering to build it again in modern idiom. But "modern idiom" entails, for him, actions without words.

When Hodgson eschewed verbal-propositional revelation on principle, it forced him to rebuild the doctrine of the Trinity from an analysis of the Christian experience of adopted sonship. Under duress, we might say, he performed admirably, and his account of Trinitarian soteriology is an abiding contribution in this field. Likewise, Rahner's deflection from verbal-propositional revelation exerted such pressure on his Trinitarianism that he forced himself to find everything he

---

67. What he did single out for criticism was the more vulnerable scholastic thesis that any person of the Trinity could have become incarnate. The scholastic thesis is, in fact, defensible if stated with due caution.

68. I have argued this rosy view in a section titled "Recentering Trinitarianism on the Economy of Salvation," in "The Trinity," in *The Oxford Handbook of Systematic Theology*, ed. John Webster, Kathryn Tanner, and Iain Torrance (New York: Oxford University Press, 2007), 39–42.

69. See Fred Sanders, "Review of Dennis W. Jowers, *Karl Rahner's Trinitarian Axiom: The Economic Trinity Is the Immanent Trinity and Vice Versa*," in *International Journal of Systematic Theology* 11:3 (July 2009): 370–72.

needed in the economy. The resulting analysis of the economic Trinity is unusually rich and well integrated, having also inspired a host of later theological projects. A great deal of late modern Trinitarian theology can be viewed as a necessary recentering on the events of salvation history, especially if we grant the assumption that this phase had been preceded by an overemphasis on the merely propositional.[70] Certainly much can be accomplished through a careful reading of the significant events that constitute the economy of salvation, and insights have abounded for theologians investigating the presuppositions and implications of that economy. But unless we are content with a decidedly nonclassical shape for the doctrine of the Trinity, we must not restrict ourselves to revelation through events without words. The doctrine did not arise in that way (this is a historical claim), because it could not have arisen that way (a systematic claim). To theologize as if it could have is to theologize in self-imposed poverty, and inevitably to beg and borrow concepts and categories from other sources.[71]

These representative projects showcase the torsions generated by theologies of revelation that are finally inhospitable to the doctrine of the Trinity. Such doctrines of revelation are inhospitable for two reasons. First, they dissolve the inner unity between act and word, a unity that constitutes revelation in general and Trinitarian revelation above all. Second, in so doing they abstract away from the actual communicative missions of the teaching Son and the testifying Spirit. We will consider both issues below. It is remarkable, however, that modern Trinitarian theologies underwritten by such doctrines of revelation have nevertheless managed to be fruitful and productive. That they have indeed been so is partly a testament to the substantial correctness and vigor of other doctrinal complexes at work in the projects that carry them, and partly a testament to the fact that theologies of this sort work hard to compensate for their anti-propositional bias by attending very closely to the meanings latent in the history of salvation or the order of salvation. Here we face trade-offs. The benefits of such reductionism are mostly concentrated in soteriology; the costs are mostly registered in the doctrine of God. Soteriology is intensified,

---

70. This is in itself a dubious enough assumption. See the evidence marshaled against it in Fred Sanders, "The Trinity," in *Mapping Modern Theology: A Thematic and Historical Introduction*, ed. Kelly Kapic and Bruce McCormack (Grand Rapids: Baker Academic, 2012), 38–45.

71. We might describe Rahner himself as an anonymous propositionalist, despite his protestations to the contrary.

but the doctrine of God is shallowed. Trinitarian theology, however, is precisely the doctrine of God correlated with the doctrine of salvation, over which it has logical and ontological priority. For this reason, we must seek theologies of revelation that are more adequate to the task of Trinitarian theology.

ACT AND WORD IN AN INNER UNITY

Fortunately, such theologies of revelation are at hand. They were not forgotten even during the peak influence of the defective modern views of revelation we have been reviewing. We now turn to some accounts of revelation that are more hospitable to the doctrine of the Trinity precisely because they show signs of having been formed by a firmer understanding of the communicative missions of the Son and the Holy Spirit.

To stay for a moment within the Roman Catholic ambit, consider Vatican II's *Dei Verbum*.[72] This document exhibits an awareness of all the dangers that so alarm Rahner: extrinsicism, mere verbalism, and a formal concept of revelation stripped of soteriological implications. But its authors opt for a very different safeguard against these dangers.[73] *Dei Verbum* defines revelation as "the action by which God freely makes known the hidden purpose of the divine will and lovingly speaks to human beings as friends, inviting them into fellowship with himself."[74] Revelation is thus the communicative constituent of a plan of salvation,

---

72. Norman P. Tanner ed., *Decrees of the Ecumenical Councils*, vol. 2 (Washington, DC: Georgetown University Press, 1990), 972.

73. As one of the *peritii* advising the bishops of Vatican II, Rahner can himself be counted among the authors of *Dei Verbum*, at least in an extended sense. For an account of the role of the theological advisers in transforming 1962's preparatory schema *De fontibus revelationis* into 1965's *Dei Verbum*, see Jared Wicks, "Vatican II on Revelation: From Behind the Scenes," *Theological Studies* 71 (2010): 637–50. In Wicks's account, it is possible to see how the acts-plus-words schema (mostly mediated from biblical theology by way of Pieter Smulders and Jean Daniélou) displaced a neoscholastic overemphasis on words, and also how an advisory document coauthored by Rahner and Joseph Ratzinger helped set the doctrine of revelation in the widest possible soteriological context. In contrasting Rahner's theology of revelation with that of *Dei Verbum*, I am making the specific point that in his post–Vatican II systematic theology as represented in *Mysterium Salutis* (that is, what became his influential work *The Trinity*) and *Theological Investigations*, Rahner's own characteristic view of revelation limited his options in the doctrine of the Trinity. Of course, Rahner's mature theological agenda, as worked out in detail, was more idiosyncratic and not something he held in common with the bishops and theologians of Vatican II, not to mention with his former coauthor Ratzinger.

74. This is Avery Dulles's paraphrase of *Dei Verbum* §2 in his "Faith and Revelation," in *Systematic Theology: Roman Catholic Perspectives*, ed. Francis Schüssler Fiorenza and John P. Galvin (Minneapolis: Fortress, 1991), 93.

which "unfolds through deeds and words bound together by an inner dynamism."[75] The inner dynamism binding these deeds and words is crucial. *Dei Verbum* carefully avoids giving any formal account of the unifying dynamism, preferring to point consistently to the salvific content itself. The accent falls on God's freedom in making known his will to save, and the definition of revelation in *Dei Verbum* is an intentionally concise placeholder for what is actually revealed, and revealed in the totality of God's economy of salvation. Since what is actually revealed is the saving presence of the Son and the Spirit, being who they are among us and teaching us the truth of salvation, the act-and-word combination is appropriate. As Avery Dulles points out, in the theology of Vatican II, act and word cannot be separated. God's acts may be foundational, but the accompanying words are also absolutely necessary for revelation. Public revelation includes by nature its initial verbalization by the first recipients, and this initial verbalization is constitutive of revelation itself.[76] The deeds underlie the words, but the words complete the deeds. Only together are they the vehicle of revelation. *Dei Verbum* may have been responding to an earlier theology of revelation that was more wooden and reductionistically verbal, but it did not veer into the opposite error of being reductionistically event-oriented. Instead, *Dei Verbum* found its way to a principled equipoise between salvation history and divine speech, God's *opera magnalia* and *locutio divina*.[77]

Many of the theologians of Vatican II later collaborated on the systematic theology project called *Mysterium Salutis*, and it is noteworthy that their reflections on revelation in those volumes were alert to the dynamics of recent biblical studies, as well as to major forces in Protestant theology. In the introduction to the first volume of this foundation of a salvation-historical dogmatics, they indicate some of the reasons behind their focused attention on the actions of God in salvation history:

---

75. Ibid., 95.

76. Ibid., 96. For Roman Catholic articulations of this principle, it is apparently necessary to assign the church, and ultimately the magisterium, a constitutive role as the recipient of this communication. This can range from Rahner's idiosyncratic "Catholic *sola Scriptura* principle" (which incorporated ecclesial reception into the doctrine of Scripture) to the argument that Joseph Ratzinger put forward in the long-unpublished first half of his dissertation on Bonaventure, now available as *Offenbarungsverständnis und Geschichtstheologie Bonaventuras* (Freiburg im Breisgau: Herder, 2009). A masterful recent treatment that states the ecumenical principle well without missing the Roman Catholic application is Matthew Levering, *Engaging the Doctrine of Revelation: The Mediation of the Gospel through Church and Scripture* (Grand Rapids: Baker Academic, 2014).

77. Wicks, "Vatican II on Revelation," 643.

As the Greek fathers say, and as is shown especially in Trinitarian theology, there is no talk about God in his inner threefold life, and therefore no *theologia* in the strong sense of the word, without reference to the *oikonomia*, the self-opening of the triune God in salvation history. And without the depth dimension of *theologia*, all talk about the *oikonomia* and salvation history becomes admittedly flat and merely foreground. What Barth said of evangelical theology holds also for Catholic: "The subject of evangelical theology is God in the history of his acts."[78]

We see here an alertness to salvation history precisely in the interest of a Trinitarian theology that could successfully refer to the eternal being of God. In *Dei Verbum*, it is also carefully elaborated as divine self-communication that takes the form of speech, and of inspired Scriptures.

The need for an adequately comprehensive doctrine of revelation was felt acutely by many in the first half of the twentieth century. One example from a Protestant quarter is J. Gresham Machen's reaction against downgrade trends in modern theology in his 1923 book *Christianity and Liberalism*. Critiquing an ecclesial mood that was hostile to doctrine altogether, Machen insists that even in its primal basis in Scripture, "Christianity is history plus doctrine, fact plus meaning." He goes on to illustrate: "'Christ died' is history, 'for our sins' is doctrine. Without these two elements, joined in an absolutely indissoluble union, there is no Christianity."[79] There is a world of difference between the theological cultures of Vatican II's renewal movement and Machen's Presbyterian conflict, but they share parallel trajectories. Both represented traditions that had recently traced a dialectic from underappreciating the role of divine actions in revelation toward so overestimating it that the role of divine speech was eclipsed, and resolving the conflict by insisting that both be recognized. The differences between their cultures makes it all the more striking that in both contexts, the doctrine of revelation was confessed as event plus word "joined in an absolutely indissoluble union" or "bound together by an inner dynamism."

We should note here a kind of expansion or elaboration of the way the doctrine of revelation is to be stated in a distinctively modern idiom,

---

78. Johannes Feiner and Magnus Löhrer, "Einleitung," in *Die Grundlagen Heilsgeschichtlicher Dogmatik*, vol. 1 of *Mysterium Salutis: Grundriss Heilsgeschichtlicher Dogmatik* (Zurich: Benziger, 1965), xxx (*sic*: this is p. 30 of the introduction).

79. J. Gresham Machen, *Christianity and Liberalism* (New York: Macmillan, 1923), 27.

though the principle itself is recognizably the same as John of Damascus's dictum that knowledge of the Trinity must come from the communicative intent of the persons of the Trinity. Already in the fourth century, Hilary of Poitiers had integrated the doctrine of the Trinity and the doctrine of revelation around the recognition that "He whom we can know only through His own utterances is a fitting witness concerning Himself."[80] Perhaps in the patristic period the idea of divine speech was so compactly fused with other aspects of revelation that it was rarely teased out from them. Not so in the modern period. Already by the sixteenth century, John Calvin was using Hilary's theology of Trinitarian revelation in a new context that required a more explicit differentiation of modes of communication. Arguing against the power of visual images to secure true knowledge of God, Calvin cited Hilary, with a special emphasis on the verbal (and not visual) element of God's self-testimony.[81] When historical modes of thought became prevalent in the period after the Enlightenment, there was a heightened awareness in theology of the fundamental importance of divine actions in history.[82] These threatened for a while to set themselves up as independent tracks of revelation, as we have seen. Perhaps God's self-testimony is, after all, a series of actions we have only been calling testimony (a verbal category) by analogy; perhaps "speech" always meant "act," and the ancient tradition was not aware of it. What takes place in Vatican II and in certain Protestant reactions against modernism is a consolidation and reunification of act and word in revelation, in a situation where history has been given its due, but not more than its due. In retrospect, the patristic principle that God is his own best witness may seem not so much naively unaware of the difference between act and word as a broad enough principle to contain within itself the coming developments. The differentiation of act and word in modern theologies of revelation is a real advance in understanding, as long as the two are joined "in an absolutely indissoluble union."

---

80. Hilary of Poitiers, *On the Trinity* 1:18.

81. John Calvin, *Institutes of the Christian Religion*, vol. 1, ed. John T. McNeill (Philadelphia: Westminster, 1960), 1.11.1, 100 n. 2.

82. The constructive case for the centrality of historical categories in all theological fields is well argued in the interdisciplinary set of essays from "the Heidelberg Circle," in *Revelation as History*, ed. Wolfhart Pannenberg (New York: Macmillan, 1961). Though the contributors position themselves too polemically over against "theologies of the word," they mostly resist the temptation to resolve all biblical claims of divine speech into metaphors for divine actions or to historicize ontology without remainder. Though the book is a bit of a period piece, the authors are already reaching out for some type of synthesis.

VERBAL REVELATION AND SCRIPTURE

Machen's point was extended, somewhat less polemically but with equal insistence, by J. I. Packer within the midcentury evangelical world. "According to Scripture," Packer wrote, "God reveals Himself to men both by exercising power for them and by teaching truth to them. Indeed, the biblical position is that the mighty acts of God are not revelation to man at all, except in so far as they are accompanied by words of God to explain them. Leave man to guess God's mind and purpose, and he will guess wrong; he can guess it only by being told it."[83]

Packer's "accompanied by words" may seem to be weaker language than Machen's "absolutely indissoluble union" or *Dei Verbum*'s "inner dynamism," but Packer's intent is the same. He insists, contra various voices calling for a total reinvestment of theological commitment into revelatory actions rather than revelatory words, that revelation is essentially but not exclusively verbal. "No historical event, as such, can make God known to anyone unless God Himself discloses its meaning and place in His plan."[84] Mere illumination of the mind of the witness is not adequate, because God himself must testify about the intended meaning of the action.[85] If providential events occur, they cannot be known to be part of God's communicative intent without God's own testimony saying so. "Their link, if any, with His saving purpose cannot be known until He Himself informs us of it. No event is self-interpreting at this level."[86] Even the exodus might have been "only one of many tribal migrations that history knows (cf. Amos 9:7)"[87] during that time period. What sets the exodus apart as the saving act in which God identifies himself with his people and identifies them with himself is that God speaks on his own behalf to explain the significance borne by the mighty act. Even the death and burial of Jesus, says Packer,

---

83. J. I. Packer, *"Fundamentalism" and the Word of God* (Leicester, UK: Inter-Varsity Press, 1958), 92.

84. J. I. Packer, *God Has Spoken: Revelation and the Bible*, 3rd ed. (Grand Rapids: Baker, 1994), 72.

85. Dissenting judgments abound, of course. An especially cogent alternative handling of the same issues in the same context is found in James Orr, *Revelation and Inspiration* (London: Duckworth, 1910). More recently, a number of alternative approaches use different means to the same basic ends. For the fruitfulness of speech-act theory in this field, see Timothy Ward, *Word and Supplement* (New York: Oxford University Press, 2002), as well as Kevin Vanhoozer, *First Theology: God, Scripture & Hermeneutics* (Downers Grove, IL: InterVarsity Press, 2002), chs. 5 and 6.

86. Packer, *God Has Spoken*, 72.

87. Ibid., 72–73.

extending the argument to the uttermost, "was only one of many Roman executions."[88]

Packer takes these actions to be meaningful events in themselves, intended by God to accomplish salvation and to be the foundation of communicating knowledge of the divine Savior to us. But in order for this inherent meaning to cross over into our sphere, divine speech must take place. "Whoever could have guessed the unique saving significance of these events, had not God Himself spoken to tell us?"[89] The inherent meaning of any particular divine act is not in suspense in Packer's view, but the communication of that meaning to us is. Redemptive actions without explanation might be salvation, but they would not be revelation, and the biblical view of salvation is that it includes awareness of salvation imparted by revelation. "We have received . . . the Spirit who is from God," wrote the apostle Paul, "that we might understand the things freely given us by God" (1 Cor 2:12).

> All history is, in one sense, God's deed, but none of it reveals Him except in so far as He Himself talks to us about it. God's revelation is not through deeds without words (a dumb charade!) any more than it is through words without deeds; but it is through deeds which He speaks to interpret, or, putting it more biblically, through words which His deeds confirm and fulfill. The fact we must face is that if there is no verbal revelation, there is no revelation at all, not even in the life, death, and resurrection of Jesus of Nazareth.[90]

There are two antitheses here that Packer may seem to have stated too sharply. The first lurks in the order he assigns to words and deeds, preferring to say that God speaks words and then confirms and fulfills them with deeds, rather than that God does deeds and interprets them with words. It seems that Packer's polemical context, which determines his characteristic tight focus on the doctrine of Scripture as a subfield of the doctrine of revelation, may account for the sharpness of the statement. He is indicating the words of the prophets and apostles. The deeds-*fulfilling*-words schema better accounts for predictive prophecy in the Old Testament, and its alternate phrasing as deeds-*confirming*-words

---

88. Ibid., 73.
89. Ibid.
90. Ibid.

better accounts for how the apostolic message was received in the New: "Our gospel came to you not only in word, but also in power and in the Holy Spirit . . . You accepted it not as the word of men but as what it really is, the word of God, which is at work in you believers" (1 Thess 1:5; 2:13; see Heb 2:3–4). Beyond this immediate application to the doctrine of Scripture, the preferred schema would run *words-interpreting-deeds*, because it recognizes the foundational character of the events. Salvation is accomplished and explained; the understanding follows on the achieving. God shows and tells, speaking forth the meaning inherent in what he does.

The other contrast that may seem overdrawn is Packer's statement that "if there is no verbal revelation, there is no revelation at all, not even in the life, death, and resurrection of Jesus of Nazareth." Surely the actions of Jesus are revelatory. Or rather, surely the one great divine action that constitutes the incarnation, life, death, and resurrection of Jesus is in itself revelation. Can we really say that the death and resurrection of Jesus are mute until accompanied by verbal and propositional truths? It seems an extreme way to make the point. But there is at least one deep reason to affirm, with Packer, the point that revelation in Christ is not reducible to revelation through act. Earlier we argued that theologies of revelation, though otherwise sound, could render themselves inhospitable to the doctrine of the Trinity in two ways. The first is to dissolve the inner unity between act and word, a unity without which the revelatory effect of the history of salvation is muffled or muted, and without which the doctrine would not have been established and cannot thrive. In the next chapter, we will examine the second way to make a doctrine of revelation inhospitable to Trinitarianism, which is to abstract away from the actual communicative missions of the teaching Son and the testifying Spirit.

The Trinity is a revealed mystery in the biblical sense of the word mystery. And it is not enough to list it alongside other mysteries, because it concerns the entire scope of salvation history and makes known the actual identity of God. As a doctrine covering territory so deep and wide, it is a mystery without peers; it is the one primordial mystery of God's being and works. The triunity of God has always been, was once concealed, and is now revealed. The manner of its revelation should establish the order and structure of the doctrine concerning it, as well as the order and structure of adjacent doctrines like revelation and salvation.

CHAPTER 3

COMMUNICATIVE MISSIONS

The Trinity was revealed when God the Father sent the Son and the Holy Spirit. When these two missions, personal and eloquently self-interpreting, are acknowledged as the actual revelation of the Trinity, all the other media of theological understanding are demoted to ministerial rather than magisterial status. Experience and tradition are manifestly subordinate to the missions, and even Scripture is ordered under the missions, though in a more complex manner.

Jesus came praying and preaching, and the Spirit bears witness. The substance of the economy of salvation is constituted by the missions of the Son and the Holy Spirit, sent in the fullness of time by the Father in fulfillment of the vast preparatory phase during which, not yet sent forth, they worked more or less anonymously.

Both missions are communicative acts in a very thick sense; they occur with and as instruction at every point. The incarnation and Pentecost are self-interpreting and mutually interpreting, and not only in the rather metaphorical sense that they are events whose meaning is apparent. They are self-interpreting in the more literal sense that the Son is the rabbi who explains his own identity and mission in his oral teaching ministry,[1] and "the Spirit is the one who testifies, because the Spirit is the truth" (1 John 5:6), the one who spoke through the

---

1. See various places in the canonical gospels, but especially Mark 13; Matthew 5–7; John 13–17.

prophets (Acts 1:16; Heb 10:15) and taught words to the apostles (1 Cor 2:13). They are mutually interpreting in that the Son gave instruction about the person and work of the Holy Spirit (John 14:15–17), and the Holy Spirit was the "Spirit of Christ" in the prophets, "predicting the sufferings of Christ and the subsequent glories" (1 Pet 1:11), as well as, after being "sent from heaven," the efficient cause of the preaching of the gospel of Christ (1 Pet 1:12). The actual, concrete, historical missions of the Son and the Holy Spirit include verbal and propositional elements. A theological interpreter could subtract those verbal and propositional elements analytically in order to get a clearer view of the divine actions underlying them, but to do so would not be to grasp the missions themselves. Another theological interpreter could distinguish the two elements precisely in order to insist on their unity, but in doing so should remain alert to the artificiality of the analysis. Yet another theological interpreter could distinguish act and word in the missions of the Son and Spirit in order to salvage the acts (as more defensible for modern sensibilities) and set aside the words (as relatively less defensible). But to do so is to turn from interpreting the actual missions to interpreting what remains after a subtractive process has been applied. The Trinitarian missions minus the words of the speaking persons are an abstraction. The missions themselves are eloquent, conversational, and word-bearing.[2]

MORE THAN WORDS, BUT NOT LESS

The point of reiterating this is, of course, a very narrow one: verbal revelation must be acknowledged at the very foundation of Trinitarian revelation. Revelatory words are not epiphenomenal to revelatory acts. Rather they are equiprimordial and unavoidable. The missions of the Son and the Holy Spirit are irreducibly verbal, though not exclusively verbal.

Because the grim shadow of merely verbal-propositional revelation still hovers over the theological landscape, at least in conservative quarters, it is worth taking a moment to abjure it. It is very bad. There is no surer way to strip the doctrine of the Trinity of all of its significance and

---

2. The senses in which the work of Christ is self-interpreting are canvassed in John Webster's interpretation of a late phase of Karl Barth's theology, "'Eloquent and Radiant': The Prophetic Office of Christ and the Mission of the Church," in *Barth's Moral Theology: Human Action in Barth's Thought* (Grand Rapids: Eerdmans, 1998), 125–50. The crucial term is that Christ is the effective prophet of his own person and work. Webster returned to some of the implications of this line of thought in his own constructive work in "Resurrection and Scripture," in *The Domain of the Word: Scripture and Theological Reason* (London: Bloomsbury, 2012), 32–49.

desiccate most of its interest than to treat it as the transferal of a set of facts about God that were revealed for their own sake as mere information. The resulting pile of Bible verses or heap of doctrinal statements is theologically and spiritually inert. In such treatments, we get the impression that "we ourselves have nothing to do with this mystery of the Holy Trinity except to know something 'about it' through revelation."[3] This dry approach, with its reduction of revelation to non-soteriological statements whose power is identical with their authority, is now uncommon in academic theology, but still fairly widespread in doctrinal writing for the churches. It would be fruitless to replace the recent overemphasis on revelatory acts with a compensating overemphasis on revelatory words.

Aside from stressing the unity of act and word, there are other defenses against this reductionistically propositionalist threat. The first is the multivalent richness that attends biblical ideas of communication and instruction. To the cognitive element of instruction we must add at least the more holistic moral element. Already in the letter to Titus, when disciples (that is, learners) are educated into the Christian *paideia*, they are told that "the grace of God has appeared, bringing salvation for all people, training [παιδεύουσα] us to renounce ungodliness and worldly passions, and to live self-controlled, upright, and godly lives" (Titus 2:11–12).[4] We can say even more about the kind of holistic education that is the intent of the divine instruction. As Scott Swain points out, "'communication,' theologically understood, involves much more than simply the exchange of words. Communication in its deepest sense is a matter of self-giving, a 'making common' of one's life. As such, it is the basis of interpersonal fellowship and communion. Nevertheless, communication, theologically understood, is never less than an exchange of words."[5] Finally, as Kevin Vanhoozer points out, "the triune God communicates not only information but life and energy as well, through

3. Karl Rahner, *The Trinity* (New York: Herder, 1997), 14. This is part of Rahner's famous lament on the deplorable state of the doctrine of the Trinity in the early twentieth century, which I have elsewhere called "the most frequently quoted passages in all of the Trinitarian literature since 1970" (my *Image of the Immanent Trinity* [New York: Lang, 2005], 56). I also called at that time for a moratorium on using Rahner's lament in the opening pages of books on the Trinity, partly because it had already become a cliché and partly because Rahner's targets were more specific than is usually acknowledged. But my voice has gone unheeded. Authors continue to start their books with Rahner's lament, and publishers continue wrapping those books in Rublev images.

4. For one angle on how the early church was organized to provide intellectual and spiritual formation for disciples, see Claire Smith, *Pauline Communities as "Scholastic Communities": A Study of the Vocabulary of "Teaching" in 1 Corinthians, 1 and 2 Timothy and Titus* (Tübingen: Mohr Siebeck, 2012).

5. Scott R. Swain, *Trinity, Revelation, and Reading* (London: T&T Clark, 2011), 8.

Word and Spirit."[6] There is more to the missions of the Word and the Spirit than instruction, but not less, because the economy of salvation is also always an economy of divine self-revelation.

If our object of inquiry is the actual, concrete missions of the Son and Spirit, there is no need to choose between word and act. Because the Son and the Holy Spirit are together the center, or the culminating point, of divine self-revelation, they are also the most conspicuous exhibit of its pervasive act-plus-word character. The absolutely indissoluble union of God's act and speech took on flesh in Christ and were poured out on all flesh in the Spirit. The incarnate Son and the outpoured Holy Spirit are divine acts that speak forth their own meanings, in person. They speak that meaning to us, because they speak it to each other. And here is a mystery.

The Trinity was revealed in person when the Father sent the Son and the Holy Spirit. They came among us speaking to and about each other as they carried out the work of salvation. One of the (perhaps unintended) casualties of the modern overinvestment in act at the expense of speech is that the conversation among the Father, Son, and Holy Spirit was for some time harder to discern in Scripture, and harder to credit when it was discerned. If God does not actually speak, it follows necessarily that the Father and the Son do not speak to each other in the Spirit. Losing our grip on the Trinity's speech to us, we dropped something even bigger, which is the Trinity's speech within itself about us, and behind that, the Trinity's own conversation above us. The eternal triune conversation behind the salvation-historical triune revelation is the dimension of depth that alone can orient us to the right interpretation of what God does and says in the economy of salvation. "Because the way God is in the economy corresponds to the way God is in himself," Vanhoozer writes, "we may conclude that the Father, Son, and Spirit are merely continuing in history a communicative activity that characterizes their perfect life together . . . Hence this triune dialogue in history fully corresponds to the conversation God is in himself."[7] That eternal interchange of light and love is the living fullness that funds the revelatory economy of redemption.[8] We know that the eternal conversation of the Trinity above

---

6. Kevin J. Vanhoozer, *Remythologizing Theology: Divine Action, Passion, and Authorship* (New York: Cambridge University Press, 2010), 177.

7. Ibid., 251. Later he states the principle even more programmatically: "The economic Trinity is, or rather communicates, the immanent Trinity" (294).

8. Elaborating the implications of this under the banner of "communicative theism" is the burden of Vanhoozer's *Remythologizing Theology*. See especially 243: "We begin, then, with a brief description of the inner life of the triune God—the eternal doings of Father, Son, and

all worlds is real because hints, callbacks, and allusions to it abound in the conversation that takes place among us when the Son and the Holy Spirit show up in person, still conversing with and about each other and the Father. As Vanhoozer says, "We come closest to understanding God's inner life by attending to the intra-Trinitarian communicative action in the economy, particularly the dialogical interaction between the Father and Son that is on conspicuous display in the Fourth Gospel."[9] As we will argue in chapter 8, there is ample reason to extend the reach of that dialogical interaction beyond the Gospels, even into the Old Testament.

But there is an obliqueness to this verbal revelation that matters a great deal for how we understand the doctrine of the Trinity to be a biblical doctrine. As Robert Jenson points out, we go amiss if we rifle through Scripture looking for sentences about the Trinity in the genre of doctrinal formulation. Instead, "if the doctrine of Trinity" is in the Bible, it may be there as a feature "of the narration, indeed, of the narrating."[10] The indirectness of the revelation, consisting in the fact that the information is transmitted not so much in the content of the sentences as in their manner, will be especially important when attending to the Old Testament, where the absence of sentences about the Trinity is conspicuous. The truth is carried in the fact that the divine characters speak to and about each other, disclosing their personal depth in a way that can only happen in interpersonal dialogue. Something of this is what Charles Gore was indicating when he famously remarked that the doctrine of the Trinity is not so much heard in Scripture as overheard:

It is important to notice that there is no moment when Jesus Christ expressly reveals this doctrine. It was overheard, rather than heard. It was simply that in the gradual process of intercourse with Him, His disciples came to recognize Father, Son, and Holy Ghost as included in their deepening and enlarging thought of God. Christ was often speaking of His relation as Son to the Father, nor did He ever allow His disciples to confuse their sonship with His. He spoke of "my Father" and of "your Father," never—except when dictating to them the words of their prayer—of "our Father." His Sonship belonged

Spirit—to the extent that it can be discerned from the communicative patterns that comprise the economy."

9. Ibid., 261. "There are three main topics in these Father-Son dialogues: mutual glorification; the giving of life; the sharing of love."

10. Robert W. Jenson, "The Bible and the Trinity," *Pro Ecclesia* 11:3 (Summer 2002): 330.

to that transcendental being of His, which in spite of all the close human fellowship which they enjoyed with Him, the disciples could not fail to recognize and to acknowledge.[11]

Jesus did not lecture on the relations of the Trinity—though we should not be afraid to admit that John "the theologian" reports in chapter 17 of his gospel something rather close to a disquisition on the three persons both in their saving missions and "before the foundation of the world." Instead, he lived out the life of the Son of the Father in the Spirit, all the while talking to the Father in the Spirit. B. B. Warfield paraphrased Gore's "overheard, rather than heard" formula into the less evocative but more accurate statement that the Trinity is "not so much inculcated as presupposed" in the New Testament.[12] But the presupposing takes the form of conversation, and readers of the New Testament encounter the Trinitarian presupposition in the form of a dialogue to which we are latecomers.

We began our inquiry into the revelation of the Trinity with the biblical teaching, summarized by John of Damascus, that knowledge of the Trinity is inside knowledge, made public in the fullness of time by the only ones who could make it public: the insiders. Those insiders, the persons of the Trinity, bore witness to themselves and each other in the process of saving the outsiders. As we pursued this theme in relation to the biblical theology of mystery (the unveiling of what was previously hidden) and the indissoluble union of act and word in divine self-revelation, we have argued that the revelation of the Trinity is not only verbal, but conversational. That conversational revelation is among the three persons, the insiders to the being of God. Much of this was already implicit in the ancient Christian conviction that the doctrine of the Trinity is a biblical doctrine, a conviction that led the church fathers to turn resolutely to the Scriptures for the testimony of the persons of the Trinity about each other. In the words of Hilary of Poitiers, "Since no one knoweth the Father save the Son, let our thoughts of the Father be at one with the thoughts of the Son, the only faithful Witness, Who reveals Him to us."[13] And all of this flows from the exclusiveness of the claim that the Trinity is known only through such revelation, not otherwise.

---

11. Charles Gore, *The Incarnation of the Son of God* (London: Murray, 1891), 131.
12. B. B. Warfield, "The Biblical Doctrine of the Trinity," in *Biblical and Theological Studies* (Philadelphia: Presbyterian and Reformed, 1952), 32.
13. Hilary of Poitiers, *On the Trinity* 2:6.

Having closed all other doors, therefore, we will take a moment to check the locks on each of them before proceeding with the substance of the argument. The doctrine of the Trinity arises from revelation, not from experience or tradition. Each of these latter two plays a helpful role in the flourishing of healthy Trinitarian theology, and each of them could plausibly be the point of access to a personal awareness of the Trinity, but neither can be the actual ground of Trinitarianism.

NOT FROM EXPERIENCE

That the doctrine of the Trinity must find some resonance in Christian experience is one of the central certainties of modern Trinitarianism in most of its forms. In itself, the desire that the spiritual reality of God's revealed triunity should register in the experience of the redeemed is laudable and appropriate. Christian salvation is, after all, Trinitarian in its deep structure.[14] Whoever has saving faith has been drawn by the Father (John 6:44) and moved by the Spirit to confess that Jesus is Lord (1 Cor 12:3). Forgiveness of sins happens because the Father puts forward his Son, the righteous one, as a propitiation (Rom 3:24–25). Furthermore, knowledge of God includes a practical aspect, because as James Ussher said, "sound knowledge is knowledge which sinketh from the brain into the heart, and from thence breaketh forth into action, setting head, heart, hand and all a-work."[15]

But in theologies where there has been a drift away from confidence that the Trinity is made known in the history of salvation, there may also be a drive toward seeking the Trinity in the experience of salvation. Such theologies are even less capable of grounding the doctrine of the Trinity than the ones we examined above that attempt to find revelatory adequacy in a wordless history of salvation. A mute economy, if it existed, would at least still be a sequence of divine actions with veiled communicative intent. That would be a more solid foundation than a series of supposedly Trinitarian experiences within the pious consciousness. Friedrich Schleiermacher's ambiguous and minimizing treatment of the doctrine of the Trinity can partly be accounted for by how clearly he understood this: Christian experience does not give

---

14. See my case for this in *The Deep Things of God: How the Trinity Changes Everything* (Wheaton, IL: Crossway: 2010).

15. James Ussher, *Archbishop Ussher's Answer to a Jesuit: With Other Tracts on Popery* (Cambridge: Deighton, 1835), 719.

clear expression to anything that is definitively Trinitarian. No set of triads that could be tracked in the ups and downs of spiritual experience stands out in such clear profile that its only possible interpretation leads to the recognition of three eternal persons in the one essence of God. As Schleiermacher famously pronounced at the end of his *Glaubenslehre*, "This doctrine itself, as ecclesiastically framed, is not an immediate utterance concerning the Christian self-consciousness, but only a combination of several such utterances."[16] As such, the doctrine could find no place within a theology constructed, like Schleiermacher's, on the consistent principles of exegeting the presuppositions and implications of the experienced fact of the consciousness of redemption. "Who would venture to say that the impression made by the divine in Christ obliges us to conceive such an eternal distinction as its basis?"[17] Insofar as theologians in Schleiermacher's lineage were able to secure the doctrine of the Trinity in the Christian confession, they had to do so by supplementing his method by recourse to other principles, chiefly Scripture and church confessions.

Karl Rahner, even in pitched battle with the extrinsicism of a merely verbal revelation, recognized that the classical doctrine could not stand without at least some correlation between inner experience and outer word. What he sought to avoid was any suggestion that the doctrine was formulated in words that were transferred to us as information to be processed intellectually (or shelved as indigestible mystery). Instead, he wanted the words of the doctrine to find their way into people who had already had a Trinitarian experience. He put the point strongly: "The Trinity takes place in us, and does not first reach us in the form of statements communicated by revelation. On the contrary, these statements have been made to us because the reality of which they speak has been accorded to us."[18] The doctrine would then serve to interpret and explain the actual reality which was in us. No doubt this approach has great pedagogical value, picturing catechumens less as Lockean blank slates on which doctrine should be chalked, and more like Socratic recollectors or the subjects of a mystagogy. But Rahner intended more by the claim that "the Trinity takes place in us," and envisaged the

---

16. Friedrich Schleiermacher, *The Christian Faith* (Edinburgh: T&T Clark, 1989), 738, sect. 170.

17. Ibid., 739, sect. 170.

18. Karl Rahner, "Remarks on the Dogmatic Treatise 'De Trinitate,'" in *More Recent Writings*, vol. 4 of *Theological Investigations* (London: Darton, Longman & Todd, 1966), 98.

correlation of the subjective and the objective (or transcendental) as the proper foundation of the doctrine. While this is better than thinking the content of the doctrine could be read off the surface of our experience, it is still inadequate for establishing the doctrine.

Herman Bavinck, describing the "incalculable importance" of the doctrine of the Trinity "for the Christian religion," argues that the Christian life "points back to three generative principles."[19] This explains why the Belgic Confession can say of the Trinity, "we know all these things from the testimony of Holy Scripture, as well as from the operations of the persons, especially from those we feel within ourselves."[20] Unless the framers of the Belgic Confession seriously intended to posit two sources of knowledge of the Trinity, we should construe "as well as" in a dependent and supplementary sense. If we do so, we can accept the invitation to consider the structured relationship between scriptural Trinitarianism and experiential Trinitarianism. Though everyone who receives the gospel has an experience whose deep structure is Trinitarian, nobody constructs the doctrine of the Trinity from the deliverances of that experience. What would result from that maneuver, if it were possible, would be a codified account of distinctions in our spiritual experience with no guarantee that it corresponds to distinctions in God. Although the doctrine of the Trinity gives rise to an experience of God, it does not derive from an experience of God; Trinity grounds experience rather than vice versa. It has to be carefully taught. Any spiritual experience we may have is bound to be too nebulous and subject to the uncertainties of interpretation. It will lack the corners, complexities, and sharp edges of the doctrine of the Trinity, and it will not be about God in a way direct enough to escape our powers of projection and assimilation. In order to capture the distinguishing features of the Trinity, we must read about them in a text greater than the book of our hearts. That text is the communicative economy of God's self-giving for our salvation, authoritatively transmitted in something that is not metaphorically, but literally, a book: the Bible.

Champions of an experiential foundation for doctrine sometimes retreat to the experience of the prophets and apostles in an attempt to suggest that an appeal to the Bible is just an appeal to earlier experience.

---

19. Herman Bavinck, *God and Creation*, vol. 2 of *Reformed Dogmatics* (Grand Rapids: Baker Academic, 2004), 334.

20. Belgic Confession, article 9, cited in Bavinck 2:334.

This retreat fails if verbal inspiration was always already at work behind the texts, and if the experiences of all biblical authors were already taking place downstream from texts that shaped them in advance. Even Paul Tillich, hardly a fundamentalist, knew this. He called experience a pervasive medium for theology, but did not admit it as a source: "The sources of systematic theology can be sources only for one who participates in them, that is, through experience."[21] Other champions of experience move from individual experience to the collective experience of the entire church, in an attempt to show that the appeal to Scripture, in fact, terminates on the church. If such an appeal is in earnest, it only succeeds in enlarging the quantity of experience rather than making any qualitative difference, so it fails for the same reason, but bigger. Some high-church forms of romanticism may indeed be attempting this kind of expansive move. Others make their appeal to the experience of the church in such a way that they are actually displacing the category of experience with the category of authoritative reception by the historical teaching office. That amounts to an appeal to tradition, on which see below.

To treat experience as the text from which we could read the doctrine of the Trinity is to treat experience as the authoritative master and instructor of Trinitarian theology, that is, to treat it magisterially. Where it fails as a magister, though, it could serve well as a minister. Recognizing the importance of experience means recognizing that this spiritual reality should secure a foothold in the depths of our being, including the depths of our consciousness. God's existence as Trinity is not a surface phenomenon of the divine action, but an essential reality that resides in the simple and absolute being and character of God. Experiential reception of the truth of the Trinity, whether experienced in prayer, illumined Bible reading, or Christian fellowship, is a connection between the depths of God and the depths of our reconciled humanity. It echoes in our hearts what is true in God's being and in his ways with us. It is a foothold in our depths corresponding to a foothold in God's depths. In teaching about the Father and the Son in words given by the Holy Spirit, the apostles were aware they were imparting "a secret and hidden wisdom of God" (1 Cor 2:7), which "God has revealed to us through the Spirit" (v. 10). Paul goes on: "For the Spirit searches everything, even the depths of God. For who knows a person's thoughts except the spirit of that person, which is in him? So also no one comprehends

---

21. Paul Tillich, *Systematic Theology*, vol. 1 (Chicago: University of Chicago Press, 1951), 40.

the thoughts of God except the Spirit of God" (vv. 10–11). The parallel here (a human person has a spirit that probes his own depths; in like manner, God has such a Spirit) is nested among contrasts (a human person's spirit is not another person; God's Spirit is both person and, by analogy, faculty or principle of depth; a human person does not, in fact, know all that is within him; God's Spirit searches all things). And the Spirit is the link from deep to deep: "Now we have received . . . the Spirit who is from God, that we might understand the things freely given us by God" (v. 12).

Freed from the improper burden of a magisterial function, the most important way experience functions ministerially is as a motive for biblical interpretation. James Denney said of the doctrine of the Trinity, "It is not a motiveless speculation; it is not the analysis of an arbitrarily chosen idea like knowledge, love, or spirit, as some philosophers and theologians have tried to show; it proceeds from the actual manifestation of God in Christ, and from the actual reception of a divine life through the Holy Spirit. When it departs from this ground it ceases to possess either significance or authority."[22]

This is especially important for the actual practice of scriptural interpretation. If we confess that the doctrine of the Trinity is in a meaningful sense a biblical doctrine, we do not thereby claim that just anybody is an apt interpreter who is likely to exhibit the intellectual virtues appropriate to reading the Bible well for its Trinitarian content. While the doctrine is not brought to Scripture from outside and imposed on the texts, nevertheless Christian believers approach Scripture with some advance indicator of what to seek there. They have been tipped off by several things, and one of those things is a spiritual experience that disposes them to notice the constituent elements of the doctrine of the Trinity distributed throughout the book with no geometric regularity. The effect of this drive or motivation can be recognized without yielding to interpretive subjectivity or eisegesis. T. F. Torrance, in Polanyian mode, described it as "the Trinitarian mind" of the church finding expression in personal experience:

> We become spiritually and intellectually implicated in patterns of divine order that are beyond our powers fully to articulate in explicit terms, but we are aware of being apprehended by divine Truth as

22. James Denney, *Studies in Theology* (London: Hodder & Stoughton, 1895), 71.

79

it is in Jesus which steadily presses for increasing realization in our understanding, articulation and confession of faith. That is how Christian history gains its initial impetus, and is then reinforced through constant reading and study of the Bible within the community of the faithful.[23]

Trinitarian interpretation of Scripture is motivated and shaped by a Christian sense of what salvation is. Note that the reading Torrance is describing is not the one-time extraction of content from Scripture in preparation for conceptual paraphrase, but "constant reading and study," that is, rereading. Readers and rereaders working from within this felt awareness of salvation are the ones who succeed in construing the texts rightly. This could, of course, be mistaken, both by practitioners and observers, for basing the doctrine of the Trinity on experience, or bringing the doctrine in from elsewhere and hunting through the text for excuses to teach it. That is precisely what must not happen if experience is ministerial rather than magisterial. The doctrine of the Trinity would not flourish without a corresponding experience of the Trinity that returned again and again as a motive and guide for perceiving the Trinity in Scripture. But the doctrine would not survive at all, nor should it, if that experience were its basis.

NOT BY TRADITION

Perhaps because the doctrine of the Trinity is not explicitly formulated in Scripture in the terms that have proven most useful for catechizing, refuting heresy, and making orderly, *wissenschaftliche* statements of the contents of Christian teaching, defenders can sometimes be found claiming that the Trinity is not so much a teaching of Scripture as an artifact of Christian tradition. Certainly the conceptual elaboration of Trinitarian theology in the early history of church doctrine is a great intellectual achievement. Nicaea alone is a mighty leap forward in doctrinal understanding, and each of the early centuries has some contribution to make. If, in grateful reception and employment of these theological tools, some advocates of the doctrine of the Trinity make unguarded statements giving the impression that the doctrine itself is the

23. T. F. Torrance, *The Christian Doctrine of God: One Being Three Persons* (Edinburgh: T&T Clark, 1996), 89.

work of the church rather than the teaching of the Bible, we may safely hear them with forbearance. But if the claim is made in earnest, it must be corrected. One reason is that it is involved in internal inconsistencies. The church fathers claimed to find the doctrine of the Trinity in Scripture. The opponents of the doctrine of the Trinity replied that it was not in Scripture, but only in the arguments of the church fathers, imposed on the Bible rather than read there. There is something perverse in latter-day defenders of the doctrine of the Trinity agreeing with the antitrinitarians of the patristic age while thinking they are defending both the Trinity and the church fathers. This, rather obviously, will not do. The way to be patristic is to learn to discern the doctrine of the Trinity in Scripture, as the fathers did, and not to blame the doctrine on churchly creativity, as their opponents did.

The doctrine of the Trinity is so central to Christian theology that it is no surprise to find it implicated at the crucial sites where the relation between tradition and Scripture were polemically negotiated. The most clarifying controversies were in the second century and the seventeenth. In the second century, theologians attempting proper doctrinal interpretation of Scripture took recourse to something called "the rule of faith." This is best understood as a summary of the key ideas in Scripture, with some indication of their connection to each other.[24] Modern scholars follow the helpful convention of calling it "the rule of faith," but in the early church, the principle was invoked using a wide range of terms: rule of piety, ecclesiastical rule, evangelical rule, rule of tradition, sound rule, the canon of the truth, and so on.[25] It is convenient to have a single name for it, but the habitual use of the term may suggest it was a document; in fact, the rule of faith was more of a principle than a document, and its actual enumerated contents could vary from time to time and place to place. Insofar as the rule of faith was an actual document or ever became one, it was the Christian creed or one of its precursors. Furthermore, it functioned with transparency by design, allowing its users to see the content of Scripture rather than the form of the rule. "So directly had the 'rule' sprung from the apostolic teaching that it was like a mirror image of the revelation itself."[26]

---

24. Eric F. Osborn, "Reason and the Rule of Faith in the Second Century AD," in *The Making of Orthodoxy*, ed. Rowan Williams (Cambridge: Cambridge University Press, 1989), 40–61.

25. Paul Hartog, "The 'Rule of Faith' and Patristic Biblical Exegesis," *Trinity Journal* 28:1 (2007): 65–86.

26. D. H. Williams, "The Search for *Sola Scriptura* in the Early Church," *Interpretation* 52:4 (1998): 359.

For example, in the first book of *Against Heresies*, Irenaeus accused his gnostic opponents of misinterpreting Scripture perniciously, because they "gather their views from other sources than the Scriptures" and then impose these views onto the words and expressions of Scripture. "In doing so, however, they disregard the order and the connection of the Scriptures, and so far as in them lies, dismember and destroy the truth. By transferring passages, and dressing them up anew, and making one thing out of another, they succeed in deluding many through their wicked art in adapting the oracles of the Lord to their opinions."[27]

Irenaeus refutes the gnostics primarily by arguments from Scripture, paying close attention to John's gospel in particular. But to make his point concisely and show how it applies to ordinary Christians, he says that any believer "who retains unchangeable in his heart the rule of the truth which he received by means of baptism, will doubtless recognize the names, the expressions, and the parables taken from the Scriptures, but will by no means acknowledge the blasphemous use which these men make of them."[28] Instead, Christians recall the main points of the Bible, including "the order and the connection" of them, which the gnostics distort. Irenaeus then composes or reports his famous proto-creedal statement, which is one of our best witnesses to the early use of the rule of faith: "The Church, though dispersed throughout the whole world, even to the ends of the earth, has received from the apostles and their disciples this faith: It believes in one God, the Father Almighty, Maker of heaven and earth . . . and in one Christ Jesus, the Son of God, who became incarnate for our salvation; and in the Holy Spirit . . ."[29]

What is Irenaeus doing here when he organizes the main points of Christian doctrine in a conspicuously Trinitarian outline? He is not claiming to bring in the doctrine of the Trinity from elsewhere and then showing how the phrases of Scripture can be drawn out to fit the outline. He is rather claiming that the true meaning of the words of Scripture, in their proper "order and connection," is the Trinitarian meaning. Speaking of the rule of faith is a kind of shorthand for this interrelated network of meanings and implications, a placeholder to indicate where connections have already been traced and decisions have been made. Its

---

27. Irenaeus, *Against Heresies* 1:8.
28. Ibid., 1:9.
29. Ibid., 1:10.

primary meaning has to do with the demonstrable meaning of Scripture; its secondary meaning recalls the fact that a classic lineage of previous interpreters have already discerned this meaning.

Writing about Tertullian, Eric Osborn once remarked that "conclusions are ambiguous without the argument which leads to them."[30] John Behr highlighted some of the implications of this observation for Trinitarian theology in particular:

> An example of this is the way in which Trinitarian theology, debated so vigorously during the fourth century on grounds already prepared during the first three, is often reduced to shorthand formulae, such as the "three hypostases and one ousia" of "the consubstantial Trinity." The reflection that lies behind such phrases is immense, yet it is often glossed over. Indeed, the very familiarity of such phrases results in their being detached from the debates that resulted in them and divorced from the content that they seek to encapsulate.[31]

What Behr is concerned about is the tendency of condensed formulas to become opaque when they should remain transparent. When this happens, the formulas become obstacles to understanding, and simplifications so drastic as to evacuate the subject of significance. That this is no antitraditionalist objection is evident from the corpus of Behr's own position as an Eastern Orthodox theologian. It is instead a recognition that when something as diffuse as the rule of faith is reified by later scholars and treated as a settled conclusion, it is bound to block the lively perception of the scriptural reasoning it should serve. Ringing one more change on the phrase, Scott Swain says that "in Christian theology at least, doctrinal propositions apart from the exegetical arguments that they summarize are at best ambiguous."[32] They are at worst idolatrous.

Some modern champions of the rule of faith have spoken of it imprecisely, even lazily. Christopher Seitz has called attention to the way the rule is reified and portrayed as if it exerted its own proper pressure on all

---

30. Eric Osborn, *Tertullian: First Theologian of the West* (Cambridge: Cambridge University Press, 1997), 6.

31. John Behr, "The Paschal Foundations of Christian Theology," *St. Vladimir's Theological Quarterly* 45:2 (2001): 135.

32. Scott R. Swain, *The God of the Gospel: Robert Jenson's Trinitarian Theology* (Downers Grove, IL: IVP Academic, 2013), 121.

sorts of biblical phenomena—when it is treated as a separable and portable gist or "a kind of creedal summary derived from Scripture, or operating independently and crucially from it, so as to provide the rationale or lens or delimiting evaluation of what the significance of Scripture might be said, perennially, to be."[33] The rule of faith is sometimes portrayed, with baleful consequences, as a hermeneutical guide that presents a truth nobody could be expected to perceive without the guidance of the rule. This does raise the question of where the rule originated, if not from a reading of Scripture. John Goldingay has called attention to the temptation of sloppiness in such appeal to the rule. He cites recent interpreters who portray the Bible as "vast, heterogeneous, full of confusing passages and obscure words, and difficult to understand," warning that "only a fool would imagine that he or she could work out solutions alone."[34] If that means new interpreters can be trained by classic doctrine to perceive the patterns in Scripture, all is well. But if it suggests that some other semi-documentary or proto-creedal source must deliver the overall plan of the doctrine of the Trinity, it is shifting the burden of Trinitarianism from Scripture to tradition. Following Irenaeus, the conventional metaphor for assembling the big picture of biblical doctrine is that of arranging mosaic tiles. But this metaphor has not functioned quite as well in modern usage. Perhaps the tesserae of a mosaic are too subject to rearrangement; there is nothing inherent in the pile of tesserae that demands any particular assembly. A more apt (though admittedly less elegant) metaphor for modern interpretation might be a jigsaw puzzle. If Scripture were a jigsaw puzzle, the rule of faith would be not so much the completed picture on the box lid, but something considerably more complex in its function: it would be a way of talking about the concrete jigsaw turnings of the undulating edges of each puzzle piece, and the way they actually dovetail with each other only when they are brought together in the one and only way they can be assembled. Gnostics smash pieces together, chop off tabs, and fill in blanks in their determination to match their own big picture. The doctrine of the Trinity emerges from fitting the pieces together as each part determines. Orthodox interpreters may also gaze

---

33. Christopher R. Seitz, *The Character of Christian Scripture* (Grand Rapids: Baker Academic, 2011), 192. The whole discussion of the rule of faith in canonical perspective runs from 192–203.

34. John Goldingay, *Do We Really Need the New Testament?* (Downers Grove, IL: IVP Academic, 2015), 170. The quotation he refutes is from R. R. Reno's series preface to the *Brazos Theological Commentary on the Bible*.

at a completed picture to see where the major blocks of color will go, but the understanding they derive from that has the character of a tip or a nudge; the perception of truth still lies in the proper relation of the pieces. In short, any appeal to the rule of faith and its use by the church fathers must make it clear that tradition is the medium, but not the source, of the doctrine of the Trinity.

"THE CONSTANT VOICE OF OUR SPIRITUAL MOTHER"

In the seventeenth century, Lutheran theologian Johann Gerhard negotiated the same tension in an elevated polemical context. Gerhard argued that "the mystery of the Trinity should and also can be proved not from the streams of the fathers nor from the murky pools of the Scholastics but from the utterly clear springs of the Holy Scriptures."[35] Gerhard, as is perhaps evident from this rhetoric, is a strong advocate and practitioner of *sola Scriptura*,[36] and he is particularly convinced it must be applied in the doctrine of the Trinity. The reason for his insistence is, in part, because sixteenth-century antitrinitarians had charged the Lutheran theologians with affirming the doctrine of the Trinity, not on good Protestant grounds, but because they had been "moved only by the authority of the Church."[37] Gerhard was adamant that the biblical evidence for the doctrine of the Trinity was necessary and sufficient, so he bristled at the suggestion that Lutheran Trinitarianism had somehow been smuggled in from Rome under false pretenses.

As for Roman Catholic theologians, Gerhard noted a curious division among them. One group of them actually agreed with the heretics: "Some of the Papists allege that the mystery of the Trinity cannot be proved from the Holy Scriptures."[38] Gerhard cites Emanuel a Vega as writing that "the Trinity does not stand unless tradition is admitted" and Johann Pistorius claiming that "the Trinity cannot be

---

35. Johann Gerhard, *On the Nature of God and On the Trinity*, vol. 2 of *Theological Commonplaces*, ed. Benjamin T. G. Mayes (St. Louis: Concordia, 2007), 274.

36. For an overview of Gerhard's attitude toward church tradition, see Benjamin T. G. Mayes, "*Lumina, non Numina*: Patristic Authority According to Lutheran Arch-Theologian Johann Gerhard," in the Richard Muller festschrift *Church and School in Early Modern Protestantism*, ed. Jordan J. Ballor, David S. Sytsma, and Jason Zuidema (Leiden: Brill, 2013), 457–70. To see how Gerhard's position harmonizes with the broader Lutheran tradition, see Quentin D. Stewart, *Lutheran Patristic Catholicity: The Vincentian Canon and the Consensus Patrum in Lutheran Orthodoxy* (Münster: LIT, 2015).

37. Gerhard, *On the Nature of God*, 278.

38. Ibid.

proved from Holy Writ but is the tradition of the Church."[39] Perhaps these theologians made such inflated claims for tradition in hopes of forcing a choice between antitrinitarianism and Roman Catholicism. But Gerhard felt no compulsion to choose between them, because he so utterly rejected their shared premise. Furthermore, he found support in the other (and, one hopes, larger) group of Roman theologians, who maintained the ancient claim that the doctrine of the Trinity was taught by Scripture. "Against this thoughtlessness of some Papists, however, we set forth the judgment of other, more sound Papists."[40] Among the "more sound Papists" Gerhard counts Cardinal Bellarmine, who he cites approvingly: "When the Council of Nicaea defined that Christ is of the same substance with the Father, it drew that conclusion from the Scriptures."[41]

Here is a key marker of ecumenical convergence in a century of deep divisions, and Gerhard gladly highlighted the agreement while marginalizing the "thoughtlessness of some Papists." He could do so because of how highly he valued the unified witness of the Christian tradition ("the constant voice of our spiritual mother, the Church"[42]), which he counted among the supporting testimonies for the doctrine of the Trinity. "We do not deny that the unanimous agreement of the early Catholic Church concerning this mystery—a consensus that the most ancient writers of the church confirm, even those who lived before the Council of Nicaea—has and also should have great weight among the devout and wise," he argued. Yet this did not change the fact that "the primary and chief foundation of our faith cannot be set on that consensus of the church." Gerhard recognized a continuum of graded authorities, which enabled him to submit appropriately to the relative and conditional authority of tradition. "It is not the case," he said, "that, if divine authority is denied them, no authority is owed to the fathers' writings. They are not judges of faith, but they are witnesses and informers [of it]. They are not divinities, but they are very bright lights."[43] The authority of tradition for Gerhard was ministerial, not magisterial, and when it came to the Trinity

---

39. Ibid.
40. Ibid.
41. Ibid. Along with Bellarmine, Gerhard cites Campianus (Edmund Campion), Gregory of Valencia, and Martin Becanus.
42. Ibid., 277.
43. Cited in Mayes, "*Lumina, non Numina*," 461. The Latin for "not divinities, but very bright lights" is *non sunt Numina, praeclara tamen lumina*, from which Mayes takes his chapter title.

in particular, he taught that "we must look for confirmation of this mystery from the only and proper principle of theology, that is, from the Word of God."[44]

If tradition is to be ministerial rather than magisterial with regard to the Trinity, it will have to serve by pointing people to the Scriptures. Wherever tradition lords it over Scripture, believers are tempted to consider the creed or the confession as a short and portable summary of the Bible's contents, full of statements that could be proved by direct recourse to Scripture. There is something backward about that. As Nicholas Lash has argued, Scripture does not so much prove the creeds as explain them. While it is true that "what the Scriptures say at length, the Creed says briefly,"[45] nevertheless:

> The Creed does not seek, in Scripture, for warrants or for "proof," but for intelligibility. If we want to find out what it *means* to confess God as "creator" or Jesus as God's "son," then the first place to which we turn is Scripture . . . against the tendency of some Christians to say: 'But we know what Scripture means; we find that in the Creed' (and may, therefore, leave the Bible safely closed), I want to emphasize that we only discover the meaning of the Creed in the measure that the Bible stays an open book."[46]

Still more could be said of the great benefits that accrue to Trinitarianism from a tradition that has humbled itself before the Word of God. As a singularly vast and comprehensive doctrinal complex, the doctrine of the Trinity thrives when it is supported by a transgenerational confessional apparatus capable of sophisticated articulation and the balancing of multiple exegetical impulses. Elaborate Trinitarianism is not the sort of thing that can be kept steadily in mind by each generation on its own. Division of labor across the centuries is a great good, and tradition can bear much weight. But here we have mainly been concerned to warn against the hypertrophic claims sometimes made on behalf of tradition, which, after all, cannot bear the full weight of the doctrine of the Trinity. Only Scripture can do that.

---

44. Gerhard, *On the Nature of God*, 277.
45. Nicholas Lash, *Believing Three Ways in One God: A Reading of the Apostles' Creed* (Notre Dame, IN: University of Notre Dame Press, 1993), 8.
46. Ibid., 9.

THE BIBLE IN THE TRINITY

Having traced the doctrine of the Trinity to God's communicative intent to make himself known in the missions of the Son and Spirit, that is, to God in the act of accomplishing salvation, we have drawn out the corollary of exclusivity: the Trinity has been revealed here and only here. We have been especially jealous to keep supporting witnesses like experience and tradition in place, not permitting them to bear the weight of establishing the doctrine. Experience and tradition both serve as placeholders, points of access, or shorthand for the biblical revelation that alone brings us to the truth of the Trinity. If we say we know the Trinity from experience, we are using a telescoped expression meaning that the Trinity made known in Scripture is also the object of our experience, though we could not have known so without Scripture. If we say we know the Trinity because the Christian tradition has taught us about it, we are using a compressed formulation that could be expanded to show that the church's tradition relayed to us what it received from Scripture.

But to be completely consistent, we can apply a similar reasoning to Scripture, insofar as Scripture is a textually transmitted report of God's actions and words. If we say we believe in the Trinity because Scripture teaches it, we are collapsing the historical works and words of God into the report that tells about them, and we could expand the statement to its full form: in the Bible we read the authoritative account of the coming of the Son and the Spirit, who themselves bring the revelation of the Trinity. That is, we ought to recognize that the appeal to biblical revelation is itself a placeholder for the actual revelation. The actual revelation of the Trinity is in the historical sendings of the two persons, the Son and the Holy Spirit. Knowledge that God is Father, Son, and Holy Spirit was communicated to us when the Father sent the Son and the Holy Spirit. The multiform prophecies of the Old Testament point forward to those sendings, and the multiform apostolic reports and interpretations look back to them.

This observation may have something of a Barthian ring to it, operating as it does with a distinction between the revelation and the scriptural witness. But in fact, the distinction is drawn specifically with regard to Trinitarianism by a theologian with a rather famously conservative doctrine of Scripture: B. B. Warfield. In his 1915 article "The Biblical Doctrine of the Trinity," Warfield argued that while the doctrine is biblical, its revelation is in this particular sense not biblical; it is a revelation made by persons acting in history, being the Son and Spirit and saying so:

> We cannot speak of the doctrine of the Trinity . . . as revealed in the New Testament, any more than we can speak of it as revealed in the Old Testament. The Old Testament was written before its revelation; the New Testament after it. The revelation itself was made not in word but in deed. It was made in the incarnation of God the Son, and the outpouring of God the Holy Spirit. The relation of the two Testaments to this revelation is in the one case that of preparation for it, and in the other that of product of it. The revelation itself is embodied just in Christ and the Holy Spirit.[47]

Warfield draws numerous conclusions from this striking fact, and we will have to return to some exegetical implications of his argument at a later point. The main thing to note in the context of our discussion of revelation is that he reserves the word *revelation* for the effective presence of the two persons, the temporal missions of the Trinity. Scripture testifies (as preparation and product) to that embodied revelation.

It is possible to make too much of this distinction, as a swarm of (what used to be called neo-orthodox) theologians once did and still do, mostly to the detriment of a doctrine of Scripture. For his part, Warfield rather famously established voluminous safeguards against any slippage in bibliology.[48] If we turned our attention from the doctrine of revelation to the doctrine of Scripture, we would have to recognize there is more going on in Scripture than just reporting or testimony. As Warfield knew, Scripture does not simply document what God said, but, through the work of the Spirit, in both its composition and its reading, it simply is what God says. Biblical texts do not just come along and alter and report on an event; the events they report on were also events that had been prepared for in previous texts. The category of witness is an indispensable one, especially when describing the relation between divine acts and divinely inspired explanations of them, but in a doctrine of Scripture we would need to add several more categories to

---

47. B. B. Warfield, "The Biblical Doctrine of the Trinity," in *Biblical and Theological Studies* (Philadelphia: Presbyterian and Reformed, 1952), 32–33.

48. See the essays on revelation and inspiration collected in B. B. Warfield, *The Inspiration and Authority of the Bible* (Philadelphia: Presbyterian and Reformed, 1948).

that of witness. Scripture's peculiar way of witnessing to divine action is by being uniquely foundational and normative, verbally inspired, and inerrant. Because God's self-testimony begins among the persons of the Trinity and extends all the way to written text (1 John 1:1–3), saying "the Trinity is revealed in the Bible" is not precisely the same type of radical shorthand as appeals to experience or tradition. The Trinity is, in fact, revealed in Scripture because in Scripture God testifies about the historical sending of the Son and the Holy Spirit. Scripture includes God's self-interpretation, so while it is ministerial vis-à-vis the missions, it is magisterial vis-à-vis the church. It serves the Father's sending of the Son and Spirit, but it canons and rules the church. Scripture is servant and lord.[49]

The distinction between event and text abides, however, and has deeper implications than simply a warning that we should police our shorthand expressions. Because the revelation of the Trinity happened in history in the coming of the Son and the Spirit, knowledge of the Trinity precedes the gathering of the documents of the New Testament. The Trinity is a biblical doctrine, then, not just because its elements are stated in the books of the Christian Scriptures, but also because the two-Testament canon of Scripture actually came into existence to bear witness that the God of Israel sent his Son and poured out his Holy Spirit. Elsewhere in B. B. Warfield's essay, he makes this point by defining the New Testament as "the documentation of the religion of the incarnate Son and of the outpoured Spirit, that is to say, of the religion of the Trinity."[50] In short, the Trinity is not so much in Scripture as Scripture is in the Trinity. When we search the Bible for its testimony to the Trinity, we should also be aware that the Bible exists because the Father sent the Son and the Spirit. The Old Testament exists because he was preparing to do so, and the New Testament exists because he did so.

If this reversal—the Bible is in the Trinity—is more than a play on words or a Chestertonian inversion, it is because in the organic hierarchy of theological truths, the doctrine of the Trinity is more fundamental and more comprehensive than the doctrine of Scripture. In fact, the doctrine of the Trinity is also more fundamental and comprehensive than even the broad field of the doctrine of revelation. It was Karl Barth who

---

49. Thanks to Matt Jenson for this formulation and to a faculty discussion group at Talbot School of Theology for helping me clarify the way the doctrine of revelation presented here influences the doctrine of Scripture.

50. Warfield, "Biblical Doctrine of the Trinity," 35.

declared that "the doctrine of the Trinity is what basically distinguishes the Christian doctrine of God as Christian, and therefore what already distinguishes the Christian concept of revelation as Christian, in contrast to all other possible doctrines of God or concepts of revelation."[51] It is inappropriate to frame a formal doctrine of revelation without constitutive reference to the content that is revealed; such a doctrine would need to be evangelized and would need to meet the Trinity. A truly Christian doctrine of revelation must borrow its character from the doctrine of the Trinity. In the preceding outline of a doctrine of revelation, we have criticized modern doctrines of revelation that float away from the concrete missions of the Son and the Spirit, especially insofar as those theologies ignore the verbal and communicative aspects of the missions. In the process, we have made numerous generalizations and methodological recommendations of a more or less formal nature for a doctrine of revelation, but our goal has been to draw these principles as directly as possible from the content of the doctrine of the Trinity. The chief safeguard was to highlight the canonical sense of mystery as the main sense in which the Trinity is to be confessed as a mystery. At the theological nexus where the doctrines of revelation and Trinity converge, along with a few elements of the doctrine of Scripture, we are touching on what Kevin Vanhoozer calls "first theology"—"treating God, Scripture, and hermeneutics as one problem."[52] It is true that the doctrine of the Trinity must be based on revelation, and that revelation must be sought in Scripture, and that in their mutual involvement these things are foundational. But it is for the health of Christian doctrine that we acknowledge "that sacred truth of the blessed Trinity of persons in unity of the God-head" to be, "as one hath it, *Fundamentum Fundamentorum*, the Foundation of Foundations."[53]

---

51. Barth, *CD* I/1, 301.
52. Kevin J. Vanhoozer, *First Theology: God, Scripture & Hermeneutics* (Downers Grove, IL: InterVarsity Press, 2002), 9.
53. Edmund Polhill, *Precious Faith Considered in its Nature, Working, and Growth* (London: Cockerill, 1675), 352.

CHAPTER 4

INCARNATION AND PENTECOST

The Bible tells a unified story of God's way with his people, reaching its center in the visible missions of the Son and the Holy Spirit. Interpreting these missions correctly as divine self-revelation is central to the exegetical establishing of Trinitarian theology. What the missions reveal about the life of God is that his life takes place in eternal relations of origin.

The most basic pedagogical decision to make in presenting the doctrine of the Trinity is whether to begin the exposition with the temporal missions and reason back from them to the eternal processions, or whether to take the opposite approach, beginning rather with the eternal processions and then working out and down to the temporal missions. Both procedures have much to commend them.

ORDER OF KNOWING AND ORDER OF BEING

The former is the way taken by Augustine in his epochal work *The Trinity*. Presupposing the absolute equality of Father, Son, and Holy Spirit, he asks how the first person can send the second and third without entailing that the sent two are somehow inferior to the sending one. How can equality and sending be reconciled? His solution is to understand the missions as visible enactments of eternal processions. For the Son, to be sent is to be known to proceed from the Father.[1] The movement of exposition is upward, reasoning back along the trajectory of the mission, into the eternal being of God. After this, Augustine gives further instructions about how we say some things about God according to the divine substance ("substance-wise") and some things according to relation ("relation-wise"). If we call this direction the Augustinian one, it is only because his *The Trinity* is such a classic and consistent working out of it, and not because Augustine invented it. A starting point in the sendings is characteristic of many pre-Nicene fathers, both Latin and Greek. Augustine perfected that method, systematized it, and solved some of the problems involved in its misuse.[2]

Chief among the considerable advantages of this approach is the way it engages the biblical witness by tracking along with the order of discovery. Scripture does not begin by instructing us on the eternal relations of origin in God and then supplementing that instruction with the account of the sending forth of the Son and Holy Spirit. The biblical epic of the triune God begins *in media res*, in the middle of the things of salvation. This holds true whether the reader of the Bible follows a canonical reading order or a chronological reading order and applies to the parts as well as to the whole of Scripture. God did not first describe the Trinity's eternal processions and then display them in missions.[3] So Augustine's presentation flows with the current of revelation, rehearsing its historical sequence as it presents the doctrine of the Trinity. The pedagogical benefit is that the mind is led from concrete actions back to their eternal presuppositions. More like a Socratic dialogue than an Aristotelian treatise, Augustine's work provokes the student by raising a question, which is answered in due course. The main pedagogical disadvantage of this approach is the mental effort it requires, as those who learn in this order must submit to the difficulty of revising their initial idea of the structure of divine unity in light of subsequent revelation. It may also run the risk of aligning with the modern historicist tendency to think that all meaningful action takes place in the economy and only in the economy.

The opposite approach, then, is to take what the missions make

---

1. Augustine, *Trinity* 4.5.29, 174.
2. I have in mind here the naive subordinationism that crept in at the edges of otherwise orthodox authors before Nicaea.
3. It is worth noting, however, that the two biblical books whose opening words are "in the beginning" do come close, if they are pondered together canonically with an eye to how John rereads the opening gambit of Genesis. This is not insignificant and did not escape the notice of the church fathers. But the fourth gospel's authorial restraint is too great for this to be counted as beginning with processions.

known about the Trinity and presuppose it from the start, beginning the exposition with the processions and working out and down to the missions. This is how Thomas Aquinas develops the vast treatise on the Trinity in the *Summa Theologica*, where it occupies questions 27 through 43 of the *Prima Pars*. The treatise begins with an article so apparently disengaged from the history of salvation that we might call it the article than which no article more abstract can be imagined: "Is there procession in God?"[4] Thomas neatly demonstrates how a clear understanding of internal processions in God eliminates in advance the major alternatives to Trinitarianism. Since language signifying procession is a scriptural given (Thomas takes his verbal cue from John 8:42, *Ego ex Deo processi*, "from God I proceeded"), our task is to understand it rightly. If the Son's procession were merely an effect going out from its cause, the Son and Spirit would be creatures rather than true God, because "proceeding as an effect from a cause" is exactly what creation does with respect to God. That is Arianism, dividing the substance. If the procession of the Son were merely a cause going out to its effect, the Son and Spirit would be nothing but the Father in action, because "a cause that makes effects" is exactly what a unipersonal God would be. That is Sabellianism, confusing the persons. In both cases, the error stems from failing to recognize a procession that is interior to God. "Careful examination shows that both of these opinions take procession as meaning an outward act; hence neither of them affirms procession as existing in God Himself."[5] It follows that the most abstract possible question is the necessary conceptual foundation for all that follows, so Thomas begins his treatise by teaching that there are processions in God.[6]

The scope and range of the treatise on the Trinity in the *Summa Theologica* is impressive. Having established the processions, Thomas goes on to ask whether there is more than one, what they are called, what relations they give rise to, and so on. Not until question 43 (sixteen questions and more than two hundred pages later in the Blackfriars

---

4. Saint Thomas Aquinas, *Summa Theologica* I, q. 27, a. 1 (hereafter *ST*).

5. Ibid.

6. The sheer abstractness of this opening question is partly a feature of the doctrine's position within the architecture of the *Summa Theologica*. In previous works, Thomas placed the treatise elsewhere and opened it differently. In his commentary on Lombard's *Sentences*, an exitus-reditus schema predominates. In the *Summa Contra Gentiles*, for apologetic purposes he postpones Trinitarian theology until the fourth book and emphasizes its character as revealed truth. See Gilles Emery, *Trinity in Aquinas* (Ypsilanti, MI: Sapientia, 2003), chs. 2–4, respectively, for the *Sentences* commentary, the *Summa Contra Gentiles*, and the *Summa Theologica*.

edition) does his discussion reach the sending of the Son and the Holy Spirit into salvation history. At long last, Thomas comes to the objection that started Augustine's project: "To be sent and to be a divine person do not seem compatible. An emissary is less than the one who sends him."[7] A mission, Thomas tells us, is "a procession in time,"[8] or an eternal procession with the addition of an effect in time.[9] So the exposition arcs from eternal processions to temporal missions and comes home to us at last. If we call this direction Thomist, it would only be because of the grandeur and thoroughness of Thomas's deployment of it. Long before Thomas, the tendency to reflect on the self-sufficiency of God was so deeply embedded in Christian doctrine that an exposition of the eternal processions naturally gravitated to the beginning of systematic teaching.

There are two major benefits of this arrangement. First, it guides the reader along the order of being by giving priority to treating what God is in the eternal divine life and then moving to the actions God freely undertakes in time. More like an Aristotelian treatise than a Socratic dialogue (no surprise in that for Thomas), it establishes first principles and then builds on them conceptually. By the time the missions are explicitly considered (they have, of course, been assumed throughout as the basis of our knowledge of the processions), a formidable array of conceptual tools has already been put in place to make sense of them. The illuminating power that the concept of procession exerts on the concept of mission is, to the attentive reader, epiphanic.

The second major benefit is the sense of proportion that accrues from handling the elements of the doctrine in this sequence. The processions are theology proper, while the missions are soteriology, and God is as much bigger than salvation as he is prior to it. In contemporary theology, John Webster has been most insistent on the great value of this ordering of topics for curing certain modern ills. Webster recommends "first contemplating the infinite depth of God in himself, out of which his temporal acts arise," in order to avoid "making the economy *id quo maius cogitari nequit*"—that than which nothing greater can be thought, a name Anselm gave to God rather than to salvation.[10]

---

7. Aquinas, *ST*, I, q. 43, a. 1.
8. Ibid., I, q. 43, a. 3, sed contra: *missio autem est temporalis processio.*
9. Ibid., I, q. 43, a. 2, resp. 3.
10. John Webster, *God and the Works of God*, vol. 1 of *God Without Measure: Working Papers in Christian Theology* (London: Bloomsbury T & T Clark, 2016), 8. The same concern looms impressively in the first four chapters, is scattered throughout the rest of them, and lurks in the volume's subtitle, which promises a treatment of "God" first and only then "the works of God."

There is one major disadvantage of this method, which should be stated precisely and not exaggerated.[11] The processions-to-missions sequence begins at such a great conceptual distance from salvation history that the exposition can be abstract and remote. It presupposes familiarity with the missions of the Son and the Spirit but does not expound them until the end. The processions-to-missions exposition is dependent on the missions-to-processions exposition; without the latter we lack the evidence to pursue the former. As Edmund Hill writes, "The *a priori* way of exposition is only valuable for those who have already been led along the *a posteriori* way of discovery." When it is instead treated "as a substitute for the way of discovery," it can bring forth the "indigestible fruits of scholasticism."[12]

In a book like the present one, which seeks to order theological language by attending to the manner of the Trinity's revelation, the former order of exposition, moving like Augustine from redemptive missions back to antecedent processions, has a natural appeal. It is not mandatory, but it is suitable—*non necessarium sed conveniens.* As long as all the material content of Trinitarian theology is made present and rightly related, however, "method is arbitrary," as the scholastic maxim holds. Because of his sustained effort to drive historicist modes of thought off the center of the stage of dogmatics, John Webster nearly always follows the strategy of beginning his exposition with the eternal life of the Trinity and then moving outward. But even when he has his polemical targets in clear view and is enjoining vigilance against collapsing God's life into world process, he can freely admit that "in its actual presentation of its subject," not even the doctrine of human salvation is required to "start from the dogmatics of the immanent Trinity. It would be quite possible to begin at some other point." He concludes that "what matters is not the starting-point but scope, scale and distribution of weight."[13] Most theologians who have invoked the proverb that "method is arbitrary" have immediately gone on to say that it is nevertheless important. Karl Barth, for example, says that the maxim "*methodus est arbitraria* . . . obviously cannot mean that the arbiter can sleep and dream, and then decide according to his fancy."[14] And J. J. von Oosterzee said

---

11. There is a cottage industry of cheap critiques of the *Summa*'s order, extending even to something that ought to have been uncontroversial: the *De Deo Uno/De Deo Trino* sequence.

12. Edmund Hill, OP, *The Mystery of the Trinity* (London: Chapman, 1985), 147, 152.

13. John Webster, "'It Was the Will of the Lord to Bruise Him': Soteriology and the Doctrine of God," in *God and the Works of God*, 151–52.

14. Barth, *CD* I/2, excursus on 861.

that it needed "to be followed by the maxim *'methodus est necessaria.'*"[15] This book is an attempt to provide dogmatic principles for Trinitarian exegesis. So here we follow the freely chosen but strategically significant method of moving from missions to processions, reflecting first on the temporal sendings that simply are human salvation and tracing them back to the eternal relations of origin that simply are God.

READING THE BIBLE AS A WHOLE

We begin with the two missions, the incarnation and Pentecost, where they are narrated and interpreted in Scripture. The Bible teaches that God the Father sent the Son and the Holy Spirit. The doctrine of the Trinity arises from the total witness of Scripture construed as a whole, considered as a narrative unity, and constituting God's progressive self-revelation. Each of the moments of this interpretive action requires a vast move of comprehension: to grasp the entire two-Testament canon, to trace its unbroken narrative arc, and to recognize that arc as a self-communicative action with God as its source.

The first step is construing Scripture as a whole. The two-Testament canon of Scripture could of course be described from the outside as a disparate body of texts with inadequate internal cohesion, bound together only externally by authority, accident, or convention. In that case, there would be no reason to read the collection together meaningfully as a single comprehensive text. That critical position, whatever arguments are offered or presupposed for it, simply amounts to a set of reasons for not taking the first step recommended here, which is construing Scripture as a whole. The modern academic discipline of biblical studies, approaching Scripture with what anthropologists would call etic principles, necessarily rejects the kind of canonical holism that can be glimpsed from the forbidden, emic perspective.[16] In that case, of course, the second and third steps would not follow, and (unsurprisingly, given our view that the Trinity is purely a revealed doctrine) there would be little reason to affirm the doctrine of the Trinity. This is not the place for a complete defense of canonical unity, much less an apologetic to

---

15. Johannes Jacobus von Oosterzee, *Christian Dogmatics: A Text-book for Academical Instruction and Private Study*, vol. 1 (New York: Scribner's Sons, 1874), 61.

16. Brevard S. Childs suggests the outlines of a truly emic and yet truly critical biblical studies in *Biblical Theology of the Old and New Testaments: Theological Reflection on the Christian Bible* (Minneapolis: Fortress, 1993), 416.

demonstrate divine authorship of the texts in that canon or a probing of the plausibility structure within which one could affirm that God has even spoken at all. Those tasks, legitimate in their own sphere, are altogether different from the one undertaken here. The only claim that would need to be established in order to underwrite our recommended initial step of construing Scripture as a whole is that Scripture presents itself, literally, as a unity.

In a full account of this contention, it would be important to ground it with as much internal evidence as possible, demonstrating, as Geerhardus Vos argued, that "the Bible gives us in certain cases a philosophy of its own organism."[17] Competence in biblical theology meant, for Vos, "making ourselves . . . thoroughly conversant with the biblical consciousness of its own revelation structure."[18] Successful interpretation on this account is a matter of giving voice to the Bible's own internal articulation of its developing canonical unity, with special attention to the way later authors interpret and incorporate earlier authors. One of the benefits Vos's method provides is removing "the unfortunate situation that even the fundamental doctrines of the faith should seem to depend mainly on the testimony of isolated proof-texts."[19] Certainly this would be a great service for Trinitarian theology, which periodically gives that isolated proof-text impression to believers and unbelievers alike. To uncover the deeper structures of Trinitarianism's exegetical basis, an awareness of Scripture's self-understanding is a summation devoutly to be wished. The anthropomorphism or personification in phrases like "Scripture's self-understanding" and "biblical consciousness of its own revelation structure" is apparently inevitable. It is also biblical: "The Scripture, foreseeing that God would justify the Gentiles by faith, preached the gospel beforehand to Abraham" (Gal 3:8). In ascribing foresight and proleptic evangelistic speech to the written narrative voice of Genesis, Paul's underlying thought pattern must be metonymic: God is the unstated agent who speaks through the stated means, Scripture. Similarly, language about "Scripture's self-understanding" should always be, on the one hand, a literary observation about intertextuality and,

---

17. Geerhardus Vos, *Biblical Theology: Old and New Testaments* (Grand Rapids: Eerdmans, 1948), 13. Vos goes on: "Paul, for instance, has his views in regard to the revelation structure of the Old Testament." Covenant is famously central to Vos's case, but it is worth noting that *mysterion*, Paul's main signifier of the "revelation structure" that spans the Testaments, is even more patent of Trinitarian interpretation.

18. Ibid., 17.

19. Ibid.

on the other hand, a polite metonymy for the doctrine that Scripture is the word of God.[20]

In contemporary academic culture, there are many obstacles to reading the Bible as a unified whole. Division of expert labor is perhaps a necessary evil. But the resulting tendency to compartmentalize the disciplines and their subject matter is reinforced by a decline in the kind of theological curiosity that would motivate experts to venture across a few disciplinary boundaries in pursuit of particular research topics. Each of those disciplinary boundaries is also policed vigilantly by border patrols. Francis Watson draws attention to the two most important territorial divisions: "One line of demarcation divides biblical scholars from theologians; a second absolutizes the division of the Christian Bible into Old and New Testaments by assigning these collections to separate interpretative communities."[21] But he goes on to argue that there is a definite relationship between these two divisions:

> In reality, the second line of demarcation is simply an extension of the first. The notion of a dialectical unity between two bodies of writing, constituted as "old" and "new" by their relation to the foundation event that they together enclose and attest, only makes sense from a theological standpoint. Where theological concerns are marginalized, the two Testaments fall apart almost automatically. The lines of demarcation between systematic theology and Old and New Testament scholarship represent more than a mere division of labour; they are ideologically motivated. They represent a collective decision of biblical scholarship that the biblical texts are to be construed as something other than Christian Scripture.[22]

There is great explanatory power in noting this causal link between a determinedly untheological account of Scripture and the resulting enforced separation of Old and New Testaments. Its implications for Trinitarian theology reach to the very foundation of the doctrine, because it is only the conviction that the God of the Old Testament sent forth his Son and Spirit in the New Testament that provides the

20. See B. B. Warfield, "'It Says:' 'Scripture Says:' 'God Says,'" in *The Inspiration and Authority of the Bible* (Philadelphia: Presbyterian and Reformed, 1948), 299–348.

21. Francis Watson, *Text and Truth: Redefining Biblical Theology* (Grand Rapids: Eerdmans, 1997), 5.

22. Ibid., 5–6.

doctrinal foundation for construing the canon of Scripture as a unity in the first place. Without the doctrine of the Trinity, there is insufficient reason to bind the two Testaments. Consider one of the earliest classics of postapostolic theology, Irenaeus of Lyons's *Demonstration of the Apostolic Preaching*. The basic argument of this little book is twofold: that God is Father, Son, and Holy Spirit, and that the Old and New Testaments belong together.[23] Irenaeus's lengthier polemic *Against Heresies* develops the same point with an even sharper opposition to gnostic attempts to separate the God of the Old Testament from the God of the New. Irenaeus speaks for the entire church when he draws the equation: one two-Testament Bible, one three-personed God. This is why it is almost a truism to say that the first step toward the doctrine of the Trinity is to read the entire Bible as a whole, and yet it needs to be said.

GLIMPSES OF CANONICAL UNITY

Irenaeus's opponents had their own reasons for refusing to construe the Bible as one book; perhaps every epoch of church history has confronted its characteristic objections. In our own period, though, the rejection of biblical unity needs not so much to be confronted as exposed. The forces that tend toward its dissolution into discrete units are nearly imperceptible, making themselves felt as common sense and scholarly decency. "Interpretive communities condition their members to regard their disciplinary structures as normal and self-evident," notes Francis Watson, "and it therefore requires a conscious effort of the imagination to perceive the coexistence of three distinct communities of biblical interpreters as the anomaly that it actually is."[24] Of course we have such conscious efforts in the form of grand gestures of opposition, insisting on the rights of theological interpretation of Scripture and a robustly canonical interpretive framework.[25] But the work of breaking Scripture

---

23. Saint Irenaeus of Lyons, *On the Apostolic Preaching* (Crestwood, NY: St. Vladimir's Seminary Press, 1997).

24. Watson, *Text and Truth*, 2. The overall goal of Watson's book is to describe biblical theology as "an interdisciplinary approach to biblical interpretation which seeks to dismantle the barriers that at present separate biblical scholarship from Christian theology" (vii).

25. In addition to the burgeoning theoretical literature, attention should be given to the proposal of "canon-consciousness" as a textual attribute offered by Ched Spellman, *Toward a Canon-Conscious Reading of the Bible: Exploring the History and Hermeneutics of the Canon* (Sheffield: Sheffield Phoenix, 2014). See also Michael B. Shepherd's innovative handling of Scripture's own internal self-summaries in *The Textual World of the Bible* (New York: Lang, 2013), and finally the argument that the New Testament creatively rereads the Old Testament in light of the Christ

apart has been prosecuted so successfully across so many centuries that in our time, any interpretive move that perceives the actual unity binding any of those parts together is a move in the right direction. The Pentateuch and its annexed texts have been picked apart and pulled asunder by any number of impressive historical- and source-critical methods; but something basic is obviously restored when an equally impressive array of redaction or intertextual methods are applied to display its abiding unity.[26] Construing that set of texts as something actually unified, and learning to exhibit its marks of unity, is an example of the kind of comprehensive act of perception required for the reading of the entire Bible as a larger unity.

To take an example from the other end of the Old Testament, there is a world of difference between serial studies on a cluster of a dozen minor prophets, on the one hand, and appreciation of the complex unity that is "the Book of the Twelve," on the other hand.[27] When the apostle Peter proclaims that "all the prophets, as many as have spoken, from Samuel and those after him, also predicted these days" (Acts 3:24 NRSV), he is generalizing in a way not obviously acceptable to modern critical canons:

> This understanding of prophecy seems to fly in the face of two of the most significant results of the study of the prophets by modern critical scholarship. On the one hand it presupposes that the prophets proclaimed a unified message, whereas any textbook on prophecy in ancient Israel is likely to concentrate on drawing out the distinctive message of each prophet or prophetic book, and on the other it makes clear that the prophets focussed primarily on a proclamation of salvation, whereas if we had to use a single word to summarize the content of at any rate the majority of the prophetic books, that word would be judgement.[28]

---

event, following the lead of Jesus' own understanding of Scripture, in Mathew Malcolm, ed., *All That the Prophets Have Declared: The Appropriation of Scripture in the Emergence of Christianity* (Exeter: Paternoster, 2015).

26. In different ways, David J. A. Clines, *The Theme of the Pentateuch* (New York: Bloomsbury T&T Clark, 1997), and John Sailhamer, *The Meaning of the Pentateuch: Revelation, Composition and Interpretation* (Downers Grove, IL: IVP Academic, 2009), both demonstrate the meaningfulness of reading this stretch of Scripture for its unified witness, and both authors show themselves fully conversant with the critical methods of earlier scholars.

27. See the essays in James D. Nogalski and Marvin A. Sweeney, eds., *Reading and Hearing the Book of the Twelve* (Atlanta: Society of Biblical Literature, 2000).

28. H. G. M. Williamson, "Hope under Judgement: The Prophets of the Eighth Century BCE." *Evangelical Quarterly* 72:4 (October–December 2000): 291.

But however self-evident it seemed during the heyday of source criticism that each prophet stood alone, later studies have reconnected the canonical twelve in subtle ways. "Even the most doom-laden prophets, such as Amos, conclude in their canonical form with a word of salvation, and regardless of the literary history which led to this circumstance . . . we should recognize that they bear witness to a pattern of interpretation which has been woven into the very fabric of the prophetic corpus."[29] To miss this is to miss something really there in the texts: what they actually have to do with each other. This is the kind of perception that resonates throughout the Christian interpretive tradition: "Holy Scripture, then, is like an immense river: the farther it flows, the greater it grows by the addition of many waters."[30]

Smaller-scale groupings like this abound within Scripture. An abiding sense that the final form of the book of Psalms matters has recently given rise to a body of scholarship that considers the Psalter as a unit of thought, with an overarching theology, an almost narrative trajectory, and a dense network of sequential linguistic connections from psalm to psalm.[31] Wisdom literature has for some time now been recognized as not only a distinct genre or tradition dispersed throughout Scripture as well as the literatures of other ancient cultures, but the canonical wisdom books as a set of texts in conscious dialogue with each other.[32] Turning to the New Testament, the General Epistles have increasingly been recognized not as a collection of disparate leftover texts, but as a literary set with a definite rationale behind their gathering and a striking thematic unity linking them internally.[33] The Gospels, too, after a long and fruitful scholarly season of being teased apart for their distinctiveness, have emerged in recent years as a set of writings whose internal correspondences, implied compositional interdependences,[34]

---

29. Ibid., 292.

30. Bonaventure, *The Breviloquium*, vol. 2 in *The Works of Bonaventure* (Paterson, NJ: St. Anthony Guild Press, 1963), Prologue, 8.

31. See the essays gathered in Nancy L. deClaissé-Walford, ed., *The Shape and Shaping of the Book of Psalms: The Current State of Scholarship* (Atlanta: SBL Press, 2014).

32. James L. Crenshaw, *Old Testament Wisdom: An Introduction*, 3rd ed. (Louisville: Westminster John Knox, 2010).

33. David Nienhuis, *Not by Paul Alone: The Formation of the Catholic Epistle Collection and the Christian Canon* (Waco, TX: Baylor University Press, 2007), and Karl-Wilhelm Niebuhr and Robert W. Wall, eds., *The Catholic Epistles and Apostolic Tradition: A New Perspective on James to Jude* (Waco, TX: Baylor University Press, 2009). To grasp the difference this makes for a classic theological locus, consider the difference between staging the old conflict of James versus Galatians, as opposed to staging a conflict between the corpus of the General Epistles versus the canonical Paul.

34. For copious historical detail, see Francis Watson, *Gospel Writing: A Canonical Perspective* (Grand Rapids: Eerdmans, 2013); for the theological implications, see his *The Fourfold Gospel: A Theological Reading of the New Testament Portraits of Jesus* (Grand Rapids: Baker Academic, 2016).

and intended audiences[35] dictate that they make the most sense when considered as a complex fourfold witness.

There are some indications that contemporary scholarship is tending away from the radically disjunctive modes of textual analysis and toward at least a season of more unitive analysis. Of course there are also counter-indicators, and the conceptual tools that make for atomization and distinctions within distinctions are always ready at hand. But every move toward comprehending larger units of Scripture as internal unities is a move toward completing the necessary first step of Trinitarian theology, which arises from the totality of Scripture rather than from a congeries of scattered texts. Every move toward accepting and interpreting the canon as a whole is a move toward the Trinity. The more we are able to gather canonical books into larger canonical units, the more attainable our ultimate task of reading all the units together will be. It will be a matter of synthesizing not sixty-six books, but a dozen or so meaningful clusters (which will themselves be found to contain internal reasons for reaching out to neighboring clusters). Of course, in intellectual cultures where historical-analytic modes of reasoning are allowed to dominate without guidance or restraint, interpreters will find themselves examining far more than sixty-six books. Each book can be discovered to contradict itself and contain multitudes. The Pentateuch's sources proliferate beyond the bounds of good taste. Three Isaiahs are not nearly enough to account for the literary seams that riddle the text. Every single proverb has its own *Gattung* and *Quelle*; "psalm" itself is a hasty generalization that fails to cover whatever these are that we have 150 of. Generations within the Q community leave the marks of their civil wars on the urtexts behind our gospels. In carnival mode, modern academic biblical studies is more likely to find itself working with a thousand texts than sixty-six. A kind of extreme philosophical nominalism sets in, mediated by historicism; it is a critical tic, a reflex act of subdividing that eliminates all meaningful generalizations. The consequences for Trinitarian theology are predictable and are all around us. The cumulative effect of the refusal to think cumulatively is the emergence of a plausibility structure inimical to big doctrines, and the Trinity is the biggest doctrine.

---

35. Richard Bauckham, ed., *The Gospels for All Christians: Rethinking the Gospel Audiences* (Grand Rapids: Eerdmans, 1997).

THE ARC OF THE BIBLICAL STORY AND SELF-REVELATION

If the first step toward the doctrine of the Trinity is to construe Scripture as a whole, the second step (especially if our goal is to understand that the Father sent the Son and the Holy Spirit) is to consider this canonical whole as a narrative unity. That is, the Scripture must be understood as a divine economy in which God is the principal agent, who acts with a consistent and unfolding plan. An economy is a wisely ordered plan that unfolds over time and whose structure manifests such wisdom that the clearer it becomes, the more it redounds to the praise of God's wisdom. Paul's letter to the Ephesians looks back over what God has done in Israel and in Christ and puzzles out the connecting thread: God's lavish wisdom and insight are shown in unveiling the mystery of his will and purpose in due course (1:8–9). That mystery is the *oikonomia* of completion, a plan to unite all things in Christ (v. 10). The grand overview of salvation history offered in such passages highlights three things: God's wisdom in the arrangement; the unity of the plan carried out across the entire range of biblical history; and the agency of the triune God. It is not an accident that a passage rehearsing the unified narrative arc of salvation history in this way falls naturally into Trinitarian cadences: God the Father has blessed, chosen, and adopted a people who have redemption through the blood of the beloved Son and are sealed by the Holy Spirit of promise for a future redemption.

Comprehending this narrative unity is a step beyond mere canonical mastery, because it specifies the central content of Scripture more helpfully. Selecting and highlighting the prominent actions out of all the details of events and realities reported in Scripture means grasping the central story line accurately and comprehending God's point of view as the author of the story and the agent behind the action. It amounts to the theological claim that God has intentionally ordered all of these words and events so that they tend toward one end, serve one overriding purpose, and can find resolution in one conclusion. It is not enough to grasp the contents of the entire canon if we misinterpret those contents as an assemblage of stops and starts unguided by a purpose. Instead of a series of Bible stories, what we have in Scripture is one vast, complex, and unpredictable Bible story, a single sweeping narrative arc in which God directs his actions and words toward human salvation. The Bible is the story of how God the Father sends the Son and the Holy Spirit to save humanity by being God's own power and presence in person.[36]

This second step gives way quickly and naturally to the third step of comprehension: recognizing the divine economy as an intentional self-revelation of God. The step is natural, but not inevitable. It is possible to imagine an economy of salvation that is not also an economy of self-revelation. Theoretically speaking, God could have accomplished a kind of salvation for us without especially communicating himself or his identity to us. There is nothing conceptually incoherent in doing the former without the latter, and in fact recognizing the possibility of this counterfactual, this redemption without revelation, turns our attention to the unexacted graciousness of God in making redemption serve the end of revelation. In such a case, God would have been the mysterious origin of salvation, the unknown power that had to be hypothesized as the worker behind the work and the speaker behind the speech. Of course, if we think more concretely about the nature of the salvation God in fact accomplished, we see it is a salvation that has the character of personal communion. Therefore this particular type of salvation, considered concretely, could not have been transmitted impersonally. "The LORD is my strength and my song, and he has become my salvation" (Ex 15:2). But if we think that concretely about the nature of biblical salvation, we must think of it as the incarnation of the Son and the outpouring of the Holy Spirit from the eternal Father, which is inherently personal, even three-personal.

That is the point of taking this third step toward the doctrine of the Trinity, which is, in fact, the largest of the three steps. It is the step from the plane of history to the transcendent plane of God's identity and character. What is required for the success of Trinitarian theology is the conviction that salvation history is an economy not only of redemption but also of divine self-revelation, in which God makes himself known in a uniquely direct way. The orthodox Trinitarian conclusion of this thought process is that God has behaved as Father, Son, and Holy Spirit in the act of saving us because in doing so, he was intentionally revealing

---

36. Wisdom on the theory and practice of discerning Scripture's narrative unity can be found in Richard Bauckham, "Reading Scripture as a Coherent Story," in *The Art of Reading Scripture*, ed. Ellen F. Davis and Richard B. Hays (Grand Rapids: Eerdmans, 2003), 38–53. Bauckham is especially helpful on how "the biblical texts themselves recognize and assert, in a necessarily cumulative manner, the unity of the story they tell" (40) and on distinguishing the various senses in which Scripture's story should be called a metanarrative.

to us that he is eternally Father, Son, and Holy Spirit in essence and eternity. The Father's sendings of the Son and the Holy Spirit were not merely the next events in a series, not even next events of greater importance. These sendings, or rather this twofold mission, only makes sense as the salvation-historical mystery toward which all other divine actions have been oriented. This twofold sending is the self-revelation of God. It was God giving himself in the gospel.

The economy of salvation is the flawlessly designed way that God administers his gracious self-giving. When God gives himself to be the salvation of his people, he does not do so in a haphazard or random way. He has a plan, and he follows a procedure that is both premeditated and perfectly proportioned. The instruction we receive from scanning the economy of God is a deliberate sequence of lessons from God. God has, in fact, carried out the central events of the economy with definite communicative intent—the intent of making himself known to us in them. Anglican theologian Francis Hall made this argument in a more pedagogic register:

> Speaking broadly, all the Sacred Scriptures subserve, either directly or indirectly, the common purpose of recording and illustrating the divine education of Israel; the process of divine self-manifestation; and the completion of both in the mystery of the Incarnate Word, and in the delivery to the Church of God of a faith which can never cease to be valid and sufficient for the spiritual welfare of mankind. Israel's education and progress in spiritual knowledge, in spite of many national back-slidings, exhibits unique and consistent meaning throughout, because determined and controlled by divine guidance. And the Sacred Scriptures not only constitute literary monuments of this progress, but are also inspired by the Holy Spirit.[37]

It is in the central events of this economy that God has actively and intentionally expressed his character and identified himself. These central events of the economy are the sending of the Son and the Spirit. The apostles met these two persons, sent by the unsent first person. Their coming is the historical event, the first aspect of revelation. But the church was also clearly told the meaning of this event in words, the form

---

37. Francis Hall, *Authority, Ecclesiastical and Biblical* (London: Longmans, Green, 1918), 174–75.

of sound doctrine that was not from human initiative, but was breathed out by God, through men moved by God. We have been notified that in these last days, God has spoken by a Son (Heb 1:2), and that the name of God into which we baptize and are baptized is the name of Father, Son, and Holy Spirit (Matt 28:18–20). We did not invent these terms as our best guess at the meaning of the economy. The first Christians received these propositions from the same God who gave himself in the acts of sending the Son and the Spirit. Filled with that knowledge and insight, classic Trinitarianism learned to interpret rightly what had occurred and took up the task of reading Scripture for further clarity about the Trinity.

WHAT DO THE MISSIONS REVEAL?

We are approaching the theology of missions and processions through these hermeneutical considerations because without these presuppositions in place, it is not possible to ask the right questions about the missions. We are trying to take up the same point of view as the church's earliest theologians, so that we can pose along with them the question that gives shape to the doctrine of mission and processions. That question is, what do the missions of the Son and the Holy Spirit reveal about God? We find this implicit question constantly present in the background of patristic theologizing about the Trinity, and wherever it becomes explicit in the theology of the church fathers, the doctrine of the Trinity emerges with clearer biblical grounding and greater conceptual precision. Presupposing that the missions reveal something about God (because, as we have just rehearsed, the economy of redemption is an economy of self-revelation), we engage in the task of considering the central events of salvation history against the background of the eternal being of God. This defines the fundamental task of Trinitarian theology. The doctrine of the Trinity poses "the question of how salvation history is to be correlated with the divine being in itself," and its systematic task is "to describe the connection between God and the economy of salvation."[38] Congregationalist theologian R. W. Dale posed the doctrinal challenge this way:

38. I have described it this way in "The Trinity," in *The Oxford Handbook of Systematic Theology*, ed. John Webster, Kathryn Tanner, and Iain Torrance (New York: Oxford University Press, 2011), 35.

The immediate question . . . is whether in the Incarnation of our Lord and in the "coming" of the Spirit and His permanent activity in the Church and in the world there is a revelation of the inner and eternal life of God. Have we the right to assume that the historic manifestation of God to our race discloses anything of God's own eternal being? But this is really to ask whether the revelation of God really reveals God—shows us what God is—manifests His "eternal life." It is to ask whether when we have seen Christ, and seen Him in His relations to the Father, we have seen the "Truth."[39]

It is possible to interpret these two incursions, the coming of the Son and the coming of the Spirit, as something other than events of divine self-disclosure or to refuse them any privileged status among the manifold saving acts of the biblical God. But if they are rightly understood as uniquely central to God's one economy of redemption and revelation, they can be grasped as the salvation-historical revelation of the triune depths of God. In this case (that is to say, in the case of the classical Christian doctrine of the Trinity), "the revealed relations of the Spirit to both Father and Son have also their eternal ground in the Godhead; they did not originate in order that God's mercy might achieve our redemption; they are revealed in the great acts by which redemption is achieved; that they are revealed implies that they already existed."[40] We must come to know what the missions reveal about God.

The sendings of the Son and the Holy Spirit have been subject to a number of interpretations in the history of theology. A range of options exists, even among those who agree that these sendings are the crucial nexus where decisive salvation and definitive self-revelation coinhere. To get some sense of the full spectrum of interpretations,[41] it is worth considering the sheer negative position, which replies to the question, "What do the missions reveal about the eternal being of God?" with the blunt answer, "nothing whatsoever." That answer takes it as given that the divine actions of incarnation and Pentecost, whatever special character they may each have, are essentially divine actions in history

---

39. R. W. Dale, *Christian Doctrine: A Series of Discourses* (London: Hodder & Stoughton, 1894), 150–51.

40. Ibid., 151.

41. See Fred Sanders, "What Trinitarian Theology Is For" in *Advancing Trinitarian Theology*, ed. Oliver D. Crisp and Fred Sanders (Grand Rapids: Zondervan, 2014), 21–41.

that are not qualitatively higher than other divine actions. On this view, God would certainly be accomplishing something in the missions, but not necessarily revealing anything. God's true identity would be made known elsewhere, but not particularly in these acts. In some theologies that give this answer, God's identity is thought of as already disclosed through verbal self-declaration in such a way that the one divine revealer is interpreted as necessarily unipersonal, no matter what he does. Indeed, there is a grain of truth in the modern worry that a one-sided emphasis on verbal-propositional revelation can undermine Trinitarianism; some of the most persistent forms of unitarianism have been biblicist in this regard. The one, unipersonal God, on this account, may look out from behind different masks as he does different tasks, but the masks and tasks reveal how the unipersonal God behaves toward us, with no implications about what he is in himself. This is a modalist form of theology, in which the Son and the Spirit are so included within the divine being as to exclude personal distinctions; they simply are the one person who is also the Father.

On the other hand, there have been vigorous forms of unitarianism that trade not on Scripture but on natural religion, considering unipersonal monotheism to be so self-evidently and inescapably rational that God's personal identity is absolutely established by general revelation. On this view, the Son and the Spirit must generally be demoted to creaturely status. Great and lofty things can be said about them, as in later Arianism, but they cannot be said to be divine, so their sendings cannot be revelatory of God in a way higher than is possible for creatures; they cannot be divine self-revelation. Approaching Trinitarian theology from the question of how much the sendings reveal about the eternal being of God, we see heresies that are practically opposites of each other (Jesus being portrayed as, on the one hand, just a name for God in action and, on the other hand, as not God) falling into the same category: they both deny that the sendings reveal God.

The opposite extreme from this minimalist answer to the question is the maximalist answer: that in the incarnation and Pentecost, God reveals everything about himself so exhaustively that we have to recognize the very being of God taking place in these events, being constituted by them, and having nothing mythologically "behind" them because divine reality itself is being historical in these events. This is a difficult view to maintain because it necessitates a complete recasting of metaphysics, and usually a metaphysics that can cover both God and creation. Georg Wilhelm Friedrich Hegel had the resources to carry out that kind of metaphysical revision and could interpret God's sending of the Son and Spirit as the absolute emerging from abstraction into concrete actuality in history, then reintegrating abstraction and actuality into the living wholeness of the Spirit. This philosophy attracts its followers. But it is very hard to disentangle what it says about the (eternal?) Son from what it says about the world. As a result, the divine nature seems to be actualized more generally and widely in the history of the world process, causing incarnation and Pentecost to recede into the universal series of historical acts that are the making-known of God. The missions reveal God on this account, but so does everything else. The economy of salvation here becomes divine self-revelation in a general way, tenuously connected to anything that could be identified as God's personal communicative intention. If the minimalist answer made the missions insignificant because God's (supposedly unipersonal) identity was too settled in advance to admit of surprising explication in the incarnation and Pentecost, the maximalist answer makes them insignificant for the opposite reason, because God's identity is not established already in itself but is utterly dependent on world process as a whole. In one regard, though, the extremes meet and agree: the missions become unimportant for knowing God.

Between these extremes, some mediating possibilities exist. Consider the hypothesis that the Father's sending of the Son and the Spirit reveals there are three persons in the being of God, but that nothing can be specified beyond this threeness. The three need not be distinguished from each other except insofar as one sends and the others are sent. In themselves, in a kind of threeness immanent to the divine being, they do not stand in relationships that map onto the economic relationships. Those economic relationships are, in fact, thought of as entirely contained within and explained by the history of salvation. The sender-sent relation has no correlate or ground within the divine life itself. This view, with its anonymous threeness corresponding to a salvation-historical threeness, is more or less congenial for those who have argued that the sonship of Jesus is a messianic title that does not attach to the second person of the Trinity but is taken on for a salvation-historical role. In fact, language like "second person of the Trinity" already has a kind of implicit bias toward this view. On this view, the question of how sender and sent can be equal is not a question that can arise. The three are stipulated to be equal, and the sending is just the difference between them.

Noting some weaknesses in this sheer threeness position, the identities of the three may be filled out with reference to some kind of eternal relationship of authority. On this view, the Father sends the Son because a father necessarily has authority over a son. Perhaps based on a biblical theology of sonship, this view argues that the first two persons of the Trinity are distinguished by personal characteristics of headship and submission.

Tending even more toward a maximalism about how much is revealed in the sendings, every aspect of the economic relations of Father, Son, and Spirit could be construed as revelatory of the divine being. What if all the complex relations that take place among these three in salvation history were manifestations of a correspondingly complex and layered set of eternal relations? On this view, the missions are revelatory, but so is the Spirit's resting on the Son or shining forth from him, and so is the mutual glorification of the persons. For that matter, if the sending of Christ reveals the eternal generation of the Son, then the ascension of Christ must also be reckoned with as some kind of revelation of an eternal receiving of the eternally returning Son by the eternal Father. Obviously what is happening in this view is an eternalizing of historical occurrence, a taking up of the Son's incarnate history into the divine nature. The most influential version of this approach can be found in theologies that take the death of Christ as revealing divine passibility or even eternal passion. Whatever else may be said about Trinitarian accounts of theopaschism, we can say that insofar as they are based on reading the cross into the being of God, they are interpretive moves that claim to know a great deal about the being of God on the basis of the central event in salvation history.

TEMPORAL SENDINGS REVEAL ETERNAL PROCESSIONS

A range of errors fall as defect and excess on opposite sides of the truth, and the truth is that the temporal missions of the Son and the Spirit make known the eternal processions of the Son and the Spirit. The Son is sent to be incarnate because he stands in an eternal relation of origin with regard to the Father, a relation called generation or begetting; and the Spirit is poured out because he stands in an eternal relation of origin with regard to the Father, a relation called spiration or breathing-out. It was in order to clarify these eternal relations that Christian theology developed, by way of contrast, a doctrine of creation out of nothing. Once they confessed that the Son and Spirit came from the Father, patristic theologians had to distinguish these comings from the way the world came from God. Thus the distinction between begetting and creating made its way into the Nicene Creed ("begotten, not made") and into the arguments of Athanasius ("Just as a man by craft builds a house, but by nature begets a son, God brings forth eternally a Son who has his own nature"[42]). All that was lacking was a more or less parallel pneumatological insight, showing that the Spirit's Pentecostal outpouring is an extension of his eternal procession from the Father, to round out the Trinitarian conceptuality and complete the doctrine of God's eternal relations. The Son and the Spirit come into our history as an extension of who they have always been. When the Father sent the Son into the economy of salvation, the relationship of divine sonship was extended from the life of God where it dwells by nature, down into human history where it tabernacles by grace. Divine sonship, having always existed, extends its line of relationality into human history and created realities. Similarly, the eternal procession of the Spirit began to take place among us when the Spirit was poured out on all flesh at Pentecost.

The judgment that these two missions are the manifestations of two eternal relations of origin is as central to Trinitarian doctrine as it is fundamental to Trinitarian exegesis. Without this judgment, the doctrine of the Trinity can never be fully elaborated and can have only a brittle and abstract structure. Without this judgment, the doctrine would never have arisen at all from the scriptural witness. The most holistic interpretive move in the history of biblical theology took place when the early church discerned that these missions reveal divine processions, and that in this way the identity of the triune God of the gospel is made known. This was the insight that manifested most clearly the relation of divine act (salvation) to divine being (triunity).

Clarity and precision on this matter were gradual accomplishments, of course, and much could be said about the various paths followed by patristic theologians arguing from their diverse theological cultures.[43]

---

42. Athanasius, *Against the Arians* 3:62.

43. In these remarks, I am using the terms provided by David Yeago, "The New Testament and the Nicene Dogma: A Contribution to the Recovery of Theological Exegesis," *Pro Ecclesia* 3 (1994): 152–64. The key point is that the same judgment can be rendered in a variety of concepts.

Any particular exposition of the doctrine's formation will necessarily be only an illumination of it from one angle. But we can catch the hermeneutical judgment in the process of formation by examining the decisions that confronted some influential interpreters of the New Testament in the formative period of classical orthodoxy. Athanasius, Augustine, and Aquinas will serve to establish the trajectory.

Athanasius, confronted with Arianism's subordination of the Son, explained how Scripture's statements about him were to be construed properly. It was clear to every interpreter that numerous passages of Scripture ranked the Son as subordinate to the Father; the Arian argument maintained that the reason Scripture spoke this way reflected actual ontological subordination. The Son, on the Arian reading, was in his essence less than the Father, even if certain other passages identified him so closely with God that he had to be recognized as highly exalted above mere humanity. Against this reading, Athanasius insisted there was good reason to distinguish between these two sorts of statements about the Son.[44] Taken as a whole and considered with its chief soteriological purpose in mind, Scripture made two sorts of statements about Jesus because there are two distinct things going on in the incarnate Son:

> Now the scope and character of Holy Scripture, as we have often said, is this: it contains a double account of the Savior; that He was ever God, and is the Son, being the Father's Word and Radiance and Wisdom; and that afterwards for us He took flesh of a Virgin, Mary Bearer of God, and was made man. And this scope is to be found throughout inspired Scripture.[45]

That "He was ever God," on the one hand, and that "afterwards for us He . . . was made man," on the other, is what Athanasius calls the Bible's "double account" of the Son. Interpreters should attend to the way Scripture distinguishes these two, and sort its statements accordingly into two categories. The categories correspond, ultimately, to the divine and human natures of Christ: "Though human things are ascribed to the Savior in the Gospel, let us, considering the nature of what is said and that they are foreign to God, not impute them to the Word's Godhead,

---

44. See John Behr's careful account of this mode of thought, under the heading of partitive exegesis (*The Nicene Faith, Part One: True God of True God* [Crestwood, NY: St. Vladimir's Seminary Press, 2004], 208–15).

45. Athanasius, *Against the Arians* 3:29.

but to His manhood."[46] What Arian exegesis took to be a conflicted witness that could only be resolved by assigning the Son a middle position between divine and human, Athanasius interpreted as a signal that different statements were being made about different natures.

Charles Kannengiesser has argued that Athanasius "was the inventor of what one can call the 'dogmatic exegesis' which became one of the principal forms of biblical interpretation throughout the great controversies of the fourth and fifth centuries."[47] Whether or not it is correct to characterize his contribution in terms of originality, the clarity of his classic theological interpretation of Scripture made an elaborate two-natures Christology all but inevitable. Nevertheless, something is missing from this twofold account with its clear, anti-Arian distinction between the divinity and humanity of Christ. We can identify the missing element by asking why this Son, this absolutely equal one, was sent to be this messenger, this inferior one. Why did the coeternal, coessential second person undertake the mission to take on a temporal, created human nature? The Arians had a clear and precise answer: this one was sent to be much less than God (incarnate) because he was already somewhat less than God (created). Having eliminated their answer, Athanasius needed to replace it. He had two explanations to offer. His favorite seems to be that "it pleased God to renew creation through the selfsame word by which he created it." Athanasius always rejoices to link creation and incarnation in this way; such a link has explanatory power in both directions and enables him to tell the story of God's wise ordering of all things.

His second answer is only sometimes made explicit, but it runs steadily in the background of everything he wrote: the second person stands in an eternal relation to the first person, which is signified by calling him Son of, Word of, image of, offspring of, wisdom of, or radiance of.[48] This relationship of derivation is even reflected in the way Athanasius consistently uses the Nicene term *homoousios* with a

---

46. Ibid., III:41.

47. Charles Kannengiesser, "Athanasius of Alexandria and the Foundation of Traditional Christology," *Theological Studies* 34 (1973): 110. Kannengiesser considers Athanasius "the man of a single battle: he refused a systematic Christology which he did not consider sufficiently inspired by Scripture" (113).

48. See *Against the Arians* 1:28 for an example of Athanasius's striking methodological awareness of how these titles need to be used in mutually corrective ways. "It is more pious and more accurate to signify God from the Son and call Him Father, than to name Him from His works only and call Him Unoriginate . . . When He teaches us to pray, He says not, 'When ye pray, say, O God Unoriginate,' but rather, 'When ye pray, say, Our Father, which art in heaven'" (*Against the Arians* I:34).

definite directionality. For Athanasius, the Son is *homoousios* with the Father, but not vice versa. He would never say the Father is *homoousios* with the Son, because in Athanasian usage, "*homoousios* with" flowed in the same direction from Father to Son as usages like "image of" or "radiance of."[49] For Athanasius, the very term that was the watchword of the Son's equality with the Father was simultaneously the term that marked the Son's relationship of origin from the Father. Why was the coessential Son the one who was sent? Because his coessentiality was that of the one who stood in a relationship of fromness with regard to the one he is eternally from.

Augustine consolidated these Athanasian insights and reintegrated them into the task of doctrinal exegesis, with a specific interest in giving a more transparent answer to the question of the sending of an equal:

> We find scattered through the scriptures, and marked out by learned Catholic expositors of them, a kind of canonical rule, which we hold onto most firmly, about how our Lord Jesus Christ is to be understood to be God's Son, both equal to the Father by the form of God in which he is, and less than the Father by the form of a servant which he took. In this form indeed he is seen to be not only less than the Father, but also less than the Holy Spirit, less, what is more, than himself—and not a self that he was but a self that he is.[50]

This is obviously the twofold account, which he has accepted from "learned Catholic expositors" as a *canonica regula*.[51] But Augustine has taken on board the need to situate the christological distinctions in a more explicitly Trinitarian context, and he also has an eye for comprehensiveness in handling the full range of biblical texts. "There are," he admits, alongside the divinity and humanity texts, "some statements in the divine utterances of such a kind that it is uncertain which rule should be applied to them."[52] The statements Augustine has in mind are those affirming that the Father is the source of the Son, or that the Son comes

49. For Athanasius, that is, "*homoousios* has some derivative force in it; sons derive from fathers, but brothers do not derive from each other" (R. P. C. Hanson, *The Search for the Christian Doctrine of God: The Arian Controversy 318–381* [Edinburgh: T&T Clark, 1988], 441).

50. Augustine, *Trinity* 2.1.2, 98.

51. See Jaroslav Pelikan, "*Canonica Regula*: The Trinitarian Hermeneutics of Augustine," in *Collectanea Augustiniana: Augustine: "Second Founder of the Faith,"* ed. Joseph C. Schnauabelt and Frederick van Fleteren (New York: Lang, 1990), 329–43.

52. Augustine, *Trinity* 2.1.2, 98.

from the Father. Culling such texts in the sixteenth century, a young John Calvin would say of them, "There are very many passages of this form in John's Gospel, which agree well neither with the divinity nor the humanity, but best fit the person of Christ in which God and man have been manifested."[53] Augustine does not jump straight to the notion of personhood, but (with characteristic leisure and thoroughness in his exposition) lingers on the notion of the Son's relation of origin from the Father. "We do, after all, call the Son God from God, but the Father we simply call God, not from God."[54] Is the Son's derivation from the Father evidence for his essential, eternal divinity, or is it something he took on for us and our salvation? It is certainly not the latter (merely economic), but it is also not quite the former (evidence of deity simpliciter). Statements about the Son's origin in the Father are not merely about the Son's divinity; rather they are about his relation to the Father, or his sonship. "From him" and "of him" and "son of" all indicate this eternal relation of origin. Thus Augustine adds to the hermeneutics of the twofold account a third category: texts indicating fromness:

> Some statements of Scripture about the Father and the Son . . . indicate their unity and equality of substance. And there are others . . . which mark the Son as lesser because of the form of a servant, that is because of the created and changeable human substance he took . . . Lastly there are others which mark him neither as less nor as equal, but only intimate that he is from the Father.[55]

If sorting biblical statements into the two categories of human and divine was a necessary clarifying move in the clash with Arian readings of Scripture, it nevertheless risked oversimplifying the identity of Jesus Christ. Specifically, the two-term partitive strategy, focused as it was on distinguishing the natures, failed to account for the person of Christ. The personhood of Christ cannot be apprehended by any amount of analysis of the two natures; it must be analyzed in terms of its relation to the Father.[56] By formally acknowledging the need for a

---

53. John Calvin, *Institutes of the Christian Religion, 1536 Edition*, trans. Ford Lewis Battles (Grand Rapids: Eerdmans, 1995), 52.

54. Augustine, *Trinity* 2.1.2, 98.

55. Ibid.

56. An abiding contribution of Wolfhart Pannenberg's Christology is his insistence that the divinity of Christ should be established not directly by identification with the preexistent Logos, but indirectly by the relation of Jesus to the Father. See his *Jesus: God and Man*, 2nd ed.

third category, interpreters like Augustine[57] were able to recognize that incommunicable aspect of Jesus Christ's identity which is the heart of the Trinitarian doctrine of God: the sonship. And by linking the Son's temporal mission (being sent by the Father) with his eternal procession (being from the Father), patristic theology offered a comprehensive, holistic interpretation of salvation history and its divine ground.[58]

The theological judgment that missions reveal processions is the proper dogmatic consequence of recognizing the incarnation and Pentecost as the central points of divine self-revelation. As such, it forms the implicit conceptual guideline for all Trinitarian interpretation of Scripture. There are other elements to be taken into account, no doubt: We should consider the various titles of the Son and the Spirit; we should consider other patterns of relationality among Father, Son, and Holy Spirit beyond those of sending; we should consider a host of verbal and conceptual links between the two Testaments. As we shall see when we turn fully to the New Testament witness, it contains not only "raw material for the church doctrine of the Trinity," but also "highly developed patterns of reflection on this material," driven by "pressure to account somehow for the distinct personhood and divinity of Father, Son, and Spirit without compromising the unity of God."[59] But before any of these phenomena can contribute to Trinitarian theology, they must all find their place within the overarching conception of a single

---

(Philadelphia: Westminster, 1977), 334–44, but more comprehensively his *Systematic Theology* (Grand Rapids: Eerdmans, 1991–1998) 1:259–80 and 2:372–79.

57. It would be no service to Augustine to pretend he originated this interpretive move. Lewis Ayres credits him with "an idiosyncratic appropriation of themes already in play among his Latin forebears," especially Hilary and Ambrose. What distinguishes Augustine's presentation of the missions-processions argument is "its systematic character" in which he "offers by far the most extensive and analytical discussion of the term 'sending' and when he has settled on the main features of his account he applies that account logically and across the board." Among other novel features of the argument, Ayres notes "the sophistication with which . . . Augustine comes to use his account of the Son's eternal generation to show how the Son's earthly nativity reveals his eternal nativity, how the visible mission is grounded in the character of the Father's eternal act of generation" (*Augustine and the Trinity* [Cambridge: Cambridge University Press, 2014], 187–88).

58. Paul Helm asks, "Is the language of begottenness and procession not a reading back into the doctrine of the Trinity *per se* of those roles which according to the New Testament each person of the Trinity adopts in order to ensure human salvation?" Oliver Crisp responds that Helm "appears to have conflated the missions of God with the divine processions . . . the divine processions are *de re* necessary relations within the divine life. There is no possible world in which God exists without this sort of internal self-differentiation" (*The Word Enfleshed* [Grand Rapids: Baker Academic, 2016], 14–15, responding to Helm's *Eternal God: A Study of God without Time* [Oxford: Oxford University Press, 2010], 286).

59. Cornelius Plantinga Jr., "The Fourth Gospel as Trinitarian Source Then and Now," in *Biblical Hermeneutics in Historical Perspective*, ed. M. S. Burrows and P. Rorem (Grand Rapids: Eerdmans), 303–21.

divine economy of redemption and revelation structured by the missions of the Son and the Holy Spirit that manifest their eternal oneness with the sending Father. The divine missions are the central point, bounded on one side by the prophetic preparation for them and on the other side by the apostolic outworking of their consequences. It is the fact that the sending schema spans the entire history of salvation that enables it to indicate the divine reality beyond or above the history of salvation. Only the pan-economic is trans-economic, and vice versa.

CHAPTER 5

GOD WHO SENDS GOD

The Father's sending of the Son and the Holy Spirit makes it possible and necessary to discern distinctions within the life of the one God. The distinctions drawn by Trinitarian doctrine are the ones that must be presupposed if it is true that the two missions are the ultimate self-revelation of God. There are, therefore, in the eternal essence of God three distinct persons.

The doctrine of the Trinity is vast, and its great scope is one of its great merits. The doctrine of God that arises from consistent and coherent reflection on God's communicative missions as set forth in Scripture exerts a powerful integrative force for Christian theology. What is already apparent in interpreters like Athanasius and Augustine becomes architectonically central in the grander scholastic projects of thinkers like Aquinas. He integrated the missions-processions line of thought more explicitly into a coherent framework, taking the conclusions of earlier exegesis as a presupposition for broader application. What becomes gradually clearer is that the missions and processions are what enable theology to distinguish between the persons of the Trinity on the basis of the history of salvation. Of course, Christians had always made such a distinction among the persons, and had done so as monotheists, "neither confounding the persons nor dividing the substance" (in the words of the Athanasian Creed). But as the logic of the missions worked its way out in doctrinal understanding, classical Trinitarian theology took its stand on the fact that what is revealed in the missions is the eternal reality that distinguishes the persons from each other: relations of origin.

THE DISTINCTION OF THE PERSONS

It is easy to overlook the crucial role the missions and processions play for distinguishing the persons of the Trinity. Consider the other possibilities. When the Father sends the Son, and then we ask about the difference between the Father and the Son, we can hardly settle for the answer that one sends the other. That answer is tautologous, telling us only what we were asking about in the first place: One sent the other because one is the sender and the other is the sent. We could answer that the Father sent the Son because in the beginning God created all things through the Word. This is a true answer, has biblical warrant, is well attested in the tradition (Athanasius used the argument to great effect), and recognizes the strong continuity between creation and redemption. But as an account of the distinction between the Father and the Son, it is inadequate. It gets us back no further than the earliest divine work, creation. It only succeeds in postponing the question of distinction by pushing it back one more step, from incarnation to creation. But why did God the Father create through the Word who is his Son?

We could distill an answer from an analysis of the given names: Father is Father and Son is Son, so it makes sense that Father would send and Son would be sent. Whether as a bare appeal to the lexicon or as a placeholder for a biblical theology of fatherhood and sonship, pressing these terms would, in fact, yield much of the content for Trinitarian theology: any Father and Son as such are characterized by equality, shared substance, personal distinction, relatedness, and irreversible order. But the names set forth in Scripture cannot serve as the basis of our knowledge of the distinction of the persons. Analysis of the names certainly has the advantage of rising above the level of the merely economic answers considered above. But the actual missions of the Son and Spirit must be recognized as the foundation of the names. To appeal directly to the names is to bypass the fact that the revealed metaphors of Father, Son, and Holy Spirit were themselves given to us as self-interpretations of the missions. They are self-interpretations because Jesus spoke of the one who sent him as Father, and of himself, the sent one, as the Son. These revealed names, as metaphorical self-articulations of the persons at either end of the missions of salvation, are actually accounts of the meaning of the missions—definitive, revealed, metaphorical accounts.

The mysterious phenomenon of sent deity needs to be explained, and so it explains itself by speaking of the Father who sent it. No less mysterious is the sending deity at the other end of that mission, who singles out this consummate case of sending by proposing the terms for identifying its unrepeatable uniqueness: "This is my beloved Son, with whom I am well pleased; listen to him" (Matt 17:5).

What we have said about paternity and filiation also applies to the series of other terms put forth by Scripture as accounts of the missions: a word and its speaker, radiance and its glorious source, an image and that which it makes present by representation. All of these images function in Scripture as explanatory illustrations of what the divine mission actually is. Athanasius recognized that Scripture proposes "such illustrations and such images [παραδείγματα and εἰκόνα] . . . that, considering the inability of human nature to comprehend God, we might be able to form ideas even from these, however poorly and dimly, and as far as is attainable."[1] Athanasius was not indulging in some sort of bottomless relativism of metaphor, nor did he think Scripture gave us only a set of raw materials we could arrange at will. For Athanasius, there were standards of judgment and a coherent structure of understanding built into the revelation, taken as a whole. For example, he treated the various images as already ranked in a kind of hierarchy, with "Son" exercising a norming function over the others. Son explained Logos more than Logos explained Son. And Athanasius was especially jealous to keep properly personal terms from being exchanged for merely economic terms:

> It is more pious and more accurate to signify God from the Son and call Him Father, than to name Him from His works only and call Him Unoriginate. For the latter title, as I have said, does nothing more than signify all the works, individually and collectively, which have come to be at the will of God through the Word; but the title Father has its significance and its bearing only from the Son.[2]

---

1. Athanasius, *Against the Arians* 2:32. Jaroslav Pelikan has shown how Athanasius appropriated these Platonic philosophical terms for exegetical ends. He calls Athanasius's method "the collation of biblical images" (*The Light of The World: A Basic Image in Early Christian Thought* [New York: Harper, 1962], 27–29, 191). Note that when Athanasius rehearses the revealed παραδείγματα, he includes among them "hand" and "power."

2. Athanasius, *Against the Arians* 1:34. Athanasius cannot resist making the application: "Moreover, when He teaches us to pray, He says not, 'When ye pray, say, O God Unoriginate,' but rather, 'When ye pray, say, Our Father, which art in heaven.'"

Above all, Athanasius handled all of the revealed metaphors so that they functioned as explanations of the sendings of the Son and the Spirit. As a practitioner of the doctrinal interpretation of Scripture, he let the usage of the revealed terms be governed by their relation to the actual missions they explain. Kept in this subordinate role, the biblical metaphors function powerfully to guide us to the right understanding of what God has done in sending his Son. They evince the basic structure of Christian revelation: event and word bound together by an inner unity. We could say that the metaphors are built up on the foundation of the missions, which is why it is best to not attempt to build Trinitarian theology directly on the names without conscious recourse to their own foundation in the missions. One of the reasons for giving close attention to this possibility of basing Trinitarian distinctions on the given names is to ward off some false impressions that classical writings on the Trinity sometimes give. Classical Trinitarian theologians often argue as if they are deriving the distinctions among Father, Son, and Spirit from the revealed metaphors. But we must remember that what they are doing is pondering the incarnation and Pentecost and asking the question, "How did God send God, and what does that entail for the eternal, essential being of God?" Facing that question, they give the biblical answers of Son and Spirit (buttressed by the other terms: word, glory, wisdom, light, etc.), recognizing that the missions are temporal fromness, for us and our salvation, which manifest eternal fromness.

In establishing the missions as the foundation of our knowledge of the distinction of the persons, we are not merely saying the difference between the Father and the Son is that the Father sends the Son. That answer would be no answer at all, since it would juggle away Trinitarian distinctions (which must be eternal and essential to God) into salvation-historical acts of God (which must be temporal and freely undertaken by God). We are instead recognizing that the revelation of the Trinity occurred primarily in the historical event of the arrival of the persons of the Son and the Holy Spirit, rather than in the communication of a set of words or a series of propositions. What preserves our distinguishing of the persons by reflection on the missions from being merely economic is the confession that missions reveal processions. Economic sendings (to reason along Augustine's trajectory) make known eternal processions. And immanent processions (to reason along Aquinas's trajectory) are extended or elongated into economic missions.

Neither of the sendings is a new relation of origin in addition to the processions. Each is instead the incorporation of a further ending point to an eternally existing procession. The whole idea of a mission, as Aquinas clarifies, involves an origin point and a termination point. The origin point of a divine mission is not different from the origin point (if we may speak this way) of an eternal divine procession. That is, the eternal Son is eternally from the Father as his origin point, and the incarnate Son is identically from that paternal origin point—unless he is two different Sons. But the Son does have two distinct termination points, one in the divine nature and one in the human nature. The Son's termination point in the divine nature is his eternal deity; his termination point in the human nature is his assumption of humanity in the finite and temporal world of the events of salvation history. In Aquinas's own words, "Mission includes an eternal procession, but also adds something else, namely an effect in time; for the relationship of the divine person to a principle is eternal. We speak, therefore, of a twofold procession—the one during eternity, the other during time—in view of the doubling, not of relation to principle, but of the terminations—one in eternity, the other in time."[3]

Aquinas speaks here of a "twofold procession," which is terminologically unwieldy because it seems to call the mission a procession. But distinguishing mission from procession is the whole point. The reason Aquinas calls this movement from the Father through the eternal generation to the incarnation a "twofold procession" is to make the point that the Son is from the Father by way of a procession that terminates in deity, and (as incarnate) is also from the Father when that procession becomes twofold by terminating in humanity. For clarity's sake, it is much more helpful to reserve the word *procession* for the immanent action, and to use the word *mission* to designate the external extension. When attending to the identity of the origin point, the single source of the fromness of the Son, we can recognize that the line from the eternal Father to the incarnate Son is a straight one—though it is the very definition of amazing grace. The line from the Father to Christ incarnate passes through the eternal generation of the Son.

It is fitting that our knowledge of the distinction of persons arises from the missions, because "distinction in God arises only through the

3. Aquinas, *ST* I, q. 43, a. 2.

relation of origin."[4] The insight that missions reveal processions is what opens up the entire realm of Trinitarian discourse, where we can speak meaningfully about the one living God whose two internal processions constitute three persons. For the sake of establishing clear exposition, theologians follow Scripture's lead in focusing attention first on the generation of the Son and then turning to the spiration or procession[5] of the Holy Spirit. But just as the mission of the Son is distinct from the mission of the Holy Spirit, it reveals an internal divine procession that is distinct. What is the difference between them? John of Damascus speaks with a reserve typical of the classical tradition: "We have learned that there is a difference between generation and procession, but the nature of that difference we in no wise understand."[6] Obviously more could be said, but it is worth recognizing how much has already been said in simply acknowledging the second difference: The Father is not the Son or the Holy Spirit, but God is one.

SONSHIP AND GENERATION

When pressed to say what differentiates the three persons, aside from the relations of origin, classical Trinitarian theologians have sometimes seemed deliberately canny. "Certain distinguishing marks," they say, but all of those distinguishing marks resolve into other ways of indicating what the relations of origin have already indicated. As early as with Gregory of Nazianzus, there is an attempt to identify and label the personal characteristics, or ἰδιοτητες, of the three persons. "The personal name of the unoriginate is 'Father'; of the eternally begotten, 'Son'; of what has issued, or proceeds, without generation, 'the Holy Spirit,'" he argued,[7] adding in due course the obvious fact that "it is their difference in, so to say, 'manifestations' or mutual relationship, which has caused the

---

4. Ibid., q. 29, a. 4.

5. The Holy Spirit's relation of origin is generally called procession (from εκπορεύω) in traditions formed by Greek usage, and spiration (from *spiratio*) in traditions formed by Latin. Texts from different periods must be interpreted accordingly. But there is some strategic terminological advantage in the Western convention of letting "procession" function as a common term for both of the internal relations, while using "spiration" to indicate the Spirit's relation, parallel to "generation" for the Son's.

6. John of Damascus, *On the Orthodox Faith*, ch. 8, "Concerning the Holy Trinity."

7. Gregory of Nazianzus, Oration 30:19, in *On God and Christ: The Five Theological Orations and Two Letters to Cledonius* (Crestwood, NY: St. Vladimir's Seminary Press, 2002), 109. In all citations referring to these orations, I will be quoting from this widely available edition and using its page numbers.

difference in names."[8] In the later scholastic tradition (both in Aquinas and among the Protestant orthodox), these personal characteristics were systematically related to a host of other categories: personal acts, personal notions, and order of subsistence.[9] Valuable as these categories might be in their own rights, they are all derived from the processions; no further information has been imported into the system when these implications are drawn regarding distinctive characteristics, notions, and order.

In this regard, W. G. T. Shedd's (1820–1894) discussion of the Trinity is especially instructive for our contemporary setting because of how well he uses missions and processions to explain the distinction of the persons. Shedd was writing in a context highly suspicious of scholastic distinctions. In fact, by his time and in his tradition, there were theological voices claiming that the doctrine of the Trinity only required confession of eternal sonship, not the relation of eternal generation that the classic tradition claimed was its foundation. In correcting this view, Shedd makes good use of the distinction between the *notae internae* by which the persons of the Trinity are differentiated, and the *notae externae* by which we can also distinguish them.[10] It is a wise ordering: the internal marks are the ones that belong to the divine essence, or rather that constitute the divine essence. They are "immanent and constitutional." The external marks, by contrast, are freely chosen divine actions: creation, redemption, inspiration, and so on. Most of the work of Trinitarian theology proper has to do with the internal marks, while a full discussion of the external marks would occupy almost the remainder of a theological system (being everything the Trinity does). To answer the question, "How is the Father a distinct person from the Son?" the theologian has to attend to the *notae internae*; without them the *notae externae* are inadequate, since external works of the Trinity are undivided.

The internal marks are the generation of the Son and the spiration of the Spirit; that is, they are the processions. After surveying some biblical

---

8. Ibid., Oration 31:9, 123.

9. For the Protestant reception of these medieval scholastic distinctions, see August Twesten (1789–1876), "The Trinity," in *Bibliotheca Sacra and Theological Review* 4:13 (1847): 25–68. See especially note 1 on page 26, where Twesten disagrees with Wegscheider, Bretschneider, and Hase, who argue that this proliferation of terms (acts, notions, attributes) arises only from considering the same phenomena from different perspectives. Twesten undertakes to refute this view, but the mere fact that so formidable a trio of that period's Protestant theologians are arrayed against him shows how contested the question is.

10. William G. T. Shedd, *Dogmatic Theology*, ed. Alan W. Gomes (Phillipsburg, NJ: P&R, 2003), 241–53. Gomes's edition has helpful glosses and comments throughout; he glosses *notae interna* as "internal marks or characteristics."

reasons for affirming these relations, Shedd offers a brief defense of the theological concepts of begetting and spiration. "Some Trinitarians," he says, "have attempted to hold the doctrine of the Trinity while denying eternal generation, spiration, and procession."[11] They concede that there are three eternal persons in the Godhead, named in Scripture Father, Son, and Spirit, but contend that to go beyond this and affirm such acts in the Godhead as generation and spiration is to go beyond the record. Shedd, however, champions the Nicene way of talking about these matters. He makes the case that in saying "Father and Son," the essential content of "begetting" has already been spoken, since "begetting" is just a way of unpacking or elaborating the content already contained in the revealed name "Son." Therefore to stop at "Father and Son" language "is inconsistent."

> These trinal names *Father, Son*, and *Spirit*, given to God in Scripture, force upon the theologian the ideas of paternity, filiation, spiration, and procession. He cannot reflect upon the implication of these names without forming these ideas and finding himself necessitated to concede their literal validity and objective reality. He cannot say with Scripture that the first person is the Father and then deny or doubt that he "fathers." He cannot say that the second person is the Son and then deny or doubt that he is "begotten." He cannot say that the third person is the Spirit and then deny or doubt that he "proceeds" by "spiration" (Spirit because spirated) from the Father and Son. Whoever accepts the nouns *Father, Son*, and *Spirit* as conveying absolute truth must accept also the corresponding adjectives and predicates—beget and begotten, spirate and proceed—as conveying absolute truth.[12]

For some theologians who want to stay closer to the language of Scripture, the terminology of begetting and spirating sounds suspiciously like more than the Bible says. But how much more is it in fact saying? Shedd claims that for anybody who affirms eternal sonship, generation is "forced upon" them; their theology is "necessitated to concede" the truth of the processions. Shedd argues that language of "begetting" is simply the translation of the nouns of revelation into the "corresponding

---

11. Ibid., 245.
12. Ibid.

adjectives and predicates" of theological understanding. The Father gives his Son: that is to say that the Father who fathers the Son, gives the Son, who is passively sonned by the Father who actively fathers him. How much more do we know about the Trinity when we have translated the nouns of fatherhood and sonship into the "corresponding adjectives and predicates" of begetting and spirating? Shedd's whole presentation can be viewed as a rhetorical minimizing of the difference between sonship and begetting, between eternal persons with revealed names and eternal relations of origin manifested in the missions. But to affirm, with the great tradition and in particular with Nicene Trinitarianism, the begetting of the Son and the spiration of the Spirit provides a much more ample foundation for the doctrine of the Trinity. We have not dispelled the mystery: "Respecting the meaning of the terms generation and spiration, filiation and procession, little can be said, because inspiration has given but few data."[13] Shedd's entire argument is explicitly grammatical, and it might be tempting to interpret him as deriving the distinctions of the persons from the revealed names. But that would be a misinterpretation. His grammatical maneuvers with the revealed names and images are all carried out on the foundation of the revelatory missions.

Suppressing the memory that the revealed names are interpretations of the missions can lead to an abstract and brittle doctrine of the Trinity. Keeping these divine words linked to those divine acts is what enables us to understand the acts correctly and to use the words accurately. "What must be observed about the names Father and Son," notes Geerhardus Vos, is "that from them one derives at times too much and at other times too little."[14] We find too much in the names if we take them so literally as to mean that the Son derives his being from the Father; too little if we take them so figuratively that they express no real relation between the persons. But we also find too little in them if we take them to be "only an expression of the unity of being or of the equality of the persons with each other."[15] Various attempts to state the doctrine of the Trinity settle all too often for a demonstration of this unity and equality, eliding the relations of origin. One of the principle causes of this impoverishment of Trinitarianism is forgetfulness that the foundation of Trinitarian doctrine is inquiry into the meaning of the missions.

---

13. Ibid., 246.
14. Geerhardus Vos, *Theology Proper*, vol. 1 of *Reformed Dogmatics*, ed. Richard B. Gaffin Jr. (Bellingham, WA: Lexham, 2012), 54.
15. Ibid., 55.

INTERNAL ACTIONS OF THE TRINITY

Having traced the temporal missions back to eternal processions, there is some advantage to talking about them as internal actions. In one sense, of course, all we are doing is translating the fundamental Trinitarian insight into a new metaphorical register, or rather two: interiority on the one hand, and action on the other. But this scholastic-sounding translation into the conceptuality of internal actions is fruitful in several ways. If we do not unpack Trinitarianism using this conceptuality, it will be hard to deal with a number of pressures. Consider the alternative. If we are to use the idiom of action or agency to talk about what God does, we will, of course, say that God is the source of all sorts of effects within the order of creation. But once we have begun talking in this way about an agent who carries out actions with effects, we will need to apply it consistently and ask about what God is doing when considered apart from these doings in the world. At that point we have a choice to make. We could say that within the divine life itself there is no action leading to effects, because the life of God, being simple, is above the kind of distinctions implied in agency. Agency, on this view, would be something God has with respect to that which is not God. As for the life of God itself, we might describe its being as a very active Be-ing. We could describe it as something very alive indeed, and as something categorically greater than action, carefully refusing to apply the word *action* to the divine life in itself because we want to save it for what God does with the world. If we were to pursue this conceptual option, we would have to answer the question, "What is God doing when God is not doing anything to the world?" with an austerely apophatic answer: God is doing nothing. But with such an answer, it would be incumbent on us to find a satisfactory way of recognizing that the nothing God is doing is not a defect of the divine life in itself. The traditional account of God as pure act would need to be replaced by an account of God as pure non-act, and one that could avoid the inference that the divine being is substantially enriched by entering into relations with the lively and active reality of the world. Perhaps such an account is possible.

But traditionally, Trinitarian theology has considered it wiser to choose the other path, which is to apply the category of action to the divine life in itself, and then to say what those actions in the life of God are. Building on what the Cappadocians called *energeia* and Augustine called *opera*, Trinitarian theology developed a distinction between the inward acts of the Trinity and the outward acts. The inward acts of the Trinity are, of course, the familiar ones of generation and procession, but now handled under the general conceptual framework of "actions" in God. Each of these actions picks out a person of the Trinity, or rather each of them has a person of the Trinity at each end. The Father begets or generates the Son, which puts Father and Son at opposite ends of the relation generator-generated. The Spirit proceeds from the Father,[16] placing Spirit and Father over against each other within the divine life. This polarity or opposing relation is why the inward actions of God cannot be called undivided. The internal actions mark the distinctions among the persons. The formula used by the Council of Florence in 1439 is what has become the classic statement of the principle: "In God all is one, where there is no relation of opposition." But precisely in generation and spiration, a relation of opposition obtains,[17] so precisely here God is not one person, but three.

This account of the relations of origin as internal actions of the Trinity enables theology to recognize the divine life as inherently active and full. Wolfhart Pannenberg identifies the distinction between internal and external divine actions as "a great gain for the actual understanding of God that God should be thought of as active," and therefore as a crucial safeguard for the doctrine of divine aseity: "Does there not have to be a world of creatures, or a relation to it, if God is to be thought of as active? Christian doctrine denies this by describing the Trinitarian relations between Father, Son, and Spirit as themselves actions. To these divine actions in the creation of the world are added as actions of a different kind, as outward actions."[18]

Pannenberg's support for the doctrine is noteworthy in part because the overall drift of his theological system is toward a very close

---

16. I am attempting to state the basic, agreed doctrine without excluding either filio-quists or monopatrists. Readers may use the margins of this book to supply the phrases "and from the Son as from one common source" or "and from the Father alone," respectively. Readers who want and need more careful argument to this effect should consult the lovely note 49 on page 294 of Richard Cross's "Two Models of the Trinity?" *Heythrop Journal* 43 (2002): 275–94.

17. The objection that two such relations would yield four persons (Son and Son-Generator, Spirit and Spirit-Generator) does not work. The Father can stand in relation to Son and Spirit without thereby becoming two persons, because both relations are characterized by nonreversible "originative order." As Richard Cross says, "One person can have two distinct 'causal' relations to two distinct things in a way that one thing cannot have two distinct and individually sufficient 'causal' origins" ("Two Models," 294).

18. Wolfhart Pannenberg, *Systematic Theology*, vol. 2 (Grand Rapids: Eerdmans, 1994), 1.

involvement of the divine being with the world process. Even within the doctrine of the Trinity proper, he tends to support revisions of the classical model in favor of connecting God more closely to the world.[19] Perhaps because the distinction between internal and external works is (by Pannenberg's lights) the one necessary safeguard for recognizing divine aseity, he calls for an absolute wall between internal and external: "God does not need the world in order to be active. He is in himself the living God in the mutual relations of Father, Son, and Spirit. He is, of course, active in a new way in the creation of the world."[20]

Pannenberg draws out another benefit of distinguishing internal from external actions of the Trinity. The distinction allows for recognition of the unity of God's work in the world, without removing our grounds for identifying the distinctions among the persons: "The acts of the Trinitarian persons in their mutual relations must be sharply differentiated from their common outward actions. This differentiation finds support in the rule that posits an antithesis between the inseparable unity of the Trinitarian persons in their outward action relative to the world and the distinctiveness of their inner activities relative to one another, which is the basis of the personal distinctions of Father, Son, and Spirit."[21]

In other words, external acts of the Trinity are undivided, while the internal acts of the Trinity are distinct relative to one another. The internal actions of the Trinity help us conceive of God in himself as the living and active God, not as a God waiting for a created, historical stage on which to be living and active. They enable a confession of dynamism as part of the divine life. Nor does this distinction illegitimately manufacture or import any new content for Trinitarian theology, because the content continues to be what it has always been: the generation of the Son and the procession of the Spirit. Anchoring the livingness and activity of God in eternal generation and eternal spiration, Trinitarianism has the necessary resources to declare the external works of the Trinity as undivided. Augustine had, of course, taught that "with reference to creation Father, and Son, and Holy Spirit are one origin, just as they are one creator and one lord."[22]

---

19. It is also interesting that Pannenberg does not insist on this distinction until the second volume of his *Systematic Theology*, when he has turned from the doctrine of God to the doctrine of creation. See Fred Sanders, "Entangled in the Trinity: Economic and Immanent Trinity in Recent Theology," *Dialog: A Journal of Theology* 40:3 (Fall 2001): 175–82.

20. Pannenberg, *Systematic Theology*, 2:5.

21. Ibid., 2:3.

22. Augustine, *Trinity* 5.3.15, 197.

By contrast, theologians who deny or downplay the eternal relations of origin are susceptible to locating the distinctions among the persons in the history of salvation. Without internal acts such as processions behind the external acts that are the missions, the historical manifestations of the incarnate Son and outpoured Spirit would have to carry all the meaning and significance of Trinitarian distinctions. Any theology with a weak grasp of the internal actions of the Trinity will be a theology under tremendous pressure to make too much of the separateness of the external actions. Such a theology is bound to overexploit the external actions, perhaps reading them as three different agents doing three distinct things. In extreme cases—for example, Jürgen Moltmann at his most drastically crucicentric—the events in the history of salvation may even be described as the actual ground of the distinctions among the persons of the Trinity.[23] The desire to point to the cross as the center of all theological action is in itself understandable, and may derive from a healthy intuition. But failure to recognize the antecedent activeness in the life of the living God is debilitating for attempts at thoroughly Trinitarian theology. As Karl Barth asked Moltmann in a 1964 personal letter, "Would it not be wise to accept the doctrine of the immanent trinity of God?"[24] For safeguarding divine aseity, the distinction of persons, and the unity of God's action in the world, it would indeed be wise.

ON THE TOP SHELF

Our argument began in chapter 4 with the claim that the canon of Scripture is a unified story centered on the definitive self-disclosure of God as Trinity when the Father sends the Son and the Holy Spirit. We then traced, here in chapter 5, the argument that those missions reveal processions, which are internal actions of God that constitute the divine life in itself, in distinction from God's free outward actions toward creation. Because this is the actual basis of the doctrine of the Trinity, we must clarify its character as an ultimate claim. It does not

---

23. Moltmann testifies that he felt "bound to surrender the traditional distinction between the immanent and the economic Trinity, according to which the cross comes to stand only in the economy of salvation, but not within the immanent Trinity." At this stage of his thought, Moltmann taught that the idea of the immanent Trinity "brings an arbitrary element into the concept of God which means a breakup of the Christian concept" (*The Trinity and the Kingdom* [London: SCM, 1981], 151).

24. Quoted in James Smart, ed., *Revolutionary Theology in the Making* (Richmond, VA: John Knox, 1964), 176.

constitute merely an angle of approach, perhaps one among others, to a doctrine that can be viewed from many angles. God sends God for our salvation, making known to us that God is the kind of God who can do so. Trinitarian theology has other kinds of arguments and analyses to correlate with this central claim, but unless this central claim is true, there is no good reason for believing that God has revealed himself as he truly is through the missions of the Son and Holy Spirit.

In the historical process of faith seeking understanding, the temptation to treat this Trinitarian revelation as something less than ultimate has been recurring. But the doctrine of the Trinity must be handled as something that belongs on the top shelf of Christian doctrine, so to speak—that is, residing on the highest conceptual level such that the claims we make about it are things that apply to the divine being. Consider why this matters for questions about our comprehension of God. Incomprehensibility is a divine attribute. That God cannot be grasped, defined, and made the object of full understanding is a statement about more than just the temporary limits of our understanding. Incomprehensibility characterizes God's essence, so anything that belongs in the divine essence shares in the incomprehensibility of God. When we approach the doctrine of the Trinity as a puzzle that ought to be solvable, we are not treating it like a top-shelf doctrine. Just as we should not expect to comprehend any of the divine attributes, we ought not to expect to comprehend the triunity of God. This is not an excuse for making incoherent statements about the Trinity, or indulging in a "theological sleight of hand" that "consists in excusing doctrinal obscurity by appealing to divine mystery."[25] Responsible theology must make clear statements. When talking about things that exceed human understanding, the theological statements about those boundaries must be clear statements. Coinherence is no excuse for incoherence. But if God's triunity is an ultimate truth about God, then our grasp of it will have the same limitations as our grasp of the divine essence.[26] To expect otherwise is to treat triunity as something less than ultimate, as something on a lower shelf of theological discourse than the top shelf.

---

25. Ted Peters, *GOD as Trinity: Relationality and Temporality in Divine Life* (Louisville: Westminster John Knox, 1993), 16–17. Peters warns further that we are on thin ice when "we are tempted to cover over our puzzles and occasional lapses in clarity by ascribing them to the infinite mystery of the divine being itself."

26. A very satisfying discussion of the parameters of rationality in Trinitarian theology is Bruce Marshall, "Putting Shadows to Flight: The Trinity, Faith, and Reason," in *Reason and the Reasons of Faith*, ed. Paul J. Griffiths and Reinhard Hütter (London: T&T Clark, 2005), 55–77.

At one of the crucial turning points in the development of the doctrine of the Trinity, Gregory of Nazianzus sharply rejected any attempt to discuss the divine processions as if they belonged anywhere except on the top shelf of teaching about God.[27] In his debate with that rationalist strand of later Arianism known as Eunomianism, he stressed the fact that the Son and the Holy Spirit belong to the essence of God, and that therefore their modes of origin from the Father are on the same level as the mystery of God's own being. His opponents were apparently willing to admit that God's being is incomprehensible in itself. Gregory's task, therefore, was to persuade them that the generation of the Son and the procession of the Spirit belong properly to that same level of divine being. If he could convince his opponents that these relations of origin from the unoriginate Father belong on the top shelf, then they would have to admit the relations of origin share in the mystery of the divine essence itself. Indeed, placing the generation of the Son and the procession of the Spirit on a lower shelf from the being of God is the definition of subordinationism. Gregory drives this point home repeatedly in his third theological oration:

> It is not the case that the ingenerate and only the ingenerate is God . . . but you must allow that the Begotten too is God. The Begotten stems from God, however fond you are of unbegottenness . . .
>
> *So what is the being of God?*
>
> You must be mad to ask the question, making such a fuss about unbegottenness! . . . If it is a high thing for the Father to have no starting point, it is no less a thing for the Son to stem from such a Father . . . That he has been begotten is a further fact about him, as significant as it is august, for men whose minds are not totally earthbound and materialistic.[28]

And in the fifth theological oration, applying the same top-shelf logic to the Spirit: "What then is 'proceeding'? You explain the ingeneracy of

---

27. Although Gregory was not especially prolific by patristic standards, his works were repeatedly copied and widely distributed, to such an extent that there are more manuscripts of Gregory's works in existence than there are for any other Eastern father, with the sole exception of Chrysostom. Some of these manuscripts were even illuminated: a detailed study of one such corpus can be found in George Galavaris, *The Illustrations of the Liturgical Homilies of Gregory Nazianzenus* (Princeton, NJ: Princeton University Press, 1969).

28. Gregory of Nazianzus, Oration 29:11, 79.

the Father and I will give you a biological account of the Son's begetting and the Spirit's proceeding—and let us go mad the pair of us for prying into God's secrets.[29]

Even allowing for Nazianzus's characteristic rhetorical bombast, we must acknowledge his point: if the Son is fully divine, then it is not for us to decide whether sonship is fitting for a person of the Trinity. Epigrammatically, Nazianzus concludes this discussion: "Sonship is no defect."[30]

If a theologian is going to assert that the eternal relations of origin belong on the top shelf with the being of God, it is incumbent on that theologian to provide the evidence that the Son and the Spirit are fully divine. These proofs should be drawn rather directly from Scripture and be as persuasive as possible. Their witness should be clear rather than ambiguous, and the relevant passages should be copious rather than scarce. A general waving of the hand in the direction of the evidence would be inadequate here. Above all, the proof from individual Scriptures must itself be based on the underlying and comprehensive logic of the two missions, incarnation and Pentecost, as the salvation-historical manifestation of eternal relations of origin. Nazianzus is aware of this, and a great bulk of *The Five Theological Orations* (especially the third and fourth orations) is made up of vigorous presentations of the biblical evidence for the deity of the Son and the Spirit, to which Nazianzus annexes explanations that had become by the fourth century commonplaces of controversial theology, along with defenses against counterarguments. Structurally speaking, this material supports Nazianzus's argument that the eternal relations cannot be placed on a lower shelf than divinity itself.

To place these Trinitarian distinctions on the top shelf is, of course, only to be consistent in affirming Trinitarian theology at all. As Khaled Anatolios recognizes, "Even Arius accorded primacy to Christ as 'first-born of all creation,' the created Creator."[31] Such a primacy—primacy merely within creation or among the ways of God with creatures—is subtrinitarian. It falls short of the high standard marked by the Nicene confession and is unable to approach "the heart of the fourth-century debates," which Anatolios characterizes as the question of:

---

29. Ibid., Oration 31:8, 122.
30. Ibid., Oration 31:9, 123.
31. Khaled Anatolios, *Retrieving Nicaea: The Development and Meaning of Trinitarian Doctrine* (Grand Rapids: Baker Academic, 2011), 156. For Anatolios's detailed presentation of these conclusions, see especially the section "Constructing a Trinitarian Hermeneutics," 108–26.

how Christ's primacy informs the Christian faith as a whole, and, in particular, the Christian understanding of absolute divine transcendence. With Athanasius, the answer is that two main scriptural routes lead us to see the very character of God as Christological. The patterns of scriptural co-naming of God and Christ lead us to conceive of the God-Christ relation as intrinsically constitutive of God. Simultaneously, the salvific work of Christ, to the point of death on the cross, manifests the character of the divine nature as merciful *philanthrōpia.*[32]

What Anatolios affirms of the theology of Athanasius holds good for Trinitarian theology in general: It is "ultimately founded on the insistence that there is no divine 'remainder' above or beyond or aside from the scriptural co-naming of God as Father, Son, and Spirit. God's creative and salvific agency is to be identified strictly within that divine interchange."[33] The comprehensive grasp of Scripture's total message as witness to an economy of revelation and redemption, combined with a soteriological impulse to link salvation to God himself, entails that Trinitarianism is fully serious in its intent to refer to God without remainder.

TRINITARIAN PERSONHOOD

If our next step is to make explicit the concept of Trinitarian persons, it is nevertheless worth noting that this will not be an especially large step. Having affirmed that relations of origin are what distinguish Father, Son, and Holy Spirit, we have already stated most of the content of Trinitarian personhood. If Trinitarian theology's overall orienting concern is what the missions reveal about God, then the discussion of personhood is simply a more precise form of that question: Since God sent God and God, what common noun should we use to mark what those three occurrences of "God" signify?[34] Three what?

---

32. Ibid., 156.
33. Ibid.
34. Occasionally a theologian will attempt to say what needs to be said about Trinitarian personhood without taking recourse to a stable noun. The boldest such performance in recent memory is David Cunningham's *These Three Are One: The Practice of Trinitarian Theology* (Oxford: Blackwell, 1998), 28: "In my own writing, I have intentionally opted out of the quest for the perfect substantive; instead, I simply use the phrase 'the Three.'" The move works fairly well for Cunningham's project because of his close attention to rhetorical effect and his strong

The answer given by church dogma is "three persons." Every short statement of the basic doctrine of the Trinity will include some reference to the ancient formula: "one being, three persons." In this formula, "one being" identifies the divine essence, which must be acknowledged as simple and single, neither divided nor multiplied (on pain of polytheism). The "one being" part of the formula should be no surprise for mono-theists of any kind. "Three persons," on the other hand, identifies the distinctions in which the one God subsists. It is not the sort of position that could have been predicated in advance as a form of monotheism—though Trinitarianism is, properly considered, monotheism concretized rather than monotheism compromised.[35]

Almost as ancient as the formula itself, however, is a tradition of apparently backpedaling from it somewhat. No sooner has the illumi-nating word *person* been offered than it is all but retracted. "Human speech," Augustine famously said, "labors under a great dearth of words. We say three persons, not in order to say that precisely, but in order not to be reduced to silence."[36] John Henry Newman made the same point somewhat more auspiciously when he wrote of the word *person* that we already knew "before we began to use it, that the Son was God yet was not the Father . . . the word Person tells us nothing in addition to this."[37] Indeed, if we were intentionally trying to say no more than what we have already said about eternal relations of origin and internal actions, we might describe the persons as relations that are themselves subsistent. That is in fact what Christian doctrine has said about the meaning of the word *person* as applied to the Trinity: "'divine person' signifies a relation as subsistent."[38]

A deft argument by Augustine showcases the conceptual tensions that led to this use of the term *person*. Augustine noted that anything said about God substantially is said about the one unchanging God, which makes it impossible to argue to Trinitarian persons from divine attributes or actions. No single attribute can pick out a person of the Trinity, unless

Wittgensteinian account of how words get their meaning from practice anyway. It would not work for most theological writing.

35. Karl Barth emphasized this so strongly that it damaged his prose: "Christian monotheism was and is also and precisely the point also and precisely in the Church doctrine of the Trinity as such" (*CD* I/1, 351). The German is not much better. For "concrete monotheism," see Pannenberg, *Systematic Theology* 1:335.

36. Augustine, *Trinity* 5.2.10, 196.

37. John Henry Newman, *The Philosophical Notebook of John Henry Newman*, vol. 2, ed. Edward Sillem (Louvain: Nauwerlaerts, 1970), 105.

38. Aquinas, *ST* I q. 29, a. 4.

we are willing to deny that the other persons possess that attribute. If the Apostles' Creed called the Father the almighty maker of heaven and earth with the intent to exclude the Son and the Spirit from the attribute of almightiness or the act of creation, it would exclude Son and Spirit from divinity.[39] Yet on the other hand, the immediately preceding word, Father, does pick out the first person alone. "Father" cannot be said substantially, or it would include Son and Spirit, rendering each of them as much Father as they are almighty. What kind of statement, then, can include Son and Spirit as God but exclude them as Father? When we consider the various things Scripture says of God, Augustine points out, we should notice that "not everything that is said of him is said substance-wise. Some things are said with reference to something else, like Father with reference to Son and Son with reference to Father."[40] These things "said with reference to something else" are said relation-wise. Of course, many things could be said of God relation-wise, if we admitted all of God's ways with the world into our discourse. But if the things to be said of God relation-wise are eternal and internal, that is, if they are actually about God and not realities outside of God, then we have entered the realm of discourse about the divine persons. This is, in fact, precisely how the treatise on the Trinity was introduced in Protestant scholastic systems. Consider the Lutheran theologian Johannes Quenstedt (1617–1688): "The consideration of God is twofold, one absolute, another relative. The *former* is occupied with God considered essentially, without respect to the three persons of the Godhead; the *latter*, with God considered personally. The *former* explains both the essence and the essential attributes of God; the *latter* describes the persons of the Holy Trinity, and the personal attributes of each one."[41]

Or see the same movement in the Reformed theologian Francis Turretin (1623–1687), who marked the transition from De Deo Uno to De Deo Trino with this conceptual turn: "The absolute consideration of God (as to his nature and attributes) begets the relative (as to the persons)."[42]

---

39. The creed is, in fact, speaking by way of appropriation. This venerable notion stands in need of some rehabilitation since undergoing critique and misrepresentation during the revisionist Trinitarian excitement of the late twentieth century. The best exposition of which I am aware is Gilles Emery, "The Personal Mode of Trinitarian Action in Saint Thomas Aquinas," *The Thomist* 69 (2005): 31–77, but a more general study of appropriation is much to be desired.

40. Augustine, *Trinity* 5.1.6, 192.

41. Cited in Heinrich Schmid, *The Doctrinal Theology of the Evangelical Lutheran Church* (Minneapolis: Augsburg, 1889), 134.

42. Francis Turretin, *Institutes of Elenctic Theology*, vol. 1, ed. James T. Dennison Jr. (Phillipsburg, NJ: P&R, 1992), 254.

Although this is the precise and rather arid language of scholastic theology (absolute versus relative, substantial versus relational), and we are
describing how two doctrinal loci relate, what the terminology actually
expresses is the transformation in our relationship to God brought about
by the coming of Christ and the Holy Spirit. Gerald Bray transposes
the discussion into a new register when he describes knowledge of the
Trinity as "inside knowledge" of God's life. The transition from God's
true self-revelation in the old covenant to his fuller self-revelation in the
new covenant cannot be understood as merely an increase in degree of
knowledge. It is the introduction of a new kind of knowledge of God,
by participation in God's own self-knowledge. "Christians have been
admitted to the inner life of God," writes Bray. "The God who appears as
One to those who view him on the outside, reveals himself as a Trinity of
persons, once his inner life is opened up to our experience. The Christian
doctrine that has resulted from this is neither nothing more nor less than
a description of what that experience of God's inner life is like."[43] To
understand God from the outside (that is, "absolutely considered") is
to leave personal distinctions out of the question. To understand God
from the inside ("relatively considered") is to note the eternal relations,
that is, the persons. Luther taught that "viewed from without, from the
point of view of the creature, there is but one Creator"; but turning to
the revelation of the Trinity, he said "here you observe how the three
Persons are to be believed as distinct within the Godhead and are not to
be jumbled together into one Person."[44] The only way to "view God"
from an inside perspective is if the eternal relations of origin, in which
the one God subsists these three ways, have been graciously made open
to us in their salvation-historical extensions—the sendings of the Son

---

43. Gerald Bray, "Out of the Box: The Christian Experience of God in Trinity," in *God the Holy Trinity: Reflections on Christian Faith and Practice*, ed. Timothy George (Grand Rapids: Baker Academic, 2006), 45–46. The whole set of distinctions introduced here provides a partial justification for using a singular pronoun to refer to God ("reveals himself as a Trinity"), and even for calling the one God a person—occasionally, loosely, and nontechnically. Considered from outside, or absolutely, he is the triune God.

44. Martin Luther, "Treatise on the Last Words of David," in *Notes on Ecclesiastes, Lectures on the Song of Solomon, Treatise on the Last Words of David*, vol. 15 of *Luther's Works*, ed. Jaroslav Pelikan (St. Louis: Concordia, 1972), 305. See also 311: "As the works of the Trinity to the outside are indivisible, so the worship of the Trinity from the outside is indivisible." Luther consistently uses the "outside/inside" language to contrast creation with redemption. Gerald Bray's argument contrasts old covenant (outside) with new covenant (inside). His distinction, if developed further, would need to be hedged with many warnings. But as long as Israel has real knowledge of the true God, of a sort that is "inside" by contrast with uncovenanted knowledge, Bray's distinction is a helpful extension of some New Testament ways of speaking.

and the Holy Spirit from the Father. Because that is what has happened, we confess three persons in the one God.

USING THE WORD *PERSON*

Two features mark our use of *person* in Trinitarian theology. First, it is used metaphysically, and second, it is used ad hoc.

Person is used metaphysically rather than psychologically or subjectively. Gilles Emery makes this point by citing the classic definition of person from Boethius ("a person is an individual substance of rational nature") and then remarking, "This metaphysical understanding of the person is not the first thing we notice in our experience of being 'persons.'"[45] Perhaps we could add certain psychological or subjective elements to our use of the word and integrate the psychological with the metaphysical. Emery points out that we can reflect on our own experience of personhood and discern, underlying it, "the deep reality that is the radical principle of free action, of openness to others, and of self-consciousness."[46] So when Trinitarian theology poses the series of questions ("What do the missions reveal? What are there three of in God?") that lead to the answer "person," the result is not a mere verbal cipher with no analogical purchase on our experience. "The metaphysical approach, it should be clear, excludes neither the psychological, moral, and relational features of the person, nor the importance of action. Rather, it enables one to integrate these aspects, and it guarantees their foundation."[47] On the other hand, the Trinitarian use of the word *person* rather spectacularly fails to satisfy the expectations of interrogators who approach it from other contexts, especially less metaphysical contexts. What greets them in Trinitarian personhood, while it has some analogical points of contact in human affairs, is mainly a restatement of the line of thought we have traced in this chapter. The God who sends God and God must be God in eternal relations that subsist.

Closely related is the second feature of our usage, which is that the word *person* as used in Trinitarian theology has an ad hoc character. It was pressed into service for this particular purpose and can only with great

---

45. Gilles Emery, *The Trinity* (Washington, DC: Catholic University of America Press), 102.
46. Ibid.
47. Ibid., 104.

difficulty be generalized or abstracted from its original context. It must pass through a zone of disanalogy, be layered over with adjustments, and ringed around with qualifications. This is why it should not be presented with a flourish, as if it introduces new material content into the doctrine: it bears all the marks of having been devised to summarize a train of thought. We cannot safely start any phase of Trinitarian theology by subjecting the term *person* to analysis and deriving information from that analysis. We must always return to the generative dynamics that resulted in our taking recourse to talking of persons in God. This is what Barth was signaling when he said that "the truly material determinations of the principle of threeness in the unity of God were derived neither by Augustine, Thomas nor our Protestant Fathers from an analysis of the concept of person, but from a very different source."[48] This has pedagogical implications, of course: it is probably unwise to present robust definitions of such terms at the beginning of a lesson. But it also has systematic implications in that it limits the usefulness of the term for other doctrinal uses.

Just how ad hoc the Trinitarian account of personhood actually is can be seen from the way it is explained in James Ussher's 1648 *Body of Divinity*. Immediately upon answering the question of what a person is (the work is written as a kind of advanced catechism, in question-and-answer format), Ussher distinguishes between persons in general, and "then what a Person in the Trinity is."[49] A person in general, says Ussher, is "one particular Thing, Indivisible, Incommunicable, Living, Reasonable, subsisting in it self, not having part of another." And he anatomizes each term in that definition briefly:

> I say that a Person is, first, one particular Thing: Because no general Notion is a Person. Secondly, indivisible: Because a Person may not be divided into many Persons; although he may be divided into many parts. Thirdly, incommunicable: Because, though one may communicate his Nature with one, he cannot communicate his

---

48. Barth, *CD* I/1, 359. Barth says this on the way to announcing his decision to eschew the term *person* and instead to use *mode [or way] of being*. I view his rejection of the traditional term *person* as one of the places where Barth made the wrong decision for all the right reasons. In general, he is seeking to obey the axiom *non sermoni res, sed rei sermo subjectus est* (word is subject to reality, not vice versa), "without adopting which we cannot really be theologians" (*CD* I/1, 367). But abandoning person-language has not resulted in clarity about the thing itself.

49. James Ussher, *A Body of Divinity: The Sum and Substance of the Christian Religion* (Birmingham, AL: Solid Ground, 2007), 67.

Person-ship with another. Fourthly, living and Reasonable: Because no dead or unreasonable thing can be a Person. Fifthly, subsisting in it self: To exclude the humanity of Christ from being a Person. Sixthly, not having part of another: To exclude the Soul of Man separated from the Body, from being a Person.

While "Thing," even when capitalized, is not exactly a technical term in English, its adjective "particular" seems to be doing most of the work. What is to be excluded from personhood is anything general. It is this (1) particularity, which dictates that personhood must also be (2) indivisible and (3) incommunicable. Incommunicability is at the heart of the mystery of personhood, and of what differentiates it from a nature. And the kind of incommunicable particular thing that is a person must be (4) living and reasonable rather than dead and unreasonable. But it is with the fifth and sixth branches of the description of personhood that the discussion becomes strikingly ad hoc. The only reason given that (5) a person must be said to subsist in itself is that otherwise the human nature of Christ would be a person and Nestorianism would be true. The human nature of Christ came into existence in order to be the human nature of the second person of the Trinity. Thus an expressly christological concern intrudes into the very definition of personhood in general, setting a limit that must be recognized in framing the general concept. A similar adjustment for the sake of doctrine occurs with the definition (6) that a person cannot have part of another, for otherwise when a soul separates from the body, the soul itself would be a person. Ussher declares that the disembodied soul is not by itself a person and draws the conclusion for the definition of personhood. In both of these cases, Ussher writes as if he has inserted an element into the definition of person just to make room for special cases like the (utterly unique) incarnation and the (common, but not normal) intermediate state of disembodied souls.

If Ussher subjects the general notion of personhood to such alteration to make room for special cases, what is a person in the Trinity? Here he makes a series of statements that are only about God and have no value for any other discussion. A person of the Trinity, Ussher says, "is whole God, not simply or absolutely considered, but by way of some personal Properties. It is a manner of being in the Godhead, or a distinct Subsistence (not a Quality, as some have wickedly imagined:

143

For no Quality can cleave to the Godhead) having the whole Godhead in it."[50] They are called "persons" because they have "proper things to distinguish them," and these distinctions are made "not in nature, but in relation and order." These relations and order are the next thing Ussher goes on to discuss, and the analogical interval between persons human and divine necessarily expands as he describes the relations among Father, Son, and Holy Spirit. The result of a fairly typical discussion like Ussher's is that we are left with a word that, carefully defined and flexibly handled, still manages to function to enable meaningful speech about what God has revealed. But it is a not-very-portable term, local and heuristic, and it is in need of careful adjusting if used outside its sphere of origination.[51]

ECONOMIC TRINITY AND IMMANENT TRINITY

The path we have traced from the salvation-historical missions to the relations of origin and back arcs across the vast distinction between God's actions in the world and God's eternal being. It could be described as connecting the Trinity we experience in salvation history (the sending Father, the incarnate Son Jesus Christ, and the Holy Spirit of Pentecost) with the Trinity of God's own eternal being (the Father who has not yet sent and will only do so by grace, the Son who has not yet become incarnate and will only do so by condescension, and the Holy Spirit who is not yet poured out and will only be so on the basis of the finished work of Christ). We could describe the entire project in other words as negotiating the relationship between the economic Trinity and the immanent Trinity. This is the conventional terminology of modern Trinitarianism, widely used and thoroughly discussed.[52] In this final section before turning to the scriptural witness, I would like to register a warning about the disadvantages of investing much in that terminology.

---

50. Ibid., 68. For biblical evidence, Ussher cites John 11:22; 14:9, 16; 15:1; 17.21; Colossians 2:3, 9.

51. Khaled Anatolios helpfully situates this discussion within recent debates about personalism and analogy in patristic scholarship in his chapter "Personhood, Communion, and the Trinity in Some Patristic Texts," in *The Holy Trinity in the Life of the Church* (Grand Rapids: Baker Academic, 2014), 147–64.

52. The distinction provided the orienting categories for my interaction with modern Trinitarianism in *The Image of the Immanent Trinity: Rahner's Rule and the Theological Interpretation of Scripture* (New York: Lang: 2005).

At first glance, discourse about the economic Trinity and the immanent Trinity seems like simply a modernized translation of the patristic distinction between *oikonomia* and *theologia*. Just as Athanasius spoke of the incarnation of the Logos as "that which is *kata oikonomia*," meaning something like "by way of dispensation" or "in carrying out the plan of God," he spoke of the eternal deity of the Son as "that which is *kata theologia*," or as referring to divinity proper.[53] Such a distinction was crucial in resisting Arians, whose denial of the deity of the Son was expressed as seeing the Son's incarnate mission (his *oikonomia*) as revelatory of his essential being (his *theologia*, or in their view, his lack of it). While the language of economic Trinity and immanent Trinity can be used to make that sort of distinction, on its own it tends in another direction, as can be seen by the peculiarity of its construction and by its hazy origins.

What is peculiar about its construction is that it verbally doubles the Trinity. While nobody thinks there are two actual trinities involved in reality, the reduplicative phrasing puts two trinities into any sentence framed by economic and immanent. If this modern way of talking simply translates the ancient way of talking, it is strange that some of the things the Greek patristic writers wanted to affirm cannot be put into the modern idiom. Would Athanasius, for instance, insist that the economic Son of God is the immanent Son of God? Or would he say that sonship is both economic and immanent? Or that there is an economic sonship and an immanent sonship? None of the permutations can quite capture his claim that the eternal Son took on human nature and came to us. The categories themselves do not quite invite such formulation.[54] One reason is that the trope of Trinity-doubling serves to construct two referential planes, each with its own network of relations. It is a schema in which many true things can be glimpsed and expressed, but it invites the mind to assume such a high level of abstraction that fundamental errors about concrete matters can go unnoticed. Seminary professors

---

53. The distinction is pervasive but not especially quotable in Athanasius. Its influence can be seen as it enters into the more concise formulations of John of Damascus, speaking of "that which relates to *theologia* and in that which relates to the *oikonomia*" (*Orthodox Faith*, II). See R. A. Markus, "Trinitarian Theology and Economy," *Journal of Theological Studies* 9 (1958): 89–102.

54. Thomas Torrance should be counted among the few moderns who managed to use this terminology without being used by it. His success stems from the rhetorical effect of his constant use of Greek patristic terms, the flexibility with which he worked *oikonomia* and *theologia* into various expressions throughout his oeuvre, and his methodological self-awareness. For the latter, see his explanation of levels of discourse in *The Christian Doctrine of God: One Being Three Persons* (Edinburgh: T&T Clark, 1996), 95.

can attest to the sort of theological blunders this particular abstraction underwrites (and no doubt partly blame themselves for retailing categories that make such mistakes easier for students to make but harder to detect). Perhaps the diastasis between the two conceptual trinities has the advantage of making room for a greater amount of data—an entire Trinity's worth of economic data in distinction from an entire Trinity's worth of immanent data, all within a comprehensive conceptual field that demands an argument about how the two are correlated. This comprehensiveness is the most evident advantage of talking about the economic Trinity and the immanent Trinity. There is something vaguely Kantian in the transcendental perspective assumed by the distinction, as if the real point of any inquiry carried out in these terms were to relate the phenomenal Trinity to the noumenal Trinity and vice versa. But that brings us to its hazy origin.

Karl Rahner, articulating what later theologians have sometimes called Rahner's Rule,[55] wrote that "we are starting out from the proposition that the economic Trinity is the immanent Trinity and vice versa," and then remarked, "I do not know exactly when and by whom this theological axiom was formulated for the first time."[56] Although even Rahner does not know the source of the sentence called Rahner's Rule, there is some consensus on the origin of the words that are used in it. Earlier writers may have compared God's eternal being with God's revealed triunity, but it was the Lutheran theologian Johann August Urlsperger (1728–1806) who put the terminology into circulation.[57] Urlsperger was an idiosyncratic thinker rather marginal to established academic circles,[58] but the polemical thrust of his arguments about the

---

55. In an academic rivalry of an unusual kind, two scholars credit each other with inventing the phrase "Rahner's Rule." Roger Olson says Ted Peters coined it ("Wolfhart Pannenberg's Doctrine of the Trinity," *Scottish Journal of Theology* 43 [1990]: 178), while Ted Peters says Roger Olson coined it (*GOD as Trinity: Relationality and Temporality in the Divine Life* [Louisville: Westminster John Knox, 1993], 213).

56. Karl Rahner, "Oneness and Threefoldness of God in Discussion with Islam," in *God and Revelation*, vol. 18 of *Theological Investigations* (New York: Crossroad, 1983), 114. I attempted to sleuth out the origin of the axiom in my *Image of the Immanent Trinity*, 47–82.

57. Several older histories of theology identify Urlsperger as the source, but the most thorough discussion of his role is Ralf Stolina, "Ökonomische und immanente Trinität? Zur Problematik einer trinitätstheologischen Denkfigur," *Zeitschrift für Theologie und Kirche* 105 (2008): 170–94. Eberhard Jüngel responded to Stolina's argument (commending his historical work, but sharply questioning his dogmatic conclusions) in "Was ist er inwerds? Bemerkungen zu einem bemerkenswerten Aufsatz," *Zeitschrift für Theologie und Kirche* 105 (2008): 443–55.

58. See F. Ernest Stoeffler, *German Pietism During the Eighteenth Century* (Leiden: Brill, 1973), 249. Stoeffler quotes Urlsperger's contemporary, Nicolai: "Mr. Urlsperger is a very well-meaning

Trinity drew responses that helped his way of talking become established in general usage even as he himself receded into obscurity.

In Urslperger's Trinitarian writings,[59] he distinguished between a Trinity of being on the one hand and a Trinity of revelation on the other.[60] He did this as a way of insisting that God was triune at both levels, in contrast to trendy rationalist modalisms that admitted, on a biblical basis, a certain revelatory threeness, but envisioned a merely unipersonal God behind those manifestations. Urslperger championed an actual threeness in the eternal being of God. But he agreed with the antitrinitarians that the whole tangle of relations made manifest in the economy of salvation (sending and being sent, fatherhood and sonship, etc.) were in fact inadmissible to the level of God's actual being. There was absolutely nothing about those relations that would remain after they had been purified of every hint of subordination, in Urlsperger's view, so they had to be restricted to the level of the economy. Determined to maintain real threeness within God, but steadfastly refusing to follow the traditional route of tracing temporal missions back to eternal processions, Urlsperger instead posited an eternal Trinity consisting of three subjects whose relations were not the revealed relations:

> For in the essence of God there is no Father, Son, and Spirit; each subsistence in this essence is equally eternal, equally necessary, indeed grounded in each other but not dependent on one another through subordination. In short: one essence, no first, no second, no third, no greater, no lesser. All alike equal, all alike necessary, all alike supremely realized.[61]

For us and our salvation, these three enter a mutual compact to be Father, Son, and Holy Spirit. It is not just that one sends the others, but

---

man but of very modest learning and intellectual powers . . . neither orthodox nor heterodox, only indefinite and unclear."

59. Over the course of five years, Urlsperger published the four-volume *Versuch in freundschaftlichen Briefen einer genaueren Bestimmung des Geheimnesses Gottes* (Frankfurt, 1769–1774), generally considered unreadable. He summarized his findings in his *Concise System of His Presentation of the Triunity of God* (*Kurzgefaßtes System seines Vortrages von Gottes Dreyeinigkeit* [Augsburg, 1777]), on which see Georg Gremels, *Die Trinitatslehre Johann August Urlspergers dargestellt nach seiner Schrift "Kurzgefaßtes System"* (Frankfurt: Lang, 1993).

60. "Wesensdreieinigkeit und Offenbarungsdreieinigkeit." See Urlsperger, *Kurzgefaßtes System*, 106, 167. Note how German prose's characteristic compound nouns make for a relatively smooth reference to two trinities.

61. Cited in Stolina, "Ökonomische und immanente," 177.

that at some point before the foundation of the world, they enter into genetic, processional relations that constitute them as Father, Son, and Holy Spirit. In a kind of economy before the economy but in preparation for the economy, they become whatever it is necessary for them to be in order to assume the functions they will manifest in the history of salvation. On this account, the economic Trinity predates creation itself, but is not identical to the essential Trinity in which "there is no Father, Son, and Spirit."

CLASHING FRAMEWORKS

A paragraph is probably already too much space to have devoted to elaborating Urslperger's curious concoction of theosophy, Eunomian Arianism, and covenant theology.[62] Nobody else in the history of Christian thought has ever believed quite what Urlsperger believed. But through his new set of technical terms, he turned the course of modern discussion of the Trinity.[63] What is especially striking is that he devised the categories of economic and immanent Trinity not simply to distinguish the two levels, nor simply to insist that God was triune on both levels, but precisely to deny that missions reveal processions. His goal was to find a way to confess an actual threeness of the eternal God, while treating all the known relations among the three as matters of the economic revelation. What, then, shall we say Karl Rahner is accomplishing when he joins the discussion on these terms and proposes that the economic Trinity simply is the immanent Trinity, and vice versa? No doubt he is repairing a breach that Urlsperger opened, and closing a gap that needed to be closed. But once we grasp that Urlsperger's project was designed to block the inference from missions to processions, we see that Rahner's intervention into the discussion ought to be evaluated on whether it succeeds in restoring that inference. That, it seems to me, is an open question, since Rahner has become the symbolic figurehead for modern use of the terms *economic Trinity* and *immanent Trinity*. Any baleful influence transmitted by the continued use of terms themselves

---

62. He had access to material from all three sources. For the theosophist connection (Oetinger and Wurtemburg pietism), see Stoeffler, *German Pietism*, 249. Urlsperger's familiarity with Eunomianism was part of his response to the eighteenth-century quest for alternatives to Athanasianism. Finally, he was steeped in Lutheran orthodoxy which included scholastic discussion of the *pactum salutis*.

63. For details on how "Trinity of revelation" and "Trinity of Being" turned into "economic Trinity and immanent Trinity," see Stolina, "Ökonomische und immanente," 174–77.

can likely be tracked to Rahner's Rule as the chief carrier. Furthermore, if the conceptual construct itself exerts a distracting or distorting effect on Trinitarian thought, Rahner's attempt to collapse the distinction may be bootless. The chief thing to attend to is whether this approach restores the missions to their central place in the doctrine of the Trinity, as revelatory of processions.

One particularly telling case study suggests not. Six years after Rahner's influential Trinity essay appeared, the Dutch Jesuit theologian Piet J. A. M. Schoonenberg published a controversial article called "Trinity: The Consummated Covenant: Theses on the Doctrine of the Triune God."[64] Schoonenberg argued that if Rahner is correct about the identity of the economic and immanent Trinity, then the question of whether God is triune *in se*, apart from the economy of salvation, is "unanswered and unanswerable. It is thereby eliminated from theology as a meaningless question."[65] Rahner's Rule is usually taken to be a radically, if not revolutionarily, Trinitarian watchword. How did its application result in agnosticism about whether God is triune *in se*? Schoonenberg reached his conclusion simply by taking up Trinitarianism's standard terminology and reworking it as a set of corollaries to the axiom of Rahner:

> The salvation-economy fatherhood of God is the inner-divine fatherhood, and vice versa.
>
> The salvation-economy filiation is the inner-divine filiation, and vice versa.
>
> The Spirit of God at work in salvation history is the inner-divine Spirit, and vice versa.
>
> The missions are the processions, and vice versa.
>
> The salvation-economy relations are the inner-divine ones, and vice versa.[66]

The problems with these corollaries are legion. We cannot spare time to give them all the swatting they deserve, but a few problems that stand out include the following. If economic filiation is immanent filiation, then God becomes Father of the Son in time rather than eternity. The

---

64. Piet J. A. M. Schoonenberg, "The Consummated Covenant: Theses on the Doctrine of the Triune God," *Sciences Religeuses* 5:2 (Fall 1975): 111–16.

65. Ibid., 112 (theses 7–8).

66. Ibid., 112–13 (theses 11–15).

entire Trinity seems to be constituted for the first time by the relations among Father, Son, and Spirit that take place in salvation history. In general, there is an economizing of God and a deflationary historicizing of triunity. Indeed, Schoonenberg claims that "Trinity" is no longer a statement about God *in se*, but is instead "a term that describes the morphology of the divine-human covenant rather than the reality of God."[67] This is a severe dislocation of the doctrine of the Trinity from theology proper to soteriology. It is also a long journey to undertake, burdened by a heavy load of jargon, in order to arrive after all at plain modalism. Perhaps the most insidious problem with Schoonenberg's radicalization of Rahner's (that is, Urlsperger's) terminology is the damage it inflicts on the link between missions and processions. "The missions are the processions, and vice versa" makes nonsense of the entire development of Trinitarian theology we have traced. It makes our chief question— "What do the missions reveal about God?"—collide with its own answer in a tautological disaster.

Blunders like this are not inevitable, nor can the blame for them simply be laid on the doorstep of a conceptual schema. There are many opportunities to turn aside from the path Schoonenberg's argument follows. We have already acknowledged that the conventional terminology of economic Trinity and immanent Trinity has certain advantages, including its comprehensiveness and its abstractness. If theologians show restraint in reaching for it, and only do so when they positively desire abstraction and remoteness, economic-immanent language might serve well. Some theologians of a traditionalist temperament have treated the economic-immanent idiom as simply another way of talking about the same thing that has long been talked about in the mission-procession idiom. Gilles Emery, for instance, says that "the reflection connected to this theological elaboration indisputably possesses a real value. And the axiom formulated by Rahner has made a notable contribution to the renewal of Trinitarian theology."[68] Nevertheless, he worries that "when the doctrine of the Trinity is posed in these terms, it leads at times to presenting Trinitarian faith in a dialectical and even wooden manner. The theological tradition shows that there are other ways of accounting for the truth of the Trinitarian revelation and of manifesting the gift that the Trinity makes of itself in the economy. One

---

67. Ibid., 115.
68. Emery, *The Trinity*, 178.

enlightening way consists, undoubtedly, in the doctrine of the 'missions' of the divine persons."[69]

This is a fairly friendly turning from one set of categories to another, with some allowance that either set of conceptual tools can be used to work toward the shared goals of Trinitarian theology (accounting for the truth of revelation and recognizing God's self-gift in the economy).[70] Emery gives the impression that Thomas Aquinas and recent Trinitarian theology are doing much the same thing, except that Thomas, of course, did it better.

Others have given a more stern warning about the limits and dangers of the economic-immanent framework. Bruce Marshall first of all laments the prominence and novelty of the terminology: "The language of 'immanent' and 'economic' has become so pervasive in Catholic Trinitarian theology that to question it might seem tantamount to questioning faith in the Trinity itself. But that cannot really be right, since Trinitarian doctrine and theology got along quite well for most of their history without thinking in these terms, still less in terms of two Trinities, one 'immanent' and the other 'economic.'"[71]

Marshall then expresses skepticism that the problems posed by the distinction, and the answers offered to those problems, are worth working on: "There is reason to think the standard strategies for showing the 'immanent' and the 'economic' Trinity to be identical are by turns self-contradictory, much ado about the obvious, or purchased at fearsome theological cost."[72] One of the costs Marshall has in mind is the neglect of the topic of divine unity, and its replacement by what is essentially a reflection on the God-world relationship. Marshall argues that "the fundamental question about God's unity" is "the question whether there can be processions in the one God." The economic-immanent apparatus does not exactly focus anybody's attention on

---

69. Ibid. The irony is considerable. Rahner's generation abominated the "dialectical and even wooden" theology of the scholastics as transmitted by their manualist epigones. It takes a retrieval-minded Thomist of Emery's stamp to expose a post-Rahnerian sclerosis with its sprawl of technical terms, thoughtless habits of expression, and deadening effect on the inquiring mind.

70. I adopted a similarly friendly approach to the terminology in *The Deep Things of God: How the Trinity Changes Everything* (Wheaton, IL: Crossway, 2010). There my concern was to correlate the strengths of the economic-immanent approach with the spirituality and church practices of evangelical Christians. The task was made easier by two commitments peculiar to that book's method: it was written at a nontechnical level, for a church audience; and it programmatically refrained from quoting premodern sources, however great their anonymous influence.

71. Bruce D. Marshall, "The Unity of the Triune God: Reviving an Ancient Question," *The Thomist* 74 (2010): 8.

72. Ibid., 12.

that question with which Thomas begins his treatise on the Trinity. Indeed, treatises on divine unity are all but absent from modern doctrines of God, and Marshall believes this absence "stems from the widespread eclipse, in nineteenth- and twentieth-century Trinitarian theology, of the carefully worked-out distinction between procession and mission by the much more malleable and imprecise distinction between the immanent and the economic Trinity."[73] These are striking criticisms, and Trinitarian theologians who continue to deploy the economic-immanent framework—judiciously, and with an awareness of its advantages and disadvantages—would do well to be alert to them. Emery's friendlier view suggests that the economic-immanent framework can be treated as a supplementary way of dealing with some of the same issues as those addressed by the mission-procession framework. Marshall's more oppositional view suggests that the economic-immanent framework competes with the mission-procession framework, posing an alternative conceptual schema. Marshall's reading gains credibility from the historical fact that Urlsperger designed the framework explicitly to avoid drawing the mission-procession conclusion. That is why even Rahner's apparently radical attempt to identify economic Trinity and immanent Trinity is, in fact, insufficiently radical. It does not get to the root of the problem. Rahner's way of putting things may be a sharp turn on the road marked out by Urlsperger, but if it is possible to go back and divert traffic from the road altogether, that would be preferable.

When Johann Urlsperger crafted the distinction between the Trinity of Being and the Trinity of Revelation, he presented it to the world with a flourish. Not everyone was impressed. One contemporary reviewer wrote a response, which at this distance seems remarkably prescient. Ludwig Spittler made several substantive points about Urlsperger's Trinitarian theology before turning his attention to the fact that "Mr. Urlsperger has seen fit to coin some new technical terms in order to express himself briefly."

> I believe I am called to speak on behalf of the feelings of every reader regarding the whole idea of these technical terms: Hereby, nothing is gained in clarity, but rather an opportunity is given for endless misunderstandings.

---

73. Ibid., 29.

The fate of these technical terms will go just as it has with all such. Our busily collecting theologians will gather them, either polemically or thetically, into a compendium.

The first user still understands the term, because he has actually read Urlsperger's text. The next, having merely heard it from his teacher in college, no longer receives it quite so loudly. A third, not even having heard it from a teacher, takes counsel from etymology. And the odds are ninety-nine to one that from now on these technical terms will be used with the significance assigned by this last fellow.

This is the most natural way for heretics to be made in all subsequent centuries. No connoisseur of church history will demand examples as evidence.[74]

It is a good warning for Trinitarian theologians in any age. In the case of Urlsperger (and Rahner by extension), it is striking how well Spittler's prediction has played out. This chapter has traversed a good number of Trinitarianism's older technical terms, commending their abiding value as helpful tools for grasping biblical revelation. In service of clarifying the plausibility structure of Trinitarian theology as a biblical doctrine, we will occasionally generate a few new ways of talking. But we will attempt to be modest in introducing new technical terms and to use the economic-immanent framework in a more limited way than has been customary in recent theology.

---

74. Ludwig Timotheus Freiherr von Spittler (1752–1810), "Ueber Urlspergers Lehre von der heiligen Dreieinigkeit," in *Vermischte Schriften über Theologie, Kirchengeschichte und Kirchenrecht*, vol. 8 of *Spittler's Sämmtliche Werke*, ed. Karl Wächter (Stuttgart: J.G. Cotta'schen Buchhandlung, 1835), 64–65. Spittler is hardly an orthodox critic, and he is in some ways criticizing Urlsperger from the left. Neither of them have a firm understanding, much less a positive assessment, of the contribution of Athanasius or of the accomplishment represented by pro-Nicene theologies.

CHAPTER 6

TRINITARIAN EXEGESIS

We believe God is Father, Son, and Holy Spirit because Scripture bears witness to the deeper self-revelation of the one God in the Father's sending of the Son and the Holy Spirit. The doctrine of the Trinity must arise from Scripture if it is to be affirmed by the church. Although the textual negotiations by which dogmatics identifies the Trinitarian revelation attested in Scripture have undergone a far-reaching change in recent centuries, the fundamental task is what it has always been: to discern the triunity of God in the biblical witness.

Is the Trinity in the Bible? It is always tempting to dispatch the question with the brief answer: the word is not there, but the idea is. Any concordance proves the first claim; any catechism the second.[1] Nevertheless, profound and perennial issues are at stake in the question, because the church has always confessed the doctrine of the Trinity as something to be believed on the grounds of revelation alone as recorded in Scripture alone. The church should continue to do so. But the last few centuries of development in theology, hermeneutics, and biblical studies have brought the old dogma into a new context. The biblical demonstration of the Trinity, accordingly, has taken on new forms and adopted new strategies in the modern period. Some of these are in line with the dogmatic principles we have rehearsed so far, while others need to be drawn into alignment and consolidated. Before turning directly to the Trinitarian witness of Scripture, therefore, this chapter surveys what the new situation means for the prospects of biblical Trinitarianism.

---

1. Except the Racovian Catechism.

155

AGRAPHON: UNWRITTEN TRINITARIANISM

Gregory Nazianzus found this question of whether the doctrine of the Trinity was explicitly in Scripture to be provocative enough to warrant serious (if not extended) attention. At the conclusion of his *Five Theological Orations*, he addresses the distinction between what is actually stated in Scripture and what must be admitted to be *agraphon*: not written. In that context, Nazianzus is specifically arguing against the pneumatomachian objection that there is not enough biblical evidence for the deity of the Spirit to warrant calling the Spirit "God." His response is not that there is any other possible source of knowledge about the deity of the Spirit (tradition, mystical illumination, pure reason, etc.), but rather that a narrowly literal approach to Scripture is unable to detect all that Scripture teaches. To this end, he presents a little didactic lecture on words, things, and meanings, concluding that Scripture can mean things that it does not explicitly formulate. "Why are you so dreadfully servile to the letter . . . following the syllables while you let the realities go?" he asks. Such syllable-mongering would not even be able to support arithmetical reasoning, he argues. "Supposing you mention 'twice five' or 'twice seven' and I infer from your words 'ten' or 'fourteen . . .' would you allege that I was talking rubbish? How could I be? I am saying what *you* said."[2]

Nazianzus's use of a numerical example is fruitful beyond his immediate purpose. Although he does not make the connection, part of the question about whether the doctrine of the Trinity is in the Bible is the question of whether the number three is in the Bible with reference to divine things. Throughout these theological orations, Nazianzus explicates "the name of the Father, the Son, and the Holy Spirit" (Matt 28:19), which he summarizes as a threefold name. He frequently uses the word *triad* in reference to God, but also in reference to the threeness in the words of the risen Lord as he gave the baptismal command. *Triad* simply is Greek for threeness, just as *thrynnysse* is Anglo-Saxon[3] and *trinitas* is Latin for threeness. Any reader of Matthew 28:19 must admit there is threeness, or trinity, in the text. The substantive question, of course,

---

2. Gregory of Nazianzus, Oration 31:24, 135.

3. For one example of the usage, see " . . . se haelend sylf on his halgan godspelle cythath tha halgan thrynnysse on sothre annysse" (p. 6): " . . . the Savior Himself, in His holy gospel, declare the Holy Trinity in a true unity" (p. 7) in Henry W. Norman, ed., *The Anglo-Saxon Version of the Hexameron of St. Basil, or, Be Godes Six Daga Weorcum* (London: Smith, 1849).

is what kind of threeness is envisioned. Subtrinitarian answers would include three titles, three modes of divine being, three manifestations, three roles, three people, three gods, three ways of talking about one God, and so on. But baptism in the name of one Father, one Son, and one Holy Spirit must signify three somethings, which puts threeness in the text, though not the word *threeness*. At the first level of analysis, then, Trinity is in Scripture as a very modest summarizing statement about how many names are to be counted in the one baptismal name in Matthew 28:19. This simple counting is in itself not much of a foothold for properly Trinitarian theology, which sees there the names of three coeternal and coequal persons related by processions revealed in the missions. But as certainly as twice seven is fourteen, the Father, Son, and Holy Spirit are related in Scripture as a threeness of some kind, though the word (*threeness, thrynnysse, triad, trinitas*) is *agraphon*. Only an exegesis "dreadfully servile to the letter," one content with "following the syllables" while letting the realities go, would recoil from the conclusion. When Scripture lists the persons and we reply that there are three (perhaps even adding that these three are one), we are saying to Scripture, "I am saying what you said."

Some elements of Trinitarian theology, therefore, are neither explicit in the words of Scripture nor ought to be expected to be. If the charge of *agraphon* Trinitarianism was brought forward as a defeater, Nazianzus treated it as no such thing. His response is echoed fifteen hundred years later in B. B. Warfield's comments on the same subject. Writing the "Trinity" entry in the 1915 *International Standard Bible Encyclopedia*, Warfield freely admitted that "the term 'Trinity' is not a biblical term"—a rather cheeky opening line for the "Trinity entry" in a Bible encyclopedia.[4] But Warfield laid out the range of doctrinal commitments contained in fully elaborated Trinitarianism (one God in three persons who are coequal but distinct) and said that the terms of that doctrine were not set forth in the words of Scripture. Instead, Warfield argued, "a doctrine so defined can be spoken of as a biblical doctrine only on the principle that the sense of Scripture is Scripture. And the definition of a biblical doctrine in such unbiblical language can be justified only on the principle that it is better to preserve the truth of Scripture than the words of Scripture."[5]

---

4. Warfield's entry is reprinted as "The Biblical Doctrine of the Trinity," in *Biblical and Theological Studies* (Philadelphia: Presbyterian and Reformed, 1952), 22–59.

5. Ibid., 22.

If "the sense of Scripture is Scripture," there need be no dichotomy between what the Bible says and what it means. But where a distinction exists, there may also exist the logical possibility of having one without the other. This is what Warfield posits: that it is possible to repeat the words of Scripture while departing from its own meaning, and conversely that it is possible to prescind from the words precisely in order to cleave to the meaning more securely. If forced to choose, the theologian would have to choose the truth of Scripture rather than the words of Scripture.[6]

Yet Trinitarian theology could not actually advance along some hypothetical path that departed from the actual words in the text of Scripture. Theology should at least keep itself on a short tether connecting itself to the words of Scripture. Karl Barth gave an eloquent account of the attitude appropriate for the preacher, and *mutatis mutandis*, it applies also to the theologian. "The right attitude," he said in his lectures on homiletics, "is that of one who is not concerned with self but with something else, who is so caught up . . . that there is no time for other things." Barth is emphasizing that the locus of attention should be the word of God rather than our own formulations; the good preacher will be asking, "What does it say?" rather than, "What should I say?" When the attention is properly fixed on the words of Scripture, "the sermon will be like the involuntary lip movement of one who is reading with great care, attention, and surprise, more following the letters than reading in the usual sense, all eyes, totally claimed."[7] The portrayal has not usually seemed flattering to preachers, let alone theologians, who enjoy the satisfactions of careful craftsmanship as much as any worker does, and who prefer not to think of their hard-earned formulations as an accidental by-product of rapt attention ("involuntary lip movement!"). And it is tempting to think these directions are for students at an early stage of development, a stage that mature theologians have so transcended that we can now multitask by putting one eye on Scripture and the other on the form of our own statements. But Barth was describing the attitude,

6. It is hard to cite brief examples, but consider the difficulty of expounding Isaiah 9:6 ("to us a child is born, to us a son is given . . . and his name shall be called . . . Everlasting Father"). A Trinitarian explanation of this passage would have to include the assertion that the Son is not the Father.

7. Karl Barth, *Homiletics*, trans. Geoffrey Bromiley and Donald Daniels (Louisville: Westminster John Knox, 1991), 76. For the considerable textual uncertainties surrounding this statement, see Angela Dienhart Hancock, *Karl Barth's Emergency Homiletic, 1932–1933: A Summons to Prophetic Witness at the Dawn of the Third Reich* (Grand Rapids: Eerdmans, 2013), 226–27.

not the thought process, of the one who ministers the word of God. And he was presenting a simile, not prescribing a method. The sermon, or the theology, will not be involuntary lip movement; it will be like it.

When Barth turns from homiletics in general to an actual dogmatics of the Trinity, he explicitly insists on the need for intelligent paraphrase. The Father's own revelation in Christ through the Spirit is the text we focus on, while our theological formulation of the doctrine of the Trinity is the commentary we speak. Our theological formulation "translates and exegetes the text. And this means, for example, that it makes use of other concepts besides those in the original. The result is that it does not just repeat what is there. To explain what is there, it sets something new over against what is there."[8] Barth always treated the work of theology as honest labor in the field of the humanities. As such, it requires creativity and innovation and is subject to assessment and peer review. None of that is denied when we take the further step of noting theology's peculiar character as a response to divine revelation.

TRINITY BETWEEN SOUND AND SENSE

Theology, therefore, does not do its work by simply repeating the words of Scripture. It answers back with what it hears there, and in giving its answer, theology may be heard making any number of noises not found in the text. This answering back is crucial to the theological task. It is what shows that something more than memorization of syllables is happening. It is what shows that one theologian has understood rightly and another has not. Anyone who is not willing to take the risks of translation, paraphrase, metaphrase, summary, and explanation has not yet crossed the threshold of theological speech. "It is one thing," said Francis Turretin, for a doctrine "to be in Scripture according to sound (*quoad sonum*) and syllables, or formally and in the abstract; and another to be in Scripture according to meaning (*quoad sensum*) and according to the thing signified (*rem significatam*), or materially and in the concrete."[9]

Turretin does not mean there is a dichotomy between the two ways for a truth "to be in Scripture," as if we always had to choose between *sonum* and *sensum*, formal and material. All doctrines must have some

---

8. Barth, *CD* I/1, 308.
9. Francis Turretin, *Institutes of Elenctic Theology*, vol. 1, ed. James T. Dennison Jr. (Phillipsburg, New Jersey: P&R, 1992), 1.

purchase on the text *quoad sonum*, even if they must then be formulated using other words which are themselves chosen and employed *quoad sensum*. The example Turretin uses is the term *theology* itself. It is not a Bible word; Turretin admits it is not in Scripture according to sound, but only according to sense. Nevertheless the component parts are found in Scripture, and are even brought into relation several times (Turretin cites "*logos tou theou*" and "*logia tou theou*" from Rom 3:2; 1 Pet 4:10; Heb 5:12). Furthermore, Scripture uses a number of other terms to indicate something like theology: teaching, the form of sound doctrine, the full counsel of God, and so on. Minting the word theology (or appropriating it from extrabiblical Greek) is a matter of listening actively to Scripture and saying back what we understand by what we are hearing.[10]

Though the nature of theology itself is at stake here, the term we are asking about is not *theology* but *Trinity*. Is it biblical to speak of the Trinity? When we use this word, are we speaking *quoad sonum* or *quoad sensum*? While the truth of Scripture is Scripture, so are the words. Theological usage must make the leap from direct biblical language to its own helpful vocabulary. It must move from "the language of Canaan" to another tongue, spawning a set of generalizations and paraphrases, associative linkages and metaleptic allusions, new verbal tags, glosses, and clusters. But the leap from one vocabulary to the other ought to be a short one, and the latter vocabulary ought to signal its dependence on the former with enough clarity to keep the next generation's language-learners from forgetting what all these terms indicate.[11] Theology, with its terminological specifying, consistent systematizing, and logical sequencing, does not make an improvement on Scripture, as if perfecting it somehow, or succeeding in saying what Scripture was unsuccessfully trying to say. It is semiotically and structurally dependent on the words of Scripture and ought to make this evident.

In the way it speaks, theology as a whole and Trinitarian theology in particular occupies a place between *sonum* and *sensum*, in regular contact with both. It shares something of the character that French poet Paul Valéry attributed to poetry in his influential aphorism: "The poem is a

---

10. For a surprisingly prolific account of theology along these lines, see Bernardinus De Moor, *Concerning the Word and Definition of Theology*, vol. 1 of *Continuous Commentary on Johannes Marckius' Didactico-Elenctic Compendium of Christian Theology*, trans. Steven Dilday (Culpepper, VA: L & G Reformation Translation Center, 2014), 45–75.

11. Recall the ambiguous career of "economic Trinity and immanent Trinity" language in chapter 5 above.

prolonged hesitation between sound and sense."[12] Trinitarian theology cultivates both the sound of Scripture's own language and the sense of those words, given new articulation by new interpreters. As a result, it ought to be compounded of both, making use of Scripture's own infallible language, as well as the fallible language of our best attempts to analyze what Scripture says. Barth described the utterly creaturely, purely responsive character of the doctrine in strong terms: "The doctrine of the Trinity is a work of the Church, a record of its understanding of the statement or of its object, a record of its knowledge of God or of its battle against error and on behalf of the objectivity of its proclamation, a record of its theology and to that degree of its faith, and only to that extent, only indirectly, a record of revelation."[13]

But he also acknowledged the fact that any adequate statement of the doctrine of the Trinity would include within itself the actual words of the biblical witness, sometimes indirectly by allusion and sometimes by explication of the concepts: "The text of the doctrine of the Trinity is at every point related to texts in the biblical witness to revelation. It also contains certain concepts taken from this text. But it does this in the way an interpretation does."[14] The central instance of this juxtaposition of text and interpretation is the mission-procession schema, and the most concrete guarantee of it is the verbal-propositional character of biblical revelation. These two principles are woven throughout the church's doctrine of the Trinity as the material and formal principles of Trinitarianism respectively: the missions-processions themselves are the material, and the divine explanation of those missions-processions is the formal. From both angles, we have something given by God and something achieved by way of human interpretive response.

THE SHIFTING FOUNDATION OF BIBLICAL TRINITARIANISM

Christians have always claimed they got the doctrine of the Trinity from the Bible itself. While acknowledging they had rendered the

---

12. "Le poème, cette hésitation prolongée entre le son et le sens." Paul Valery, "Rhumbs," in *Oeuvres Completes*, vol. 2 (Paris: Gallimard, 1960). One indication of the aphorism's influence is its use in the title of the widely used textbook now continued by Thomas Arp and Greg Johnson, *Perrine's Sound and Sense: An Introduction to Poetry*, 14th ed. (Belmont, CA: Wadsworth, 2013).

13. Barth, *CD* I/1, 308.

14. Ibid., 309.

doctrine more explicit, and also admitting they had manufactured a set of extrabiblical terms to help them articulate it with greater clarity and conciseness, they insisted the reason they believed in the Trinity is that they found it in Scripture. In some periods of theological history, it may have seemed that most of the work to be done was the work of elaborating the metaphysical implications of the revealed doctrine, or of illustrating the principles involved, or of extending the analogical footholds for the belief. But in our own time, it has become crucial for Trinitarian theology to demonstrate as directly as possible that it is biblical. The doctrine of the triune God must be known to be biblical and shown to be biblical. We cannot settle for claiming the doctrine merely harmonizes in some way with other biblical themes. If the suspicion has arisen that there are many ways of stating the gist of what is in Scripture, it may be tempting to present Trinitarianism as one of many possible legitimate trajectories that can be seen as emerging from the fullness of hermeneutical possibilities. We might win acceptance for Trinitarian theology as something relatively unobjectionable precisely because we present it as nonmandatory and contingent, a kind of semi-playful option among many, though graced with the favor of deep tradition. The time for these softer demonstrations and more allusive performances is not now. Again, in cultures marked by faith and docility toward the church's teaching, it may have been possible to rest the burden of proof on the church's tradition. But tradition was always a temporary resting station, a placeholder for revelation and the authority of Scripture. In contemporary intellectual culture, the full evidential weight of Christian faith in the triune God must fall on Scripture. If the doctrine is to thrive and serve its proper function in the Christian doctrinal ecosphere, it must be on the basis of Scripture. An adventurous theological critic once posed the question, "Has Christianity a revelation?"[15] We might say the question for our age is, "Has Christianity a revelation of the Trinity in Scripture?"

Although there has been no change in the material content of the doctrine of the Trinity, the epochal shifts in biblical interpretation in the modern period have greatly altered the available arguments for Trinitarianism. Indeed, the doctrine of the Trinity stands today at a point of crisis with regard to its ability to demonstrate its exegetical foundation. Theologians once approached this doctrine with a host of biblical proofs, but one by one, many of those venerable old arguments

---

15. F. Gerald Downing, *Has Christianity a Revelation?* (London: SCM, 1964).

have been removed from the realm of plausibility. The steady march of grammatical-historical exegesis has tended in the direction of depleting Trinitarianism's access to its traditional equipment, until a prominent feature of the current era is the growing unpersuasiveness and untenability of the traditional proof texts that were used to establish and demonstrate the doctrine. "Most theologians no longer expect to find in the New Testament a formal Trinitarianism, only an elemental Trinitarianism,"[16] remarked conservative Jesuit theologian Edmund Fortman in 1972. The heightened historical consciousness of modern scholars has made the very idea that Trinitarian theology has a foothold in the documents of the New Testament seem laughable: "Whatever Jesus did or said in his earthly ministry," wrote R. P. C. Hanson in 1985, "he did not walk the lanes of Galilee and the streets of Jerusalem laying down direct unmodified Trinitarian doctrine."[17] The presupposition has become widespread that the doctrine of the Trinity is a local phenomenon in the realm of systematic theology, with no provenance in the territory of New Testament scholarship. So deep has this presupposition sunk into the practices of the field that Ulrich Mauser could write in 1990, "The historically trained New Testament scholar will today proceed with the task of interpretation without wasting a minute on the suspicion that the Trinitarian confessions of later centuries might be rooted in the New Testament itself, and that the Trinitarian creeds might continue to function as valuable hermeneutical signposts for a modern understanding."[18]

We may succeed in countering any particular taunt and in raising objections to the hardening of categories that attends the overwhelming consensus of the guild. Nevertheless, a great deal of the assured results of modern scholarship in this area simply must be accepted, even when the result is the partial removal of the traditional way of demonstrating the exegetical foundation of Trinitarian theology. A complete catalogue of examples would approach a survey of the entire discipline of biblical studies in its bearing on the doctrine of the Trinity.[19] Perhaps no development in biblical studies has left the foundation of Trinitarianism

---

16. Edmund J. Fortman, *The Triune God: A Historical Study of the Doctrine of the Trinity* (Philadelphia: Westminster, 1972), 291.

17. R. P. C. Hanson, *Studies in Christian Antiquity* (Edinburgh: T&T Clark, 1985), 296.

18. Ulrich Mauser, "One God and Trinitarian Language in the Letters of Paul," *Horizons in Biblical Theology* 20:2 (1998): 100.

19. No such survey has been undertaken to my knowledge since Richard J. Knowling, "Some Recent Criticism in Its Relation to the Doctrine of the Holy Trinity," in *Messianic Interpretation and Other Studies* (London: SPCK, 1910), 38–84.

unaffected, partly because the long Christian exegetical tradition had at various times delighted to find the Trinity in nearly every layer and every section of Scripture. If the doctrine of the Trinity had come to be at home in every verse of the Bible, it was more or less implicated in revisionist approaches to every verse.

At any rate, the overall trend of sober historical-grammatical labors has been toward the gradual removal of the Trinitarian implications of passage after passage. Some of these proof texts evaporated because they were, in fact, never anything but Trinitarian mirages: 1 John 5:7's "three that bear witness in heaven," for example, withered away at the first touch of "the lower criticism," textual criticism. By overwhelming consensus, the *comma johanneum* is judged not to have been in the original manuscript, and therefore it should not be used as biblical support for Trinitarian theology, though it has some value as early Christian commentary on John's letter. The discarding of the Johannine comma is perhaps the clearest example of the helpful, clarifying, and destructive work of biblical scholarship. Even the fustiest traditionalists gladly admit that this text has been reassigned to its proper place in the margins of our Bibles.[20] Nor is this cutting-edge research; it was seen and affirmed in the eighteenth century and disseminated in the early nineteenth. Bishop Thomas Burgess (1756–1837) not only waved aside the Johannine comma but also lamented the fact that retrograde attempts to prove the Trinity by it had the opposite effect. "The doctrine of the Trinity I really believe," he assured his readers, asserting that Socinian arguments against the doctrine could be "evidently overthrowne, though not by this text, yet by plaine Scripture-proofes." Burgess generalized to a broader principle:

> I could heartily wish that orthodox men would not build good conclusions upon bad principles, nor lie the weight of such great positions on such weak proofes; for a bad defence makes a good cause suspected; and when the adversary finds the premise false (as the Socinians often doe) they are soe far from being confuted, that they are confirmed in their errors, because noe better are brought.[21]

---

20. Though see Pohle-Preuss's remarkable Vatican I–era Roman Catholic defense of 1 John 5:7. Even with its text-critical foundation admittedly undercut, Pohle-Preuss treats it as "a pregnant and clear *textus per se dogmaticus*" whose authority is guaranteed by its reception into the Vulgate and its centuries of liturgical use (Joseph Pohle, *The Divine Trinity: A Dogmatic Treatise*, ed. Arthur Preuss (St. Louis: Herder, 1930), 31.

21. Quoted in Crito Cantabrigiensis [pseudonym of Thomas Turton], *A Vindication of the Literary Character of the Late Professor Porson* (Cambridge: Deighton, 1827), v–vi. For one example of

Burgess's warning is perhaps even more appropriate now than when he wrote it, because now the complex clashes of premodern, modern, and postmodern modes of interpretation have left the field of Trinitarian exegesis in extensive disarray. Many arguments that once seemed foundational to Trinitarianism no longer apply.

Trinitarian theology has frequently conducted itself with exegetical candor and, on the academic side at least, has shown an openness to criticism and an eagerness to be instructed by fresh work in biblical studies. This candor has been interpreted as weakness and confusion by antitrinitarian writers, whose work is an interesting mirror in which to regard the transformation we are describing. Unitarian John Wilson published in 1845 *The Concessions of Trinitarians,* citing nearly six hundred pages of instances where scholars committed to the doctrine of the Trinity nevertheless overturned Trinitarian readings of various biblical passages.[22] But the polemical mirror is a distorting one, not least because it assumes that Trinitarianism is an inherited dogma foisted on Scripture or read back into it by hermeneutical force, and that orthodox interpretation requires a "dogmatizing eisegesis rather than exegesis."[23] In fact, there is abundant evidence in early modern Trinitarianism of a desire to examine every text on its own terms. In the sixteenth century, Cardinal Cajetan famously departed from conventional exegetical judgments about a range of Trinitarian proof texts such as messianic psalms.[24] Partly because of his similarly nontrinitarian interpretations of these same psalms, John Calvin even developed an undeserved reputation for being an antitrinitarian exegete.[25] Certainly he refused to insert the doctrine of the Trinity into every place it had traditionally been found. In showing this sort of restraint, Cajetan, Calvin, and a host of later

an antitrinitarian polemicist gleefully seizing on the passage as evidence of mendacious conspiracy, see *Some Trinitarian Forgeries Stated by a Monotheist* (New York: Grafton, 1906).

22. John Wilson, *The Concessions of Trinitarians: Being a Selection of Extracts from the Writings of the Most Eminent Biblical Critics and Commentators* (Boston: Munroe, 1845). Wilson's strategy was inspired by John Locke, who noted that "there is scarcely one text alleged to the Trinitarians which is not otherwise expounded by their own writers" (see Lord King, *The Life and Letters of John Locke, with Extracts from His Journals and Common-Place Books* [London: Bell & Daldy, 1864], 297).

23. This is Richard Muller's characterization of Frederic Farrar's suspicious view of Protestant scholastic interpretive culture, in *The Triunity of God*, vol. 4 of *Post-Reformation Reformed Dogmatics* (Grand Rapids: Baker Academic, 2003), 411.

24. Jared Wicks, "Cajetan," in *Dictionary of Major Bible Interpreters*, ed. Donald McKim (Downers Grove, IL: IVP Academic, 2007), 283–86.

25. See G. Sujin Pak, *Judaizing Calvin: Sixteenth-Century Debates over the Messianic Psalms* (Oxford: Oxford University Press, 2009), and for further Reformed developments, Benjamin Merkle, *Defending the Trinity in the Reformed Palatinate: The Elohistae* (Oxford: Oxford University Press, 2015).

theological interpreters of Scripture have only been putting into modern practice the ancient principle articulated by the fifth-century Isidore of Pelusium: "If ye strive with violence to draw and apply those texts to Christ which apparently pertain not to him, we shall gain nothing but this, to make all the places that are spoken of him suspected; and so discredit the strength of other testimonies."[26]

Was early modern Trinitarian exegesis basically in continuity or discontinuity with premodern conventions? This is the sort of question Richard Muller has traced carefully with regard to post-Reformation Reformed theology. Although he notes the "alteration of patterns of interpretation away from the patristic and medieval patterns that had initially yielded the doctrine of the Trinity and given it a vocabulary consistent with traditional philosophical usage,"[27] he also detects a clear intention on the part of the Protestant scholastics to maintain the traditional doctrine of the Trinity on a biblical basis more solid than ever. Their commitment to the authority of Scripture combined fruitfully with their commitment to Trinitarianism; either commitment without the other would, of course, have been disastrous for the continuous identity of Christian doctrine. "The orthodox task of building the primary justification of the doctrine of the Trinity on exegesis was made more difficult" by conflict with Socinian exegesis, which was expelled from the churches but increasingly found its way into the academy. Muller notes that "the orthodox found themselves in the very difficult position of arguing a traditional view of the Trinity against an antitrinitarian exegesis that appeared, in a few instances, to represent the results of text criticism and, in a few other instances, to represent a literal exegesis of text over against an older allegorism or typological reading."[28] The early modern disputation of the exegetical basis of Trinitarianism was a battle on multiple fronts.

THE DIFFICULT TASK OF FORGETTING TRINITARIAN EXEGESIS

The sifting and rearranging of traditional Trinitarian exegesis, as early modern theology maintained essential continuity with premodern doctrine, could be told as a fairly peaceful story. Perhaps a gardening

26. Quoted in Edward Bickersteth, *The Christian Student: Designed to Assist Christians in General in Acquiring Religious Knowledge* (London: Seeley and Burnside, 1832), 79.
27. Muller, *Triunity of God*, 62.
28. Ibid.

metaphor could be used, with disturbances no more traumatic than the horticultural: pruning, weeding, irrigating, and turning over the soil. But as Muller shows, what could have been a relatively straightforward readjustment of the patterns of appealing to Scripture for proof of the Trinity was greatly complicated by the rise of militant antitrinitarian exegesis. The broadly Socinian style of interpretation and many of its conclusions have become such central conditions of modern Bible interpretation that it is easy to forget how much work and argument it took to establish them. The centuries-old patterns of traditional Trinitarian exegesis did not fall away; they were pushed. And they required considerable pushing not only to overcome the inertial state of tradition. The reason the older patterns of Trinitarian demonstration stayed in place so stubbornly was that, for all their hermeneutical naiveté and inadequacy in the details, they were fundamentally correct as apprehensions of the total witness of Scripture. Being right about something as comprehensive as the holistic meaning of God's self-revelation in the sendings of the Son and the Spirit, the great tradition of Trinitarian interpretation could survive a few thousand negligible errors, the occasional illegitimate totality transfer, and some premature fusion of horizons.[29] We might say the Trinitarian interpretation of the Bible flourished because it is true, while the antitrinitarian interpretation, with all its demonstrable rigor, is false.[30]

When the Socinian movement arose in the sixteenth century, the churches rejected its theology as being a late revival of the same old antitrinitarian heresies that had circulated since the fourth century. But Socinianism was different from earlier varieties of antitrinitarianism in important ways. As a development of early modern thought, it was more rationalist, more literalist, and more committed to the liberationist task of breaking ecclesial authority than any of the ancient heretics could have been. It was also, as a movement of biblical criticism, more hermeneutically self-aware. As Klaus Scholder has argued, "Socinian criticism was aimed less at the content of dogma than at its presuppositions. And to the degree that the alteration to these presuppositions penetrated consciousness generally, the danger and influence of Socinian ideas

---

29. I genuflect toward James Barr, Hans-Georg Gadamer, and other vigilant watchers of interpretive correctness, having learned not to perpetuate these hermeneutical blunders, though I reserve the right to excuse them in the fathers.

30. This is to appropriate the language, but not the actual argument, of David C. Steinmetz, "The Superiority of Pre-Critical Exegesis," *Theology Today* 37:1 (April 1980): 27–38.

increased."[31] The Socinians were not just finding different doctrines in the Bible; they were generating entirely new ways of reading the Bible.

The alternative approaches to the Bible scouted out by the Socinians were at length perfected by Hermann Samuel Reimarus (1694–1768), a German writer whose biblical criticism, published posthumously (and at first, anonymously), was a major event in Enlightenment biblical criticism.[32] From this distance, what stands out most prominently about Reimarus's criticism is the way it drove a wedge between Jesus and the apostles. According to Reimarus, Jesus was an admirable teacher who, in general, taught and practiced what Reimarus taught and practiced. The apostles, on the other hand, overlaid his simple message with a mess of metaphysics, church authority, and priestcraft. The distinction makes all the difference: "I cannot avoid revealing a common error of Christians who imagine because of the confusion of the teaching of the apostles with Jesus' teaching that the latter's purpose in his role of teacher was to reveal certain articles of faith and mysteries that were in part new and unknown, thus establishing a new system of religion."[33]

In fact, however, what Jesus actually taught was not "articles of faith and mysteries," but "nothing more than purely moral duties, a true love of God and of one's neighbor."[34]

Reimarus is very clear about the reason for driving a wedge between Jesus and the apostles. His target is the "main articles and mysteries of the Christian faith," that is, "the doctrine of the trinity of persons in God and the doctrine of the work of salvation through Jesus as the Son of God and God-man." Of course, Reimarus knows that terms like "trinity of persons" or "God-man" are not to be found in the mouth of Jesus. What he undertakes to explain are the basic biblical terms that orthodoxy has misconstrued. He explains "in what sense [Jesus] is called Son of God, what the Holy Spirit signifies, and finally, what it means when Father, Son, and Holy Spirit are joined together during baptism."[35] In each case, Reimarus has to project a meaning that offers a clear alternative to the inherited dogmatic meaning.

31. Klaus Scholder, *The Birth of Modern Critical Theology* (Harrisburg, PA: Trinity Press, 1990), 28.
32. Charles H. Talbert, ed., *Reimarus: Fragments* (Philadelphia: Fortress, 1970). See Talbert's introduction for the intrigue surrounding the Wolfenbüttel Fragments. The quotations below are from "Concerning the Intention of Jesus and His Teaching."
33. Ibid., 71.
34. Ibid.
35. Ibid., 76.

What does "Son of God" mean? Reimarus declares that it means simply "loved by God," and since Jesus was especially that, Jesus was especially the Son of God. "Son of God" language should always signify, at its fundamental level, "loved by God" in Scripture:

> This meaning is so obvious that any other interpretation is unscriptural, new, and unprecedented if it makes the Son of God a person whom God begot out of God's being in eternity, and who in turn with the Father who begot him produces yet a third divine person. The Old Testament, the Jews, the evangelists, do not know such a Son of God, and Jesus himself does not present himself as such; it is, rather, the apostles who first sought something greater in this term.[36]

What led the apostles to seek "something greater" in the biblical language? Reimarus's answer is a pervasive demystification of biblical language, which he finds quaintly oriental. It is characteristic of the Eastern mind that it expresses itself in grand and poetic ways that seize the imagination. This grandiloquent Jewish manner of talking must be borne in mind, says Reimarus, or later interpreters will systematically misinterpret the Bible's expressions, making metaphysics of what was originally only an ancient culture's hyperbolic manner of speech:

> How easily, from ignorance of the Jewish expressions, thought, and allegories, one can be misled into a completely unfounded interpretation and system. For one can be certain of this much: the Hebraic expressions of the Jews sound swollen and bombastic in the Oriental manner, and one might marvel at what great things seem to be hidden beneath them, but they always mean less than the words seem to imply. So one must learn to divest and strip them of their magnificence; then he will at last understand their speech correctly, and the history of the ideas that prevailed among the Jews will confirm that we have hit upon their meaning.[37]

Reimarus subjects all the relevant language to the same stripping and divestment, showing that it means less than it seems to. He takes

---

36. Ibid., 84.
37. Ibid., 88.

apart the term "Holy Spirit" into its component parts: "Spirit" points to special talents and aptitudes of the human spirit; "Holy" indicates their origin in God. When Reimarus reassembles all these trimmed-down linguistic parts, the results are similarly unspectacular. At the baptism of Jesus in the Jordan, the descent of the Holy Spirit and the voice from heaven saying "this is my beloved son" signify "nothing more than Jesus' extraordinary spirit or gifts imparted to him by heaven."[38]

What stands out in the example of Reimarus's pioneering work is how difficult a task he has set for himself. He has to devise explanations, practice them, and put them in place so plausibly that when a believer turns to Matthew 28 and reads, "Baptize them in the name of the Father, the Son, and the Holy Spirit," his readers will not see the Trinity right in front of them. If they have learned their Reimarus lexicon properly, they will instantly translate that formula into a command to baptize converts in the name of the one God, who Jesus respects so much he calls him "Father," and in the name of the man who is especially beloved by God, and the unique charisma that God gave that man.[39] Taking up a New Testament that seemed to bristle with Trinitarian indicators on every page and at every level of analysis, he labored to disenchant it. Readers who sometimes wish the elements of Trinitarian theology were clearer and more numerous in the New Testament may take courage from considering it from Reimarus's antitrinitarian angle: how full of difficulties this text is for him, how much of it needs explaining away, how brimming it is with passages that might lead his readers back into the ruts of Trinitarian theology.

Reimarus's views were an international shock to his era. Today, while much of his exegesis is dated, and almost none of it rises to the standards of scholarly argument in the guild, many of his conclusions have nevertheless become utterly commonplace in academic biblical studies. Francis Watson has noted "the antipathy towards the doctrines of the trinity and the incarnation which the historical-critical tradition has inherited from its Socinian roots."[40] Many of the major strategic

---

38. Ibid., 95.
39. Breaking the hold of the Trinitarian baptismal formula is, Reimarus admits, a task that requires more labor. He announces on page 91 of *Fragments* his intention to explain it and works steadily toward that goal until page 117.
40. Francis Watson, *Text, Church, and World: Biblical Interpretation in Theological Perspective* (Grand Rapids: Eerdmans, 1994), 256. Watson introduces this topic as an illustration of the way a Trinitarian hermeneutic that presents itself as speaking about reality must "show itself to be capable of responding to objections proceeding from a different understanding of reality."

decisions about how to read the Bible in the academy—decisions that still guide the field of academic biblical studies today—were made early in the Enlightenment period and were made by antitrinitarians motivated by their unorthodox doctrinal commitments. The tools and techniques themselves—atomizing, dissecting, deflating, culturally locating—may be neutral enough to be used in a wide range of investigations. Competent scholars today routinely use some combination of them in studies that tend to support Trinitarian doctrine rather than some competing doctrine of God. But as Helmut Thielicke once remarked, "We need to remember that Biblical Criticism emerged in the form of a mortal attack, not merely on the mythical clothing of biblical faith, or on the excesses of popular piety, but more radically on the Christian message itself."[41] It takes a lot of work to remove all traces of the Trinity from the New Testament.

PIECEMEAL PROOF

One of the principal tactics Reimarus used was to break apart the larger unities of Scripture, the better to handle the discrete parts. For him, everything depended on the untrustworthiness of the disciples of Jesus. Reimarus used their incomprehension of the Old Testament to separate the two Testaments from each other; he used their metaphysical perversion of the teaching of Jesus to fracture the New Testament between gospels and epistles. This technique of dissolution is vital for obscuring the Trinity. We have argued above in chapter 4, and will show again in the next section of this chapter, that a crucial element of renewing Trinitarian exegesis is to reverse that process and restore the connections among the various parts of Scripture.

In his classic 1915 essay on the biblical doctrine of the Trinity, B. B. Warfield wrote:

> The doctrine of the Trinity lies in Scripture in solution; when it is crystallized from its solvent it does not cease to be Scriptural, but only comes into clearer view. Or, to speak without figure, the doctrine of the Trinity is given to us in Scripture, not in formulated definition,

On the Socinian roots of modern biblical studies, see further Scholder, *Birth of Modern Critical Theology*, 26–45.

41. Helmut Thielicke, *Modern Faith and Thought* (Grand Rapids: Eerdmans, 1990), 103.

but in fragmentary allusions; when we assembled the *disjecta membra* into their organic unity, we are not passing from Scripture, but entering more thoroughly into the meaning of Scripture.[42]

Warfield's image of assembling scattered parts into organic unity, or of crystallizing something that has been dissolved, is ambiguous. It could suggest that a lost unity is being restored, or that a new unity is being achieved, or that a concealed unity is being understood. We might conceive of the task of Trinitarian theology as getting the right perspective on the biblical evidence to see its unity, or we might conceive of the task as assembling the right structure from a set of materials. What is at stake is not so much the connotations about the theologian's attitude (viewing seems more reverent than building) as the indication of what kind of argument the theologian will undertake. In either case, Trinitarian theology will be formulating statements that allow for "entering more thoroughly into the meaning of Scripture." In this book, we are mainly seeking to give dogmatic guidelines for Trinitarian exegesis, which is more a matter of viewing biblical Trinitarianism from the right angle, in the right light, at the right distance. We are explaining the "fragmentary allusions" as glimpses of a bigger picture. To this end, we are retrieving some classical dogmatic themes on the one hand, and inquiring after larger structures of the Bible's own meaning-making on the other hand.

But there is also a venerable tradition of assembling the case for the doctrine of the Trinity in a constructive move, in which the component parts of the doctrine are identified and assembled. This piecemeal proof is a deeply traditional mode of demonstration. Those who practice it announce in advance the basic elements of the doctrine and then prove each of the various elements seriatim. This way of proceeding, while it can be carried out in a disjointed and pedestrian way (here a verse, there a verse), does not have to be. In fact, it is in one particular way congenial to the character of Trinitarian revelation, since the various propositions of the doctrine of the Trinity are not assembled thematically in any single passage of Scripture. The doctrine of the Trinity is a vast doctrinal complex containing numerous ideas, summarizing vast stretches of biblical revelation, integrating them, and holding them

---

42. B. B. Warfield, "The Biblical Doctrine of the Trinity," in *Biblical and Theological Studies* (Philadelphia: Presbyterian and Reformed, 1952), 22. "*Disjecta membra*" is an allusion to the Roman poet Horace's first Satire. The phrase is used there to indicate that a poet torn to pieces still has poetic parts.

together so they can be taken in at one mental glance. For this reason, it will always be appropriate to demonstrate, in serial fashion, that the Son is divine, then that the Spirit is a distinct person, then that they are not the Father, and to conclude by reestablishing that there is only one God. These arguments then combine to yield a set of propositions that are reconciled with each other, resulting in a doctrine of one God in three persons. There is a wide range of variations in its popular use. Sometimes it is presented with as few as three points (one God, each person divine, persons not interchangeable) and sometimes with as many as nine (enumerating each relation by specifying that the Father is God and the Son is God but the Father is not the Son, nor the Son the Spirit, etc.).

An admirable instance of the piecemeal proof is the way Augustus Hopkins Strong (1836–1921) arranges the treatment of the Trinity in his 1907 *Systematic Theology*.[43] He begins his fifty-page discussion by summarizing the doctrine in six statements:

1. In Scripture there are three who are recognized as God.
2. These three are so described in Scripture that we are compelled to conceive of them as distinct persons.
3. This tripersonality of the divine nature is not merely economic and temporal, but is immanent and eternal.
4. This tripersonality is not tritheism, for while there are three persons, there is but one essence.
5. The three persons—Father, Son, and Holy Spirit—are equal.
6. Inscrutable yet not self-contradictory, this doctrine furnishes the key to all other doctrines.

"These statements," he says, "we proceed now to prove and to elucidate."[44] Under each heading, Strong brings forth biblical evidence to demonstrate its truth, and material from the history of theology by way of amplification. The result is a teaching on the Trinity that is clear, concise, and comprehensive, especially apt for classroom use.[45]

---

43. Augustus Hopkins Strong, *Systematic Theology: A Compendium Designed for the Use of Theological Students* (Valley Forge, PA: Judson, 1907). This is the final edition, revised and enlarged, of the three-volume system that Strong originally published in 1886.

44. Ibid., 304.

45. Roger Olson relates the story that when he was taught theology from Strong's book, his teacher pointed out that the six points can be rephrased to spell T R I U N E (Three recognized as God; Regarded as three distinct persons; Immanent and eternal, not merely economical or

For these reasons, the piecemeal proof is probably the most common way of teaching the doctrine of the Trinity at the popular level today. This is no small matter, because after worship, catechesis (rather than evangelism, apologetics, or cultural analysis) is the chief end that the doctrine of the Trinity serves in the Christian church. Whatever academic theologians may be doing, the future health of the doctrine of the Trinity is, humanly speaking, in the hands of catechists. If they are all using variations of the piecemeal proof, its explicit and implicit lessons will determine the way Christians approach the doctrine of the Trinity. Theological instruction on the Trinity in the standard textbooks of evangelical systematic theology tends in this direction: the doctrine of the Trinity emerges for its readers as the product of rightly combining the scattered propositional evidence. The impression of proof texting is inescapable, and when the procedure feels arid, it provokes among evangelical Christians a craving for a few extra paragraphs about "Why This Doctrine Really Matters at All." That is to say, the piecemeal proof does not seem to carry its own sense of relevance along with it and may contribute to a heightened demand for personal or social application.

If we are keeping a watchful eye out for the eternal relations of origin, it may be the case that the piecemeal proof has a built-in tendency to de-emphasize them. Strong's *Systematic Theology*, for example, does include instruction about the generation of the Son and the procession of the Holy Spirit, but this instruction appears as a subpoint to statement 5, on the equality of the three persons. "Generation and procession," he says, are "consistent with equality."[46] There follow several pages on eternal generation, well-argued though mostly double-negative in form: it is not creation, not a commencement of existence, not an act of will, not analogous to physical derivation. We would probably be exercising undue suspicion to charge Strong with underemphasizing the relations of origin by folding them into his system in this way. At most, we might hazard the warning that the relations of origin do not play a structural role in Strong's Trinitarianism, or rather that their substantive structural role is concealed by the pedagogical arrangement of the material. Students who learn their Trinitarianism from Strong's

---

temporal; United in essence; No inequality; Explains all other doctrines yet itself inscrutable). This does not seem to have been Strong's own intention. See Roger Olson, *The Mosaic of Christian Belief: Twenty Centuries of Unity & Diversity* (Downers Grove, IL: IVP Academic, 2002), 140.

46. Strong, *Systematic Theology*, 340.

six statements will eventually have questions that only further reflection on missions and processions can answer.

Something has gone wrong, however, when B. B. Warfield makes a briefer use of the piecemeal proof in his influential 1915 article quoted above. Nestled between fine statements of the pervasive yet indirect character of Trinitarian truths in Scripture, Warfield says that "when we have said these three things then—that there is but one God, that the Father and the Son and the Spirit is each God, that the Father and the Son and the Spirit is each a distinct person—we have enunciated the doctrine of the Trinity in its completeness."[47] Warfield's omission of the relations of origin in a statement that manifests doctrinal "completeness" might be attributed to oversimplification. In fact, however, Warfield's abbreviated piecemeal proof is the first signal he gives his readers that he is not enthusiastic about the idea of relations of origin; he makes his reservations more explicit before he is done. The great failing of this otherwise helpful article is its weak treatment of the processions, driven by a fear of subordination.[48] Warfield's misstep is not dictated by his use of the piecemeal proof, though. He could have added more points. In fact, even the three points he selects are in themselves absolutely unobjectionable. Warfield's points are a kind of compression of the Athanasian Creed.[49] But the Athanasian Creed goes on to call God the Father "neither created, nor begotten," the Son begotten, and the Holy Spirit "neither made, nor created, nor begotten; but proceeding." This is precisely the language Warfield avoids. As a result, his claim of completeness is compromised, since the doctrine of the Trinity stripped of the eternal processions is brittle and abstract.

Warfield's weakness on the doctrine of eternal processions came from motivations more substantive than the pedagogical device he used to communicate them. There is no reason the piecemeal proof cannot be used to organize a more robust Trinitarian theology around the divine processions. However, it is worth remembering that the piecemeal proof has a naturally fragmentary tendency; its strength is in the way it breaks a larger complex down into discrete parts. As a result, its form

---

47. Warfield, "Biblical Doctrine of the Trinity," 36.

48. Ibid., 53–55.

49. The structure of the Athanasian Creed is also similar to the medieval "Shield of the Trinity" diagram, which relates the three persons to deity by the word *is*, and to each other by the phrase *is not*. This diagram has long been helpful in teaching, and it works especially well as visual support for the piecemeal proof. It is subject to the same limitations, however, and it especially tends to eclipse the relations of origin.

colludes with the spirit of the modern age in a way that does not fully support the health of Trinitarian theology. Emphasizing one subtopic at a time, it can only with difficulty climb back up to the level of the comprehensive judgment necessary to affirm the doctrine of the Trinity. It should be supplemented with other strategies that help to reinstate the large, comprehensive structures of meaning. These are needed to indicate how the parts should be assembled. The doctrine of the Trinity requires such comprehensive patterns of thought and does not thrive unless those patterns are cultivated. Trinitarianism was at its lowest ebb in modern theology when it was thought to stand or fall with a series of individual arguments, or even to await the conclusions drawn from the inductive gathering of numerous exegetical fragments.[50] A case in point is the Anglican philosopher and priest Samuel Clarke (1675–1729), whose 1712 book *The Scripture Doctrine of the Trinity* undertook an exhaustive investigation of every verse of Scripture that provides evidence for Trinitarianism. Clarke printed and commented on these verses in his massive book and gathered them under the headings of fifty-five propositions constitutive of his construal of scriptural Trinitarianism. This method, though bearing some resemblance to earlier projects, was characteristically modernist: it was the kind of inductive approach one would expect from a philosophical member of Newton's circle during the period of the exhilarating rise and formulation of modern science. Clarke's approach to the Trinity is an instance of an early modern tendency to press the methods of the natural sciences into service in every field, including fields where they are not methodologically appropriate. The doctrine of the Trinity is a particularly integral doctrine that cannot be formulated in the fragmentarily inductive way Clarke or other critical moderns attempted. Orthodox theologians of the period tended to be highly impressed by his method, though chary of his conclusions.[51] They should have been more alert to the bias built into his method. Anybody making use of the piecemeal proof ought to be vigilant about communicating the larger relational structures that bind together the individual theses of Trinitarianism.

---

50. A good analysis of the shift in temperament that brought this about can be found in Jason Vickers, *Invocation and Assent: The Making and the Remaking of Trinitarian Theology* (Grand Rapids: Eerdmans, 2008). Vickers's argument is that because the doctrine ceased to function as means of grace, it became instead a topic of dispute. The book fruitfully applies the characteristic argument of the canonical theism movement to the history of modern Trinitarianism.

51. See, for example, George Hill, *Lectures in Divinity* (New York: Carter, 1856), 382–89.

INSIGHT FOR THE RECONSTRUCTIVE TASK

The service that systematic theology can provide in the present state of disorder is not to do the exegesis itself, nor to dictate in advance what the exegetes are required to find. The lines of authority in the shared, interdisciplinary task of Christian theology do not run in that direction, nor with that directness. But the theologian can draw attention to the larger structures within which the exegetical laborers might do their skillful work. By offering dogmatic guidelines for Trinitarian exegesis, this book intends to highlight where meaningful work is to be done by qualified investigators. It is these larger structures that make sense of the individual bits of information that go into the doctrine of the Trinity. We have already seen how a Christian doctrine about revelation must be formed and normed by the central facts that constitute revelation itself, the communicative missions of the Son and the Holy Spirit. We took care not to exclude verbal revelation from the total matrix of God's communicative strategies, so we would not need to extract the entire doctrine from mute divine acts. We have construed the entire canon of Scripture as bound up in a single narrative unity, and taken the further step of acknowledging that unified witness as an element of God's economy of redemption and communication. All of this has been underwritten by the recognition that the Father's sending of the Son and the Holy Spirit reveals the divine life of eternal processions. This divine vantage point, made available to us by revelation, gives us the necessary remoteness and perspective from the details of Scripture that we can keep our bearings as we carry out Trinitarian exegesis of Scripture's manifold unity.

The doctrine of the Trinity is not just one doctrine among many, but is rather a conceptual foregrounding of the entire matrix of salvation-historical revelation and must be approached from a place in which all the events of the economy and all the words of Scripture hang together with an inner unity. It is senseless to try to retain the result of the early church's holistic interpretation of Scripture—the perception of the biblical doctrine of the Trinity—without cultivating, in a way appropriate for our own time, the interpretative practice that produced that result. The one premodern interpretive practice that is crucial for the doctrine of the Trinity is attention to the economy of salvation as a coherent whole. This is where attention must be focused. Many of the other hermeneutical moves of the premodern fathers—based on elaborately multilevel readings, and free-range allegorical exegesis in particular—are more to be admired than imitated (as Bonaventure said of the extreme humility of St. Francis).[52] Certain techniques of interpretation are so temporally bound and culturally located as to be unavailable to modern academics, and appropriately so.[53] But recognition of the coherence of the economy of salvation is both available to us and necessary for the practice of Trinitarianism, whether in the mode of dogmatics or exegesis.

Because of the uniquely integral character of the doctrine of the Trinity, it is never quite at home when formulated bit by bit from fragmentary elements of evidence. Atomistic approaches can never accomplish the necessary transposition of the biblical evidence from the salvation-history level to the transcendent level of the immanent Trinity.[54] Such a transposition requires first the ability to perceive all of the economic evidence at once, including the intricately structured relations among the three persons. That economic information, as a coherent body of evidence, can then be interpreted as a revelation of God's own life. To make the jump from salvation history to the eternal Trinity, the interpreter must perceive the meaningful form of a threefold divine life circulating around the work of Jesus Christ. What psychologists of perception call a gestalt, a recognizably unified single form, is what the Trinitarian interpreter must identify in the history of salvation. This triune form, once recognized, can then be understood as enacting among us the contours of God's own triune life. He is among us what he is in himself: Father, Son, and Holy Spirit. Karl Barth describes this reality from the other direction: "To the involution and convolution of the three modes of being in the essence of God there corresponds exactly their involution and convolution in his work."[55] God's unity and salvation history's unity mirror each other in a precisely Trinitarian manner.

---

52. Bonaventure, *The Life of St. Francis*, 6:2. Available in the *Bonaventure* volume of *The Classics of Western Spirituality*, trans. Ewert Cousins (Mahwah, NJ: Paulist: 1978), 230.

53. The modern retrieval of patristic exegesis has perhaps passed through its enthusiastic phase and is entering a period of more critical, though still appreciative, reception. A book instructively located at the boundary between the two phases is John J. O'Keefe and R. R. Reno's *Sanctified Vision: An Introduction to Early Christian Interpretation of the Bible* (Baltimore, MD: Johns Hopkins University Press, 2005).

54. I am using "economic and immanent" language here sparingly, but deliberately, to show that it can signal comprehensiveness and distanciation. This sort of usage should, I hope, be safely within the guidelines offered in chapter 5 and perhaps also reassure readers that I am not a total language cop.

55. Barth, *CD* I/1, 374. The unusual words "involution and convolution" translate *Ineinander und Miteinander*.

If our situation is that biblical scholarship has removed formerly cherished Trinitarian patterns of interpretation, what are we to do? It is no good to seek shelter in a precritical mind-set. Even if we are persuaded that in certain details the modern consensus is wrong, there is no road back. If the tools, techniques, and standards of modern biblical studies are warranted and legitimate, the way forward must be to use them better, more fully, and more strategically. The concepts and the vocabulary of Trinitarian theology need to be chastened and held to scriptural standards, and critical scholarship has helped greatly in pressing this demand. Nor is the role of modern scholarship merely negative or restrictive. Among its many positive contributions, we must count its enhanced literary sensibility and alertness to narrative reasoning. After noting how "the methodological moves of the older proof-texting approach occlude the theological significance of the surface shape of Scripture," including such basic elements as its existence in discrete books, C. Kavin Rowe offers a balanced assessment of modern interpretive moves: "If modern biblical studies has anything crucial to teach us in this respect, it is that engagement with the literary texture of Scripture's surface forms a critical part of fruitful interpretation in our time."[56] But whatever blessings modern historical critical scholarship brings, we will not find among them a holistic apprehension of what God says in the inscripturated economy of his self-revelation. And whatever weaknesses may have hobbled patristic and medieval interpretive practices, and however unusable some of those techniques may be for us, their great virtue was always their grasp of the overall meaning of Scripture. The doctrine of the Trinity is a large doctrine, and its formulation and defense have always required a certain ampleness of reflection on the revealed data.

There is something disconcerting in maintaining a doctrine while replacing many of the arguments for it. If Trinitarian theology can arise using one set of arguments, but then discard many of those and set about seeking better ones by which to maintain its claims, does this imply that Trinitarians intend to go on believing what they are believing, no matter what? The Stoic philosopher Chrysippus described his philosophical approach in the words, "you give me the doctrines, and I will invent the proofs."[57] Proof-switching could signal that a system of orthodoxy

---

56. C. Kavin Rowe, "The Pauline Corpus and Hebrews," in *The Oxford Handbook of the Trinity*, ed. Gilles Emery and Matthew Levering (New York: Oxford University Press, 2011), 43.

57. Chrysippus the Cilician (279–206 BC). Cited in J. H. Randall, *Hellenistic Ways of Deliverance and the Making of the Christian Synthesis* (New York: Columbia University Press,

is functioning like what Marxist analysis calls an ideology: a set of power relationships concealed behind ideas that really defend them by rationalization. Proof-switching could also, however, be an example of renegotiating the "justified" part of what epistemology sets forth as the definition of knowledge: justified true belief. We all have many beliefs; some of them are true; some of those are justified. A belief can continue to be true during the phase when a thinker has rejected one justification for it and is casting about for another. The thinker cannot demonstrate its truth during this phase, but that is the whole point of pursuing convincing arguments.[58] Buildings that have always stood firm can, on inspection, be found to have less than optimal support, and undergo seismic retrofitting without ever coming down. After the tectonic shifts of biblical criticism, Trinitarian theology is due for some seismic retrofitting.

But there is a deeper explanation for why it is legitimate to transfer our allegiance to another set of arguments while continuing to affirm the original doctrine, an explanation that has to do with the unique character of the doctrine of the Trinity. Trinitarian theology is a complex discourse based on an insight into the overall meaning of Scripture. The church fathers, as the earliest theologians to discern its truth, draw it out of the scriptural materials, and render it explicit, did their work in the light of a profound spiritual apprehension of the subject matter itself. They were aware of God's own triune presence to them as they scanned the texts and labored to formulate what they understood in it. They did not claim that their utterances were divinely inspired, but they did acknowledge that in the interpretative relationship between *res* and *signa*, the thing itself was impinging on them as they sifted through the signs. "We are saving the Trinity," wrote Gregory of Nazianzus, "and by the Trinity can be saved."[59] His sharp transition from the doctrine he was arguing for to the God he was serving shows his awareness of theologizing in the presence of the triune God.

Many of the church fathers used a moral and ascetic vocabulary to

1970), 41. There are, of course, noncynical ways of construing this boast. Consider how perfectly it would work as a pedagogical method in geometry, for example.

58. Recall Socrates's description of "tying down" beliefs in Plato's *Meno*.

59. This is how Frederick Norris translates the phrase from Oration 29:21 in *Faith Gives Fullness to Reasoning: The Five Theological Orations of Gregory Nazianzen* (Leiden: Brill, 1991). Lionel Wickham's translation is perhaps less daring with Gregory's wordplay (*sozoimen* and *sozoimetha*): "We have the Trinity in our safekeeping and by the Trinity can be saved" (Oration 29:21, in *On God and Christ*, 89).

express the spiritual insight required for Trinitarian theology. At the end of *On the Incarnation*, Athanasius exhorts his reader Macarius that while he has made a good beginning by reading this book, he should now turn to Scripture itself to see the truth of what Athanasius has argued. He sets out the requirements for reading Scripture correctly:

> But for the searching and right understanding of the Scriptures there is need of a good life and a pure soul, and for Christian virtue to guide the mind to grasp, so far as human nature can, the truth concerning God the Word. One cannot possibly understand the teaching of the saints unless one has a pure mind and is trying to imitate their life. Anyone who wants to look at sunlight naturally wipes his eye clear first, in order to make, at any rate, some approximation to the purity of that on which he looks; and a person wishing to see a city or country goes to the place in order to do so. Similarly, anyone who wishes to understand the mind of the sacred writers must first cleanse his own life, and approach the saints by copying their deeds. Thus united to them in the fellowship of life, he will both understand the things revealed to them by God and, thenceforth escaping the peril that threatens sinners in the judgment, will receive that which is laid up for the saints in the kingdom of heaven.[60]

The shift in register is jarring to modern sensibilities: a good life, a pure soul, virtue, holiness, purity, and imitating the good deeds of the sacred writers. Athanasius prescribes a spiritual and ascetical training that will result in communion with the mind of Scripture's authors (being "united to them in fellowship of life") and promises hermeneutical insight as one of the two benefits. The other benefit is going to heaven rather than hell. This is not the course of study modern theologians expect to enroll in when they inquire after the biblical evidence for the doctrine of the Trinity.

But what if some process of intellectual and spiritual formation like this were in fact the prerequisite for "the searching and right understanding of the Scriptures" in regard to "the truth concerning God the Word"? And what if a school of teachers in the early centuries of Christian theology undertook this course of study, gaining insight thereby into the meaning of Scripture as a unified message and then

---

60. Athanasius, *On the Incarnation*, sect. 57.

spelling out the hermeneutical and exegetical arguments for what they had come to perceive? If this is what happened, then these patristic generations must have been faced with the difficulty of training their own disciples not only to repeat the arguments but also to undertake the spiritual formation required to apprehend the same spiritual reality that funded the arguments. We see Athanasius making reference to all three moments in his closing remarks to Macarius: having (1) drawn out his theological arguments, he (2) exhorts his student to read the Scriptures and (3) to "cleanse his life" so he can "understand the mind of the sacred writers." No doubt some students would do so, and would themselves become teachers who had the arguments, the formative preparation, and the insight into Scripture's total message. No doubt some other students would repeat the arguments, but fail to achieve the insight. Something like this is what has happened in the mixed process of transmitting the doctrine of the Trinity across the centuries.

EINSTEIN AND ALTERNATE EXPLANATIONS

An extended illustration of this sort of process will lend concreteness to the observation. Consider the case of Albert Einstein, whose work in theoretical physics can only be followed by people who have themselves had advanced training in physics. But Einstein repeatedly undertook to make his theory and its implications understandable to a wider audience than physics students. Reflecting on the challenges of translating his thought for a generally educated audience, he mused:

Anyone who has ever tried to present a rather abstract scientific subject in a popular manner knows the great difficulties of such an attempt. Either he succeeds in being intelligible by concealing the core of the problem and by offering to the reader only superficial aspects or vague allusions, thus deceiving the reader by arousing in him the deceptive illusion of comprehension; or else he gives an expert account of the problem, but in such a fashion that the untrained reader is unable to follow the exposition and becomes discouraged from reading any further.[61]

61. Albert Einstein, in the foreword to Lincoln Barnett's 1948 popularization of the theory of relativity. Cited in Shulamit Kapon, "Bridging the Knowledge Gap: An Analysis of Albert Einstein's Popularized Presentation of the Equivalence of Mass and Energy," *Public Understanding of Science* 23:8 (2014): 1013–24.

Einstein had grasped a truth and wanted to communicate it without obfuscation or oversimplification. To this end, in 1946 he wrote a short article titled "E=mc²: The Most Urgent Problem of Our Time." In a recent analysis of this article, Shulamit Kapon noted several unusual features of Einstein's popular presentation of his theory of relativity. In his attempt to explain "an advanced, central and counterintuitive principle in physics" (that is, the equivalence of mass and energy) to a popular audience, Einstein was confronted by the problem that his audience did not have the background information crucial to understanding the argument. Kapon lists among the prerequisites things like the Maxwell-Hertz equations about empty space and the Maxwellian expression for the electromagnetic energy of space. All of them require the ability to represent physical entities mathematically so that the mathematical representations (not the actual physical entities, nor mere conceptual representations of them) can be manipulated. None of this is available to readers unless they have undergone a sequential, multiyear training in mathematical physics. Without that training, the grounds of the demonstration are simply unavailable. In this situation, readers could simply accept the conclusions based on bare authority. But Einstein wanted more. He wanted to persuade his readers by offering them an alternative argument and convincing explanatory devices. He wanted to invite nonspecialists into the process of sense making.

To this end, Einstein gave an account of recent scientific history, describing how he came to wonder how to move from the traditional idea of the conservation of mass to the new idea of mass as a form of energy. In this narrative of discovery, the crucial component was radioactive disintegration, which steps into the story as the first observable proof. In his popular-level article, Einstein completely glossed over the reasons from mathematical physics that he would suspect mass and energy were theoretically convertible in the first place. As Kapon writes, "In this alternative argument, Einstein replaced the deductive derivation of the principle with a historical argument driven by the nature of scientific inquiry."[62] There is nothing in this historical sketch that actually adds to the reader's grasp of relativity. But it "forms the necessary skeleton on which a variety of explanatory devices are coherently employed to enhance and support the reader's sense making."[63] For example, Einstein

---

62. Ibid., 1016.
63. Ibid., 1017.

generates a number of analogies, including the analogy of heat being a form of energy, which has the advantage of being perceivable (in contrast to mass as a form of energy). On top of such analogies, Einstein actually tells a parable: Once upon a time there was an incredibly rich miser, but nobody could tell how rich because he never spent money. But upon his death he leaves his money to his two sons, with the stipulation that they give a small part of their money away for the good of society. Since the sons are misers too, the only gauge of the original fortune is the fraction given to society. Being interpreted, this parable is about the release of energy from the split atom. Finally, Einstein gathers up all that he has explained and gives it ethical urgency. Since the new science can produce nuclear bombs, coming to terms with it is the "most urgent problem of our times."

Kapon summarizes Einstein's success as an explainer of physics to the uninitiated:

> One of the main claims made [in the field of the public under-standing of science] is that some advanced ideas in science and particularly in physics are hard to popularize because what is left of the formal explanation after the mathematical formalisms and the advanced conceptions are "stripped" from them is a very thin statement that might be significant to the professional scientist, but cannot make much sense to a person with no academic background in the sciences. Einstein directly confronted this challenge when he explained the equivalence of mass and energy to the general public by generating an alternative argument that bypassed the core of the formal derivation and instead provided a sense of derivation through an argument that is based on the history of science and the nature of scientific inquiry.[64]

Did Einstein surrender to the temptation to give his readers the "deceptive illusion of comprehension" that he had earlier warned about? Was he so afraid that the untrained reader would be "unable to follow the exposition" that he veered into explaining something else—something they could grasp? No, it seems he communicated many true things about his work by using an alternative explanation more widely accessible.

This is a parable, and it applies to the transmission of Trinitarian

---

64. Ibid., 1021.

theology since patristic times, especially the use of scriptural arguments. If one of the conditions of the church fathers' insight into Scripture was that they had undergone the Athanasian discipline, it seems they would be in the situation of only being able to pass it along to others who had undertaken the same regimen of formation. But to communicate it further, they devised alternative explanations, constructing conceptual frameworks on which they could hang analogical arguments from Scripture. These arguments would be the proof texts they often employ. No wonder we cannot use them. And it follows that when we set them aside and seek new arguments, we are doing so on the basis of insight into the thing itself.

GOOD PROBLEM, GOOD PRESSURE

A major task of this book is to make our knowledge of the Trinity more secure by ordering our language about it more accurately. To this end, it has sometimes been helpful to use the word *revelation* with an unusually tight restrictiveness, in which it refers only to the actual historical sending of the Son and the Spirit in the incarnation and Pentecost. The writings of the New Testament, then, are not Trinitarian revelation proper, but inspired attestation of the revelation that had already occurred "between the Testaments" (in B. B. Warfield's phrase). Of course, our only reliable point of access to the truth of the revelation is through the attesting documents, which accounts for a certain perspectival collapsing of revelation into its attestation. But if for clarity's sake we maintain the precise distinction, it sharpens the question we began this chapter with: In what sense is the doctrine of the Trinity in the Bible?

In 1962's *The Trinity in the New Testament*, Arthur Wainwright gave a carefully balanced answer that has served interpreters well. Wainwright says that what can be found in the New Testament attestation is not so much a formulated doctrine of the Trinity as an awareness on the part of some of its authors that they are facing "the problem of the Trinity." By using the category of problem, Wainwright draws attention to the presence of two bodies of evidence: on the one hand, there is only one God; on the other hand, Jesus is God and so is the Father. These two facts, given as such in the New Testament, need to be adjusted to each other. They demand explanation, and all the more so when the Holy Spirit is introduced. This demand for explanation is what Wainwright calls "the problem of the Trinity" in the New Testament. "Whether the problem is binitarian or Trinitarian in form, the crucial issue is the relationship of Father to Son, because the problem would not have been of practical importance if there had been no Incarnation. If the Word had not been made flesh, there would have been no stumbling-block for Jewish monotheism."[65]

Having reframed his task as a quest for the problem of the Trinity rather than the doctrine of the Trinity ("a statement of doctrine is an answer to a doctrinal problem"[66]), Wainwright surveys the various authors of the New Testament to see how far each of them goes. His conclusion is that, taken as a whole, the New Testament surfaces the problem but does not formulate the answer. This conclusion does justice to the fact that there are no stretches of the New Testament that undertake to explain the Trinity. The prominently didactic or argumentative sections of the New Testament are about things like the implications of Israel's election (Rom 9–11), or the logic of the new covenant (Heb 9–10), or the inclusion of Gentiles in the community of the Messiah (Acts). Nowhere in the New Testament do we find the elements of the doctrine of the Trinity laid out on the table and being made a matter of doctrinal reasoning and formulation. Wainwright claims that "the problem of the Trinity was in the minds of certain New Testament writers, and that they made an attempt to answer it. None of their writings, however, was written specifically to deal with it," and he goes on tellingly: "most of the signs that a writer had tackled the problem are incidental."[67] So is the doctrine of the Trinity in the New Testament or not? "In so far as a doctrine is an answer, however fragmentary, to a problem, there is a doctrine of the Trinity in the New Testament. In so far as it is a formal statement of a position, there is no doctrine of the Trinity in the New Testament."[68] If "doctrine of the Trinity" means the word *Trinity*, that does not appear in Christian writing until the second century, in authors like Theophilus (*trias*) and Tertullian (*trinitas*). If it means the philosophical method of adjusting the various truth claims to each other within a comprehensive framework, that does not happen until Irenaeus and Origen. If it means the set of technical terms that grow up around these basic moves (person, essence, etc.), that is a much

65. Arthur W. Wainwright, *The Trinity in the New Testament* (London: SPCK, 1962), 3.
66. Ibid., 4.
67. Ibid.
68. Ibid.

more extended conversation with semantic shifts occurring in each usage over the course of several centuries.

The decision to say "the problem of the Trinity" is in the Bible is in part a rhetorical decision, a judgment about how to order and present the truth artfully, considering the effect it will have for the audience. Any presentation of the truth will raise certain questions and tend to suppress others. One of the questions Wainwright's "problem" terminology raises is whether the New Testament knows there is a challenge of consistency, or even a paradox, to be dealt with in monotheistic worship of Jesus. Can we say we detect in the New Testament an awareness of tension between these truths? Emil Brunner drew a sharp line between what he considered the "simple testimony" of the apostles and the *mysterium logicum* of the One and the Three posed by later Trinitarian theology, a *mysterium* that "lies outside the message of the Bible."[69] This way of talking suggests that the authors of the New Testament were unaware of the strongly contrasting nature of the vast realities they were writing about. Wainwright admits "the words 'paradox' and 'antinomy' do not occur in the New Testament," but rightly points out that "there is in the Prologue of the Fourth Gospel a clear awareness of the paradox of the relationship between Father and Son. The man who wrote 'The Word was with God, and the Word was God,' knew that his statement contained a paradox."[70] We could say similar things about the men who wrote that God sent his Son and Spirit, and yet that sent ones were coequal with the sending one. The authors of the New Testament registered at the very least a problem that required a solution, a set of facts that could only be set alongside each other against a wider horizon of meaning.

But perhaps a bit more can be said. Writing in 1991, Cornelius Plantinga argued that the gospel of John stood out from the rest of the New Testament as a major source of Trinitarian theology because "among all the New Testament documents the Fourth Gospel provides not only the most raw material for the church doctrine of the Trinity, but also the most highly developed patterns of reflection on this material—particularly, patterns that show evidence of pressure to account somehow for the distinct personhood and divinity of Father, Son, and Spirit without compromising the unity of God."[71]

---

69. From Brunner's *Dogmatics* I:206; cited in ibid., 8.

70. Ibid.

71. Cornelius Plantinga, "The Fourth Gospel as Trinitarian Source Then and Now," in *Biblical Hermeneutics in Historical Perspective*, ed. M. S. Burrows and P. Rorem (Grand Rapids:

We can count three elements here: (1) raw material, (2) patterns of reflection on it, and (3) pressure. All three elements, according to Plantinga, are there in Scripture. The raw material must include things like the characters of Father, Son, and Holy Spirit in a narrative framework, with the words they speak to and about each other. But this material is hardly raw. Thus Plantinga also indicates that we have in Scripture "highly developed patterns of reflection" on the data. John's gospel goes far beyond narrating the adventures of three characters; it also poses questions, gives answers, and makes claims about how they are related to each other. And third, there is "pressure to account somehow for the distinct personhood . . . without compromising the unity."[72] Taken together, the material, the patterns, and the pressure are enough to support a bolder claim that we can find a doctrine of the Trinity in the New Testament. Of course, having said this, we must distinguish it from the elaborated form that Trinitarianism took on in the developing tradition of Christian doctrine. That form of the doctrine, with its panoply of technical terms, summary judgments, and philosophical distinctions, is obviously not in the New Testament.[73] But a doctrine of the Trinity is. To say less is not to say enough. As long as "the sense of Scripture is Scripture," and the sense is present in its raw material, its patterns of reflection, and the pressure it exerts, there is such a thing as biblical Trinitarianism.

The problem of the three persons, the patterns of reflection, and the pressure of the text are productive of the doctrine of the Trinity, whether in its biblical form or in its classically elaborated form. But they are not automatically productive of it. Trinitarian theology, as Athanasius would remind us, was worked out in the presence of the risen Christ and therefore in the domain of the triune God. Whenever we focus on the interpretive task with its attendant challenges, we risk making our conclusions sound like something that could be achieved by

Eerdmans, 1991), 303–21. For excellent commentary on this statement, see Andreas J. Köstenberger and Scott R. Swain, *Father, Son, and Spirit: The Trinity in John's Gospel* (Downers Grove, IL: InterVarsity Press, 2008), 19–24.

72. For much closer analysis of such "pressure," see C. Kavin Rowe "Biblical Pressure and Trinitarian Hermeneutics," *Pro Ecclesia* 11:2 (2002): 295–312. Rowe traces the category to Brevard Childs, calling it "one of the most important contributions of his *Biblical Theology* taken as a whole" (308).

73. David Yeago's essay on judgments that can be rendered by various concepts is very helpful in increasing the plausibility of such claims ("The New Testament and Nicene Dogma," in *The Theological Interpretation of Scripture: Classic and Contemporary Readings*, ed. Stephen Fowl [Oxford: Blackwell, 1997], 87–100).

competent readers following general rules. As much as we need to say the Trinitarian interpretation of the Bible is the correct interpretation, and can be shown to be, nevertheless something more was at work in the Trinitarian construal of the biblical revelation. John Henry Newman noted that "though the Christian mind reasons out a series of dogmatic statements, one from another, this it has ever done, and always must do, not from those statements taken in themselves, as logical propositions, but as illustrated and (as I may say) inhabited by that sacred impression which is prior to them, which acts as a regulating principle, ever present, upon the reasoning, and without which no one has any warrant to reason at all."[74]

Newman thought this "sacred impression" that inhabits the faithful helped account for "the mode of arguing from particular texts or single words of Scripture, practiced by the early Fathers, and for their fearless decision in practicing it."[75] The presence of "the great Object of Faith on which they lived" also helped explain why some of their arguments seem to overreach, or to make far too much of a small bit of evidence. "Never do we seem so illogical to others, as when we are arguing under the continual influence of impressions to which they are insensible."[76] The problem, the patterns, and the pressure are good. But the presence is best, and it influences the Trinitarian interpreter as we do our work with the other elements.

---

74. John Henry Newman, *Sermons, Chiefly on the Theory of Religious Belief, Preached Before the University of Oxford* (London: Rivington, 1843), 335–36.

75. Ibid, 336.

76. Ibid.

CHAPTER 7

NEW COVENANT ATTESTATION

The New Covenant presence of the Son and the Holy Spirit on their visible missions gave rise to the apostolic witness of the New Testament. In the story of Jesus Christ, the record of his authoritative teaching, and the understanding of salvation applied to believers by the Holy Spirit, the documents of the New Testament contain a clear and sufficient testimony to the identity and works of the triune God.

If we are consistent in reserving the word *revelation* for what occurs in the actual sending of the Son and the Holy Spirit, we will look to the Scriptures of the New Testament not for Trinitarian revelation but for the written attestation of that historical revelation. Turning to an examination of the New Testament attestation of the Trinity, we would therefore expect a certain obliqueness in what it has to say. And that is, in fact, what we find in the New Testament: the indirect Trinitarian theology of a witness that presupposes revelation, rather than the straightforward announcement of something only now being made known in words. This chapter is incomplete even as a high-level survey of the types of New Testament witness to Trinitarianism. But it indicates the main lines of a biblical Trinitarian theology that presupposes the missions of the Son and the Spirit, expects oblique testimony that refers back to them, and receives revelation as act and word having an inner unity.

THE TRINITARIAN LIFE OF JESUS

The plotline of the New Testament, presupposed in even its nonnarrative documents,[1] but rendered explicitly as story in the Gospels, is the salvation accomplished by Jesus Christ. Any reader can see this. The story told in the New Testament is the story of the Acts of Jesus, "all that Jesus began to do and teach, until the day when he was taken up" (Acts 1:1–2). Behind those acts stands the agent, "the personal and unsubstitutable center that is Jesus, his personal uniqueness."[2] This central character is surrounded by a host of other figures, whose stories precede his (as in the constant, manifold allusions to the history of Israel such as we find in the opening words of Mark or in the birth narratives provided by Matthew and Luke), are intercepted by his (consider the disciples, especially the narratives of their calling), and go on after his ascension (as in the Acts of the Apostles, of course, but recall also John's open-ended "If it is my will that he remain until I come, what is that to you?" [John 21:22]). A reader of the Gospels asked to pick out a handful of main characters would obviously start with Jesus and then face the question of who else could belong alongside him in the category of main character. The Father and the Holy Spirit present themselves as ready answers.

The Apostles' Creed may be one of the earliest postbiblical attempts to make a theologically significant list of the main characters in the plot of the New Testament. It names Jesus Christ as "our Lord," and in its radically compressed sketch of his story, it goes on to identify two other characters by their proper names: the Virgin Mary of whom he was born, and Pontius Pilate under whom he suffered. Mary and Pilate are the named parentheses of the life of Christ as condensed in the creed, the personal placeholders for his birth and death. But the creed also directs our attention to that other pair of names mentioned above as bracketing the central character, when it identifies Jesus as the "only Son" of "God, the Father Almighty," and says he is born of "the Holy Spirit," who is also the object of our faith. The creed reads the story of Jesus as the story of the Son in the midst of the Father and the Holy Spirit. This is why Henri de Lubac argued that

---

1. Even the epistolary Paul operates with an often overlooked "narrative substructure," as Richard Hays points out (*The Faith of Jesus Christ: The Narrative Substructure of Galatians 3:1–4:11*, 2nd ed. [Grand Rapids: Eerdmans, 2002]). For a cautiously optimistic assessment of this claim, see the set of essays in Bruce W. Longenecker, ed., *Narrative Dynamics in Paul: A Critical Assessment* (Louisville: Westminster John Knox, 2002).

2. Hans Frei, *The Identity of Jesus Christ: The Hermeneutical Bases of Dogmatic Theology* (Philadelphia: Fortress, 1975), 63–64.

"above all, this Creed teaches us the mystery of the divine Trinity."[3] The creed has a Trinitarian shape precisely because it serves as a summary of the three main characters in the story of salvation.

While Jesus is the focal point of the New Testament's attention, he is presented as the one who is always to be understood in reference to the Father who sent him and whose work he is carrying out. The Synoptics tend to offer the connection between Jesus and the Father as the answer to an implicit question about what makes Jesus who he is. John's gospel radicalizes this tendency by reporting a constant stream of Jesus' words of self-interpretation that place him directly in relation to the Father. Similarly, while remaining the focal point, Jesus is consistently depicted as surrounded by the person and work of the Holy Spirit. The Spirit's work precedes his (consider the virgin birth and the formation of his human body, Luke 1:35; Matt 1:20) and also follows it (consider the resurrection, Pentecost, and the ongoing spiritual presence of Christ in the church). The work of the Spirit is especially prominent at the beginning and end of Jesus' life, but these narrative brackets alert us to the Spirit's presence throughout the entire ministry. The story of Jesus is thus the concrete and observable core of a story that includes the Father and the Holy Spirit as the less observable collaborators in the work of Jesus. The actions of the three are sometimes so involved and convoluted with each other that they are indistinguishable, while at other times their actions seem to stand over against each other in such a way that the agents seem to be almost competing or taking turns. There is no simple summary formula that comprehends all the ways the work of Jesus interacts with that of the Father and the Holy Spirit in the gospels, but there are helpful interpretive norms. The salvation they accomplish is one salvation. It is not three salvations merged into one, but a single event with internal differentiations. Making the right distinctions about the actions and characters in this story is what summoned the theologians of the Christian church to do their nimblest and noblest work.[4] Too

---

3. Henri de Lubac, *The Christian Faith: An Essay on the Structure of the Apostles' Creed* (San Francisco: Ignatius, 1986), 10. The whole book is an evocative argument from the form of the creed, on the supposition that "far from being only a list or collection or series or catalogue, it is a strongly organized whole. It has a structure" (57). See, however, Barth's characteristic demurrer ("The arrangement of the three Articles is not to be understood genetically, i.e., it does not represent the way in which faith gets its knowledge.") in *Credo* (New York: Scribner's Sons, 1962), 40.

4. The road from the Synoptics to early Christian doctrine runs through John's gospel, which formulated the story of Jesus in ways most obviously congenial to dogmatic exposition. "The problem which St. John's Gospel set for the church in the succeeding centuries was the

much unity would render Christ as his own Father and Spirit; too much distinction would portray three divine people collaborating in a shared undertaking. The correct answers are correct because they cut the narrative material at the right seams, making judgments the church would eventually recognize as Nicene and Chalcedonian.[5]

The life of Jesus is bracketed by phenomena that exceed the narrative frame of a gospel, but which each evangelist finds his own way to indicate. His conception in the womb of a virgin and his resurrection from the dead are astonishing but still narratable, at least obliquely. But stretching out before his conception and looming infinitely above it is his sending from the Father. This sending precedes "the days of his flesh" (Heb 5:7); it should not be reduced to a way of characterizing his sense of mission or his posture of sentness. When Jesus offered the explanation "for this reason I was sent," he was making use of a formula more appropriate to the embassy of a heavenly messenger than the vocation of a prophet, though he outstripped both offices.[6] If Jesus' sending from the Father is the bracket that precedes his earthly life, his return to the Father and his sending of the Holy Spirit on the basis of his completed work is the bracket that follows. It was once considered mandatory to distinguish between the functional Christology of the New Testament and the ontological categories of early Christian doctrine. This rule in biblical studies dictated the possibilities of Christology during a period when the missions-processions schema was not prominent, even in Trinitarian systematic theology. But the sendings of Son and Spirit break the bounds of supposedly functional categories and demand a metaphysical interpretation of some kind.

Because the Father sent the Son, the whole duration of the life of Jesus was the extended actualization of that sending. Everything he did and taught was from God. His very life was the divine life taking up a

complex problem of formulating a doctrine of God and of the person of Christ which would keep the paradoxical balance between the essential unity of the Son with the Father and the distinction between them, and the paradoxical balance between the divinity and the humanity of Christ, while at the same time keeping in proper perspective the threefold nature of the mediatorial role of the Son" (T. E. Pollard, *Johannine Christology and the Early Church* [Cambridge: Cambridge University Press, 1970], 22).

5. For some details on how conciliar Christology and Trinitarianism assist evangelical interpretation, see Fred Sanders, "Chalcedonian Categories for the Gospel Narrative," in *Jesus in Trinitarian Perspective: An Introductory Christology*, ed. Fred Sanders and Klaus Issler (Nashville: Broadman & Holman, 2007), 1–41.

6. Simon Gathercole has made this case for the Synoptics, where it is less explicit than in John (see *The Preexistent Son: Recovering the Christologies of Matthew, Mark, and Luke* [Grand Rapids: Eerdmans, 2006]).

real human life in the person of the Son. The Synoptics make this point in various ways appropriate to their own narrative strategies, but the gospel of John takes it up as a constant topic for open discussion. His resurrection from the dead was the event in which the life the Father eternally gave to the uncreated Son was given to incarnate Son: "As the Father has life in himself, so he has granted the Son also to have life in himself" (John 5:26) is a statement of Trinitarian ontology, as well as about the inevitable resurrection. Although a new and decisive thing happened then and there at the Easter moment in history, the life that the Father gives the Son is not a life that started there at Easter. The life by which the Son lives is the life he shares in common with the Father. What we read in the gospels is the true account of how that life that was from the Father to the Son came among us, showed itself to us, and carried out its decisive conflict with everything that opposes it. John Webster makes the point with even more theological freight:

> The resurrection of Jesus is the temporal enactment of the eternal relation of Father and Son . . . It is this inner-Trinitarian reality, the eternal relation of paternity and filiation, intrinsic to the divine perfection, which is the ultimate ontological ground of Jesus' resurrection. Jesus' risen life is divine life, and his resurrection is the elucidation and confirmation of his antecedent deity, by virtue of which he is the one he is.[7]

As for the Holy Spirit, though he is less prominent in this part of Jesus' story, as the giver of life (John 6:63) he is the divine point of contact wherever new life is taking place. He is the inner secret of the Father's giving of life, both to the eternal Son and to us in salvation history. The same power that raised Christ from the dead is at work in believers—to co-quicken, co-raise, co-exalt, and co-enthrone (Rom 8:11; Eph 2:5–7).

EPIPHANY AT THE JORDAN

One episode stands out in the New Testament witness as a uniquely rich locus of Trinitarian interpretation. Jesus' baptism in the Jordan River

---

7. John Webster, "Resurrection and Scripture," in *The Domain of the Word: Scripture and Theological Reason* (Edinburgh: T&T Clark, 2012), 33.

by John is widely recognized as a Trinitarian manifestation of a special character. It is commemorated in the Eastern churches as epiphany or theophany, precisely because the one God is manifested there in a three-fold way. "The primitive Christians used to say to any that doubted of the Trinity, *abi ad Jordanem et videbis*, Go to Jordan and you will see it."[8]

Austin Farrer praises the theological richness of the story of Jesus' baptism:

> When St. John came to write the story of Christ's baptism, he connected it with Jacob's dream of the ladder from heaven to earth, on which the angels of God ascended and descended (John 1:32, 51). And certainly the Baptism has so many levels of meaning in it, that without ever going outside it we can run up as though by steps from earth to heaven and down again. At the height of it is the bliss of the Trinity above all worlds, in the midst is the sonship of Jesus to his Heavenly Father; at the foot of it (and here it touches us) is the baptism of any Christian.[9]

The baptism of Christ draws attention to the interaction between Christ and the Holy Spirit in the economy of salvation and spurs investigation into the eternal Trinitarian ground and implications of their relationship within salvation history. Reflecting on Christ in his baptism opens a spacious region between the moments of the incarnation and the crucifixion. Without distracting from the incarnation or the crucifixion, concentrating on the event of Christ's baptism highlights the historical activity of the fellowship among the three persons. Many modalisms have drowned in the Jordan because it is very difficult to explain what a merely unipersonal God would be doing as a man, a voice, and a dove.

In fact, the threeness of the persons is so evident at the Jordan that it has sometimes drawn interpreters rather too far in the direction of multiplicity and difference. In modern theology, this tendency has been expressed as a thickly social Trinitarianism. The three persons are considered as separate centers of personality converging on the event; it is a

---

8. Edmund Polhill, *Precious Faith Considered in its Nature, Working, and Growth* (London: Cockerill, 1675), 354.

9. Austin Farrer, *The Triple Victory: Christ's Temptation According to St. Matthew* (Cambridge: Cowley, 1965), 345. The baptism of Jesus may play an exaggerated role in Farrer's Trinitarianism because his idiosyncratic theology of revelation through images drew him to this narrated event as tableaux.

kind of committee convening for baptism. In ancient theology, before strong social Trinitarianism was an option, the greater danger posed by overinterpretation of the Jordan event was that three distinct agents could be picked out. An impressionistic reading of the event, inadequately attending to the implications of rigorous monotheism, heard behind the voice of the Father the distinct causal agency of the first person of the Trinity, and likewise a distinct act of the Spirit above the dove. The problem with this line of analysis is that, depending on how seriously it is argued, it puts the three persons of the Trinity into salvation history as distinct efficient causes. Even before Nicaea, the details of this view were felt to be disturbingly similar to the way three Homeric deities could appear in a story together. A strong commitment to the unity of the biblical God always more or less restrained Christian theologians from going too far in the direction of identifying three distinct divine interventions in the story.

But after the Nicene elevation of theological discourse had begun to work its way out, Augustine provided a more differentiated account of the work of the Trinity in the baptism of Jesus. He is no less impressed than earlier interpreters by the clarity of the Trinitarian manifestation. In a sermon on the story as found in Matthew, he writes, "So we have the three, somehow or other, clearly distinguished: in the voice the Father, in the man the Son, in the dove the Holy Spirit. There is no need to do more than just remind you of this; it's easy enough to see."[10] But having established the distinction of the persons on the grounds of the eternal relations of origin, Augustine also maintains that their external works are undivided. For this reason, we should not think of the Father as being the efficient cause of the voice from heaven that speaks his message, nor of the Spirit as the efficient cause, among the other efficient causes operating in the world, of the dove. On the contrary, Augustine says, "the trinity together produced both the Father's voice and the Son's flesh and the Holy Spirit's dove, though each of these single things has reference to a single person."[11]

In part, Augustine's judgment stems from his conceptual clarity about God's oneness: persons act through their natures, so if any person of the Trinity acts on creation, the action passes through the one divine

---

10. Augustine, Sermon 52.1, in *Sermons III (51–94) on the New Testament*, vol. III/3 of *The Works of Saint Augustine: A Translation for the 21st Century* (Brooklyn, NY: New City Press, 1991), 50.

11. Augustine, *Trinity* 4.5.30, 175–76.

nature that belongs equally to the three persons. But in part, Augustine's judgment stems from the compactness of his doctrine of creation as a nexus of efficient causality. Each divine act in creation must be the work of the one God, the Trinity, bringing something about. The movement of air that carries the voice of the Father is a movement of air caused by the Father, Son, and Holy Spirit, even though the words that it forms ("this is my beloved Son") refer back only to the Father. The man being baptized was, of course, the incarnation of the eternal Son only, and not of the Father or the Holy Spirit. But his human nature, as a created effect, was something caused by the entire Trinity, the one God. The dove of the Holy Spirit is a character about whom Augustine's candor is refreshing: we do not know if it was a local dove deputized for the afternoon, or a dove spoken into existence for this purpose, or an angel in dove form, or an apparition, or any number of other possibilities. We can be more certain that it was not a hypostatic union between the third person of the Trinity and dove nature,[12] nor was it an instance of the Holy Spirit intervening unilaterally to cause a dove effect. The Trinity made a dove that signified the Holy Spirit; the Holy Spirit did not become a dove. On this view, which has some claim to be the classic view, the Trinity is uniquely manifested at the Jordan, but in an economy of signs and referents rather than in a physical or local presence of three distinct persons on the stage of creation.[13]

Augustine's counsel is to regard the epiphany of the Trinity at the Jordan as a special instance of instruction and illumination rather than a distinct work or event in the history of the three persons among us. The three persons of the Trinity are made known there by a set of signals created by the one triune God. We might expect a theologian like Martin Luther to be unsatisfied with Augustine's reduction of the event to an educational event. But in fact, Luther is quite content to read it in much the same way. "Here we find a dove," he writes, "a creature which not only the Holy Spirit but also the Father and the Son had created." He reminds his readers of the Augustinian principle of inseparable operations of the Trinity: "As I was saying, 'The works

---

12. If these were words, we might speak of the columbiformity of the Holy Spirit, but not of his encolumbination.

13. Augustine's interpretation of the baptism of Christ became controversial in the twentieth century when the notion of inseparable external operations of the Trinity came to be considered dangerously subtrinitarian. See Robert Jenson, *The Triune Identity: God According to the Gospel* (Philadelphia: Fortress, 1982), 117, 127.

of the Trinity to the outside are not divisible,' whatever is creature has been created by God the Father, the Son, and the Holy Spirit as one God."[14] And yet the dove is not called Trinity, but only Holy Spirit. Luther draws out the lesson we are to learn from this by exploring the possible predications we can make of the dove:

> The Christian Creed would by no means tolerate that you say of the dove: That is God the Father, or: That is God the Son. No, you must say: That is God the Holy Spirit, although God the Father, the Son, and the Holy Spirit are but one God. You may say very correctly of the dove: That is God, and there is no God beyond that one. And yet it would be incorrect for you to say: That is God the Father; that is God the Son. You must say: That is God the Holy Spirit.[15]

He goes on to make parallel points regarding the voice of the Father ("That is God the Father") and of the human nature of Christ ("That is God the Son"). In this epiphany, Augustine's distinction between signs and things is important. Each creature is both "a reality and a symbol," says Luther. It is a reality as itself, created by the one God. But it is also symbol as "at the same time a sign of something else, something which it is not but which it indicates and reveals."[16] The distinction holds good for all creatures used by God for revelation, "but here in this sublime subject it means more. For the humanity of Christ is not a mere sign or a mere figure, as the dove and the voice also are not empty figures or images."[17] Where we might expect Luther to lean into the incarnation as a special case that bursts the bounds of mere signification, he bypasses that fact and keeps strictly to his main point: the creaturely signs given to us at the Jordan instruct us about the Trinity without being the Trinity. Luther does distinguish between the humanity of Christ and the appropriation of the dove: "The humanity in which God's Son is distinctively revealed is complete, it is united with God in one Person, which will sit eternally at the right hand of God . . . The dove is a figure

---

14. Martin Luther, "Treatise on the Last Words of David," in *Notes on Ecclesiastes, Lectures on the Song of Solomon, Treatise on the Last Words of David*, vol. 15 of *Luther's Works*, ed. Jaroslav Pelikan (St. Louis: Concordia, 1972), 304.

15. Ibid.

16. Ibid., 308.

17. Ibid.

assumed for a time by the Holy Spirit to reveal Himself, but it was not united with Him forever."[18]

Augustine and Luther represent a tradition of Trinitarian interpretation that is extremely disciplined about keeping its focus on the sending of the Son and the Holy Spirit in the culminating events of the incarnation and Pentecost. Even in the interpretation at the baptism of Jesus in the Jordan, the supreme verbal icon of our knowledge of God's triunity, this tradition recognizes the presence of the Trinity as more a matter of verbal or intentional presence, for the purpose of instruction. The deep instinct behind this move is the instinct to maintain the proper visible missions of the Son and the Holy Spirit as the revelations of the Trinity. The epiphany at the Jordan is a special case of Trinitarian manifestation, and in one sense the two missions are actually on display there. The Incarnate One is truly present in more than mere signification, and the Spirit's descent on him stands in a proleptic relation to the public outpouring at Pentecost. But for all its special character (about which much more could be said),[19] it can only serve as a focusing event for the broader reality of the two economic sendings that make known the eternal processions.

THE THREEFOLD NAME

At the conclusion of the gospel of Matthew, the risen Lord commissions his disciples to "go and make disciples of all nations, baptizing them in the name of the Father and of the Son and of the Holy Spirit." This dominical utterance is the central text of Trinitarian theology for many reasons, but primarily because it picks out the three divine characters from the gospel narrative and names them in a striking and concise fashion. The three names are grammatically absolute: not "Father of the Son" or "my Father," but "the Father" and "the Son," complete with definite articles. This way of speaking is rare outside of the gospel of John, having occurred in Matthew only at 11:27 to prepare readers for its climactic statement.[20] The phrase serves as a foundation for any

---

18. Ibid.

19. See the remarkably full study by Kilian McDonnell, *The Baptism of Jesus in the Jordan: The Trinitarian and Cosmic Order of Salvation* (Collegeville, MN: Liturgical Press, 1996).

20. The most complete attempt to trace the Old Testament background of the formula is still Jane Schaberg, *The Father, The Son and the Holy Spirit: The Triadic Phrase in Matthew 28:19b* (Chico, CA: Scholars Press, 1982).

statement of the doctrine of the Trinity, and even modern theologians who invest heavily in revelation through act rather than word have recognized the importance of these particular words.

In fact, the role this threefold name played in the development of the doctrine of the Trinity is one of the things that called into question the post-Rahnerian overinvestment in revelation through act that we traced in chapter 2. Writing in 1982, Walter Kasper warned that "we cannot deduce the immanent Trinity by a kind of extrapolation from the economic Trinity."[21] And even if we could:

> This was certainly not the path the early church followed in developing the doctrine of the Trinity in the form of confession and dogma. As we have seen, the early church's starting point was rather the baptismal confession of faith, which in turn was derived from the risen Lord's commission regarding baptism. Knowledge of the Trinitarian mystery was thus due directly to the revelation of the Word and not to a process of deduction. This revelation in word is for its part the interpretation of the saving event that takes place in baptism, through which the saving event accomplished by Jesus Christ is made present by the power of the Spirit.[22]

Kasper also connected this revelation of the Trinity, "due directly to the revelation of the Word," to a more comprehensive conception of revelation in general. "Like all revelation" he said, "the revelation of the Trinitarian mystery of God is given not in words alone nor in saving acts alone but in word and act, which are inter-related."[23] The coalescing of word and act (as traced above in the discussion of Vatican II) is crucial for Trinitarian doctrine. It is how the biblical doctrine of the Trinity is found in its New Testament attestation, and it provided the guideline for the elaboration of the church's dogma.

There is one classic patristic text in which we can see the unique force of the threefold name contained in the baptismal command. That text is Gregory of Nazianzus's *The Five Theological Orations*,[24] in which his

---

21. Walter Kasper, *The God of Jesus Christ* (New York: Crossroad, 1984 [German original 1982]), 276.

22. Ibid., 276–77.

23. Ibid., 277.

24. For a thorough discussion of the authenticity of the orations and a review of the manuscript evidence and contested issues, see Frederick W. Norris, *Faith Gives Fullness to Reasoning: The Five Theological Orations of Gregory Nazianzen* (Leiden: Brill, 1991), 71–80. In this section,

frequent recourse to the "Father, Son, Holy Spirit" triad manifestly satisfies his Trinitarian instincts as an interpreter. Though he does not provide an extended analysis of the phrase, he uses it seven times,[25] and each of these instances is a special climactic or summative moment in his argument.

First occurrence: In the opening of the second oration, Nazianzus says, "Well now let us go forward to discuss the doctrine of God, dedicating our sermon to our sermon's subjects, the Father, the Son, and the Holy Spirit, that the Father may approve, the Son aid, and the Holy Spirit inspire it—or rather that the single Godhead's single radiance, by mysterious paradox one in its distinctions and distinct in its connectedness, may enlighten it."[26]

Since the first oration was a short exhortation to humility in theological reasoning, the second oration is the real opening of the Trinitarian subject matter of the work. This is, therefore, a Trinitarian benediction on the sermons on the Trinity. Here at the beginning, Nazianzus names God and invokes his approval, help, and inspiration in Trinitarian cadences. Shortly, Nazianzus will also refer to God using the actual word *triad*,[27] which is something he tends to do after using the Father-Son-Spirit formula. The formula, it seems, functions for Nazianzus as a kind of consolidating point that he has reference to when he is summarizing or telescoping an argument. He may wander far and wide in these orations, but when he wants to bring things to a point, he flourishes the baptismal formula and the word *triad*. This usage also seems to bring to Nazianzus's awareness the distinction between the doctrine of the Trinity on the one hand, and God the Trinity on the other hand, leading him to make puns and rhetorical reversals that play off of the distinction: Here he says, "Let us go forward to discuss the doctrine of God, dedicating our sermon to our sermon's subjects," and at the end of the third oration, he will even say that in defending this doctrine, "we are saving the Trinity, and by the Trinity can be saved."[28]

Second occurrence: In a notoriously difficult section of the third oration, Nazianzus says that the three persons rule all things as one "single

I again quote from Gregory's *On God and Christ: The Five Theological Orations and Two Letters to Cledonius* and use its page numbers.

25. On pages 37, 70, 118, 123, 138, 141, and 143 of Gregory's *On God and Christ*.
26. Ibid., 37.
27. Ibid., 39.
28. Ibid., 89.

governing principle," and he says rather delphically: "For this reason, a monad is eternally moved into a dyad and comes to rest at a triad."[29] He immediately advances a paraphrase: "meaning the Father, the Son, and the Holy Spirit." We will not pause here to unpack Nazianzus's monad-dyad-triad expression, or the inner-divine movement and rest that he immediately qualifies as "passionless, non-temporal, and incorporeal." It is worth noting, however, that immediately after making a difficult statement framed in seductively speculative terms, Nazianzus touches home base, as it were, with the traditional formula.

Third occurrence: The remaining occurrences are all within the fifth and final oration, because it is only when due consideration is given to the Holy Spirit that Nazianzus can talk consistently about a triad and make the fullest use of the three persons. In section 3 of the fifth oration, as Nazianzus proves the deity of the Holy Spirit and ostentatiously applies "identical expressions to the Three,"[30] he applies the term *light* to all three, following the cadence of the baptismal formula: the Father is the true light that enlightens everyone coming into the world; the Son is the true light that enlightens everyone coming into the world; and the Comforter is the true light that enlightens everyone coming into the world.

Fourth occurrence: In a crucial summation of Nazianzus's arguments about eternal relations, he says, "The very facts of not being begotten, of being begotten and of proceeding, give them whatever names are applied to them—Father, Son, and Holy Spirit respectively . . . The three are a single whole in their Godhead and the single whole is three in personalities."[31] Note here again the sweeping rhetorical move of expansion and contraction: Nazianzus extends his language to the personal characteristics of relations of origin—unbegotten, begotten, proceeding—and immediately retreats to the scriptural language of the baptismal formula and the word *triad*. This has the effect of reassuring the listener that the unusual language is intended to be harmonious with the traditional formula.

Fifth occurrence: In an especially climactic move, Nazianzus appeals

---

29. Ibid., 70. This passage was early recognized as difficult and important. Its language about the monad and the dyad, rest and motion, is the basis of one of the most fascinating of the Ambigua of Maximus. See Andrew Louth, *Maximus the Confessor* (New York: Routledge, 1996), 94–154.

30. Nazianzus, *On God and Christ*, 118.

31. Ibid., 123.

to the formula after arguing that the Spirit's fully divine authority was gradually revealed. He anatomizes the Spirit's sending thus: The Father will send the Comforter; the Son will ask for him to be sent, saying also "I shall send" him; and finally the Spirit's own authority and initiative are disclosed in the phrase "he shall come."[32]

Sixth occurrence: This occurrence is provoked by Nazianzus's modest foray into the realm of offering analogies for the Trinity. He mentions "a source, a spring, and a river" and asks himself whether they correspond with "the Father, the Son, and the Holy Spirit." Here Gregory uses the threefold name to underline the inadequacy of Trinitarian analogies and once again to assure the reader that his analogical triad is intended to refer to the known triad.[33]

Seventh occurrence: On the last page of the *Orations*, Gregory vows that to "the best of my powers I will persuade all men to worship Father, Son, and Holy Spirit as the single Godhead and power, because to him belong all glory, honor, and might forever and ever. Amen."[34] Just as he has used the formula to consolidate, summarize, and bring to a climax the various parts of the discussion, he concludes the entire set of orations with the same formula.

Nazianzus's use of "Father, Son, and Holy Spirit" is frequently referred to in commentaries as an allusion to the rule of faith or to the baptismal formula used in contemporary churches. No doubt it is that. But it is also Scripture, and the words of the risen Christ. In its rhetorical deployment, it plays the steadying role of clarifying difficult passages of the argument and of reassuring the listener that Nazianzus is not speculating freely. Hermeneutically, this deployment of the threefold name of God, associated as it is with the term *triad* and the number three, keeps the long discussion from ever seeming like an open-ended search for characteristics of an unknown God. Nazianzus uses it as shorthand to signal the fact that a Christian interpreter knows what he is looking for when he sifts through the biblical statements and scrutinizes the events they report. He is looking for the Trinity, the three, the Father, Son, and Holy Spirit. He, the Christian theologian, has been told to do so by the tradition and liturgy of his church, by the gospel of Matthew, and therewith by the risen Lord himself. The whole development of

---

32. Ibid., 138.
33. Ibid., 141.
34. Ibid., 143.

Trinitarian doctrine in the church thus stands on the verbal foundation of this passage.

PAUL AND THE PRESUPPOSITIONS OF SALVATION

With the letters of Paul we truly confront the phenomenon of the obliqueness of New Testament Trinitarianism. We have been prepared for this obliqueness by the hermeneutical considerations of chapter 6 and have had occasion to notice it already several times. But nowhere are we confronted by Trinitarian assumptions, always backgrounded and not quite stated, as much as in Paul. The task of "showing how [the doctrine] is assumed in the exhibitions which Scripture has given of the plan of mercy for fallen man"[35] is a central task for Pauline interpretation. "This redemption," nineteenth-century Presbyterian minister and author George Patterson adds, "is the central subject of revelation; and just as it is unfolded, so, we believe, there will be found taken for granted the distinct personality of the three members of the Godhead, and their concurrent yet distinctive action in the economy of man's salvation." One of the prominent characteristics of Paul's literary style is the way he proceeds on the basis of presupposed common ground, or reacts to a rhetorical situation by engaging it midstream. This habit of Paul's is what gives his letters some of their distinctive pace and energy. In his earliest surviving letter (and therefore probably the earliest document in the New Testament), Paul reestablishes rapport with the Thessalonians by alluding to knowledge they already share, saying "you know" no less than ten times (1 Thess 1:5; 2:1; 2:2; 2:5; 2:9 [remember]; 2:11; 3:3; 3:4; 4:2; 5:2 [are fully aware]). In his study of Paul's Christology, Gordon Fee remarks that "we are seldom reading Paul's *argued* Christology, but rather his *assumed* Christology."[36] Fee cites similar observations from Larry Hurtado ("Paul characteristically seems to presuppose acquaintance with the christological convictions that he affirms") and Douglas Moo ("Paul and his churches apparently were in basic agreement about who Jesus was").[37]

---

35. George Patterson, *The Doctrine of the Trinity Underlying the Revelation of Redemption* (Edinburgh: Oliphant, 1870), 7.

36. Gordon Fee, *Pauline Christology: An Exegetical-Theological Study* (Peabody, MA: Hendrickson, 2007), 4.

37. Ibid.

Paul never intentionally frames a discussion about the nature of God or of the relation of Father, Son, and Spirit. He is always in pursuit of one of his characteristic themes, such as salvation, fellowship in Christian community, apostolic authority, or the spread of the gospel, when his speech falls into a three-beat rhythm or a Trinitarian cadence. In Galatians 4, he describes salvation history as the Father's sending of the Son and Spirit: "when the fullness of time had come, God sent forth his Son . . . to redeem those who were under the law, so that we might receive adoption as sons. And because you are sons, God has sent the Spirit of his Son into our hearts, crying, 'Abba! Father!'" (vv. 4–7). In a crucial passage of Romans, there is an inevitably Trinitarian sequence to his reprise of salvation: "Since we have been justified by faith, we have peace with God through our Lord Jesus Christ . . . We rejoice . . . because God's love has been poured into our hearts through the Holy Spirit who has been given to us" (Rom 5:1–5). He is not concerned to draw together the three names very closely, as in the Matthean baptismal formula. Sometimes they sprawl across the whole surface of an extended argument. The structure of Galatians, for example, involves Paul proving that his gospel of faith is incompatible with salvation by works. He does so in a three-part argument that is roughly Trinitarian: the Galatians received the Holy Spirit by faith and not by works; God the Father promised Abraham that he would justify the Gentiles by faith and not by works, and Christ redeemed us from the curse of the law. Similarly, the trajectory of the argument in Romans runs from the Father's judgment from heaven in the opening chapters, through the Son's propitiation in the next section, to the Spirit's deliverance in chapter 8. A Trinitarian subplot or baseline seems to underlie everything Paul does.

Johann Albrecht Bengel (1687–1752) had a keen eye for the doctrinal presuppositions underlying Paul's work. Commenting on Ephesians 1:4 ("he chose us in him before the foundation of the world, that we should be holy and blameless"), Bengel writes, "These things presuppose the eternity of the Son of God; for the Son, before the world was made, was not merely the future, but even then the present object of the Father's love; John 17:24; John 17:5, otherwise the Father would not have loved Him in Himself, but likewise through another."[38]

Bengel was famous for the terseness of his comments, cramming as

38. Johann Albrecht Bengel, *Gnomon of the New Testament*, vol. 2 (Philadelphia: Perkinpine & Higgins, 1862), 385.

much insight into as few words as possible. What he does in this brief comment on Ephesians 1:4 is explain what must be true if the gospel is true: these statements about salvation in Ephesians can only be true and effective if, in the deep background, the person in whom we were chosen was really and actually present. Unless we take this interpretive step back into the eternity of the Son of God, we have to imagine some other way we could have been chosen "in him" from before we existed. The other possible answers are either unworthily weak (we were present in the mind of God with an ideal rather than actual preexistence, which, by the way, would be all that the Son of God shares: a merely ideal preexistence), or require some sort of coeternal preexistence of all creation (everything is actually there with God in eternity past, and merely manifests itself in the course of history). These are both bad options. The easy solution is the one Bengel points to: "These things presuppose the eternity of the Son of God." The gospel works because the depth of the life of the Trinity supports it. Not only does that presupposition make sense of 1:4; it also explains why the rest of Ephesians unfolds as an exposition of our adoption into the family of God: Because the Son is eternally with and from the Father, our adoptive sonship by redemption is a gracious assimilation of our creaturely reality with the eternal love that is God.

If Bengel mined the presuppositions behind Paul's assertions, John Davenant (1606–1668) brought to the exegetical task a solid grasp of the overall coherence of biblical doctrine. Commenting on Colossians 1:3 ("we give thanks to God and the Father of our Lord Jesus Christ" [KJV]), he explained how Paul can refer to God as both "God" and "the Father" of Christ. "Here the person is described to whom thanks are presented by the Apostle. And he is described as well by his absolute name, that it is God; as by his relative title, that it is *the Father of Christ*. The Apostle employs both with the best design."[39] Here we see the Augustinian distinction between God considered absolutely (the one triune God, and therefore the God of Jesus Christ) and considered relatively (God the Father of the Son). Davenant was very concerned to draw out the implications of this Father-Son relation even from the smallest bits of Paul's language. Commenting on Colossians 1:15 ("he is the image of the invisible God"), Davenant poses the same sort of question: "How is

---

39. John Davenant, *An Exposition of the Epistle of St. Paul to the Colossians* (London: Hamilton, Adams, 1832), 55.

Christ called the image of God when he himself is God?" The answer draws on the same Trinitarian distinction:

> The word *God* is, in this place, taken with reference to person, not to essence, for it designates the Father only, not the Divine nature in general. Christ, therefore, is the image of the Father, not of the Godhead. The person of the Son bears the likeness of the person of the Father; but the Essence or Divine nature in the Son is altogether the same as in the Father: *I and my Father are one.* Christ therefore cannot be the same *in person* with Him of whom he is the image; but there is no reason why he may not be same *in essence.*[40]

We might describe Pauline Trinitarianism as a doctrine of the deep presuppositions of salvation, reaching all the way to the being and identity of God. A venerable tradition of Lutheran dogmatics organizes systematic soteriology around the three principles, or sources, of salvation:

> I. Of the benevolence of God the Father towards fallen man, who is to be delivered and blessed;
> II. Of the fraternal redemption by Christ;
> III. Of the grace of the Holy Spirit in the application of redemption.[41]

In organizing its teaching on salvation in this way, the Lutheran theologians were following a profoundly Pauline schema.

This brief survey only indicates some of the leading characteristics of the New Testament's attestation of Trinitarian revelation in the Son and the Holy Spirit. We turn now to the more difficult question of how the Old Testament contributes to Scripture's Trinitarian witness.

---

40. Ibid., 175–76. He goes on to entertain an even more scholastic question: Why, then, do we not call the Holy Spirit the image of God? His answer is Thomist: "The Spirit proceeds by mode of the will, the Son by mode of the nature."

41. Heinrich Schmid, *The Doctrinal Theology of the Evangelical Lutheran Church* (Minneapolis: Augsburg, 1899), 269.

CHAPTER 8

OLD COVENANT ADUMBRATION

God is and was always Father, Son, and Holy Spirit, but did not make this known until the fullness of time, because the revelation of the Trinity was bound up with the accomplishment of Trinitarian salvation. Therefore the triunity of God is not an open phenomenon of the Old Testament, but can only be found there retrospectively, after the fact of the sendings of the Son and the Holy Spirit.

The final step in ordering Christian language about the Trinity is identifying the status of the Old Testament in our knowledge of the triune God. We have chosen to use the word *revelation* for the personal communicative missions of the Son and the Holy Spirit, and give the name *attestation* to the inspired reflection and documentation of that revelation in the New Testament. For the Old Testament we will use the word *adumbration*, which is literally a shadowing-forth (*ad umbrae*), to indicate the dimly lit character of the Trinitarian reality of God in the time before the Messiah and in the pages of the Old Testament. Adumbration is a kind of attestation. Taken as a whole, the Old Testament could be called the prophetic or proleptic attestation of the Trinity and could be paired with the apostolic attestation. Thus, one side of the canon looks forward to the coming of the Son and Spirit, while the other side looks back on it. But for clarity's sake, we will reserve the word *attestation* for the New Testament witness, which works without the burden of its subject matter's unrevealedness. And if adumbration is not yet proper attestation, it is certainly not yet revelation. God did not yet reveal his triunity until the fullness of time had come. The Trinity is a mystery in the biblical sense: always true, once concealed, now revealed.

DARK SAYINGS

"When anyone in the endeavor to prove the faith brings forward reasons which are not cogent, he falls under the ridicule of the unbelievers, since they suppose that we stand upon such reasons, and that we believe on such grounds."[1] Thomas Aquinas made this observation, with its implied warning, in the *Summa Theologica,* brushing aside the periodic attempts of theologians to demonstrate the Trinity on purely philosophical grounds. Because the doctrine of the Trinity is a revealed doctrine, we should take our stand where it is revealed, rather than incur the *irrisionem infidelium* by pretending to establish it where it is not revealed. This principle applies especially to demonstrating the doctrine of the Trinity from Old Testament texts. There is no weaker strategy for commending Trinitarianism than the attempt to conjure the doctrine from the scattered allusions, obscure phenomena, and puzzling textual features of the Old Testament read in its own light. The God of Israel was always triune, but did not undertake to share that fact until, the fullness of time having come, the Father sent forth the Son and Holy Spirit on their salvation-constituting missions (Gal 4:4–6). Before that, knowledge of God's triunity was shadowy, allusive, and indirect. We do not stand on such reasons, nor believe in the Trinity on such grounds. Nevertheless the adumbrations of the Trinity in the Old Testament are in their own proper way crucial to the doctrine's stability. How should they be incorporated into a mature Trinitarianism normed and formed by its manner of revelation?

The Old Testament is a clear book of divine self-revelation, except when it isn't. Some things about God are made extremely plain in the stories and oracles recorded in these Scriptures, and stand out as successful communication events with their origin in the God of Abraham who wills to be known. The triunity of God is not among these things. Instead it belongs among the secret things of God, sometimes making its presence felt but never announcing its character, and not stepping forward into the light until the fullness of time—the time of the events

---

1. Aquinas, *ST* I, q. 32, a. 1c.

in the New Testament—had come. William Greenhill (1591–1671), writing about the mysterious book of Ezekiel, noted that theology had its difficult topics and dark passages just as surely as any field of inquiry did:

> In most arts and sciences are difficulties; in divinity are depths. Plato, Aristotle, Euclid, have their *nodos*, and the Scriptures have their δυσνόητά. In them are dark sayings (Ps 78:2); riddles (Ezek 17:2); parables (Matt 13:35); wonders (Ps 119:18); great things (Hos 8:12); things hard to be uttered (Heb 5:11); hard to be understood (2 Pet 3:16); mysteries (Matt 3:11); hidden and manifold wisdom (1 Cor 2:7; Eph 3:10); the deep things of God (1 Cor 2:10).[2]

With this in mind, a doctrine of the Trinity that draws on the Old Testament may need to take the form of a noctuary or a sciagraph, with an admission that darkness and obscurity are key ingredients of the message. The recognition that parts of the Bible are difficult to understand is completely compatible with confessing the clarity of Scripture. In fact, one of the clear teachings of Scripture is that some passages of Scripture are not clear (2 Pet 3:16, along with all the passages cited by Greenhill above), at least not at all times for all audiences.

There are a few structural options for an outline of Trinitarian theology that consistently recognizes that the Trinity is adumbrated in the Old Testament, revealed in the coming of the Son and the Holy Spirit, and attested in the New Testament. The present book represents a choice that is evident even in the order of chapters in the table of contents. Our preliminary exercises were a call to worship (chapter 1) and a strategic revision of the doctrine of revelation (chapters 2 and 3). We began our treatise on the Trinity proper with a thick dogmatic description of the events of incarnation and Pentecost, that is, the actual revelatory interventions of the Son and the Holy Spirit into the economy of salvation (chapter 4), and then traced its implications for the being of God (chapter 5). We then proceeded, after some hermeneutical considerations (chapter 6), to the New Testament's attestation of the Trinitarian revelation (chapter 7) and finally to the Old Testament's adumbration (chapter 8). *Methodus est arbritraria* (see chapter 4), but we

---

2. William Greenhill, *An Exposition of the Prophet Ezekiel with Useful Observations Thereupon* (Edinburgh: Nichol, 1864), iv. *Nodos* are knots, or difficult passages; δυσνόητά are "things . . . that are hard to understand" (2 Pet 3:16).

have chosen a path calculated to reinforce formally our material judgments about the revelation of the Trinity by rehearsing the order of the mystery's unveiling. There are disadvantages to this method, but at least the method reverses the unhappy trend of treatises on the Trinity that begin by canvassing the shadowy evidence of the Old Testament. That conventional sequence risks putting an intolerable burden on the exposition of the Old Testament texts, squandering its evidential power by premature exposure. The doctrine of the Trinity did not arise and cannot stand without the Old Testament, but the Old Testament's usefulness for Trinitarianism is retrospective and dependent on the light provided by the fullness of revelation. We cannot set aside the Old Testament, but we can put it off until the salvation-historical mystery of the Trinity has emerged and the light of the New Testament has arisen.

THE TRINITY IN THE OLD TESTAMENT

William Burt Pope (1822–1903) made a programmatic statement of the status of the Old Testament for our knowledge of the Trinity:

> The doctrine of the Trinity, like every other, had, in the mystery of the Divine education of the Church, its slow development. Remembering the law that the progress of Old Testament must be traced in the light of the New Testament, we can discern throughout the ancient records a pre-intimation of the Three-One, ready to be revealed in the last time (1 Pet 1:5). No word in the ancient records is to be studied as standing alone, but according the analogy of faith, which is no other than the one truth that reigns in the organic whole of Scripture.[3]

It is, of course, a kind of canonical reading strategy, treating the Bible as a unified whole and refusing to study the Old Testament on this subject "as standing alone." Pope uses the awkward term *pre-intimation* to signal that he is reading the progressive revelation of the Old Testament "in the light of the New Testament," after a revelation that was in the future of the prophets but in the past of the apostles.

This pervasive Old Testament pre-intimation of the mystery was

---

3. William Burt Pope, *A Compendium of Christian Theology*, vol. 1 (London: Wesleyan Conference Office, 1877), 260.

made up of a certain body of textual and literary phenomena that came to be more or less conventional in discussions of the Trinity in the Old Testament. An especially good representative treatment of them is found in the posthumously published *Reformed Dogmatics* of Geerhardus Vos (1862–1949). Vos is best known for his work in biblical theology, and the *Dogmatics*, which he wrote at a young age, is informed by the nascent sensibility of biblical theology. It is set in a question-and-answer format, with the questions themselves very carefully crafted. Vos opens his entire treatise on the Trinity with the complex question, "Why must we not seek a decisive proof for the Trinity in the Old Testament?" If one must begin a treatise on the Trinity by turning to the Old Testament, this is perhaps the safest way to do it: with a self-disabling opening question that points away from the Old Testament to something greater. Vos offers three answers to his own question:

> (a) Because Old Testament revelation was not finished but only preparatory. The perfect comes only at the end.
> (b) Under the Old Testament's dispensation the concept of the oneness of God had to be deeply impressed upon Israel's consciousness in the face of all polytheistic inclinations.
> (c) We must not imagine that the Old Testament saints were able to read in the Old Testament everything that we can read there in the light of the New. Yet, what we read in it is clearly the purpose of the Holy Spirit, for He had the Scripture of the Old Testament written not only for then but also for now.[4]

Answer (a) deploys Vos's strong doctrine of progressive revelation and high view of what is groundbreakingly novel in the manifestation of Christ and the Holy Spirit. Answer (b) appeals to the cultural and historical background in which the Old Testament revelation took place (the polytheistic ancient Near East). But it may also indicate the logical order of the Christian doctrine of God: *De Deo Uno* followed by *De Deo Trino*. Read left to right from cover to cover, the Bible depicts a monotheism that turns out to be Trinitarian monotheism, not an initial threeness that turns out to be unified. Answer (c) gives the Christian reader permission to find Trinitarian theology in the Old Testament,

---

4. Geerhardus Vos, *Theology Proper*, vol. 1 of *Reformed Dogmatics* (Bellingham, WA: Lexham, 2014), 38.

without claiming that such a theology could have been read from the same texts before the advent of Christ and the Spirit. Answer (c) is the tricky one, because it attempts to do justice to the Old Testament's character as, in the words of B. B. Warfield, "a chamber richly furnished but dimly lit."[5] All the Trinitarian furniture was in there the whole time, but the lights were not on until the finished revelation—that is, answer (a).

What is some of the Trinitarian theology that can be found in the Old Testament by those who read it with the advantage of its fulfillment in Christ and the Spirit? Vos lists nine "traces of the doctrine of the Trinity," which can be thus discovered in the Old Testament.[6]

1. The distinction between the names Elohim and Yahweh.
2. The plural form of this name Elohim.
3. The concept of the angel of the Lord.
4. The concept of wisdom personified.
5. The concept of the Lord's "word" personified.
6. The doctrine of the Spirit of God in the Old Testament.
7. Old Testament passages in which God speaks of himself in the plural.
8. Old Testament passages where more than one person is expressly named.
9. Passages that speak of three persons (especially the Levitical blessing in Num 6).

Readers eager to find traces of the Trinity in the Old Testament have, in this list, a pretty full set of phenomena to investigate and instruments with which to carry out their investigations. But they should keep steadily in mind Vos's starting point: We should not expect to find a decisive proof for the Trinity in the Old Testament, even with this equipment in hand.[7]

5. B. B. Warfield, "The Biblical Doctrine of the Trinity," in *Biblical and Theological Studies* (Philadelphia: Presbyterian and Reformed, 1952), 22.

6. Vos, *Reformed Dogmatics*, 38–41.

7. This discussion was somewhat stormier in Lutheran scholasticism, for complex reasons including the hotter conflict in those quarters between rationalism and pietism. The flashpoint was theologian George Calixt (1586–1656) and his 1649 *Dissertatio de mysterio trinitatis, an ex solius Veteris Testamenti libris possit demonstrari* (Treatise on the mystery of the Trinity: whether it can be demonstrated from the books of the Old Testament alone). His answer, negative and inclined toward rationalism, provoked many responses and may be responsible for an overcorrection in the opposite direction among Lutheran interpreters.

REREADING

What is required for doctrinal interpretation of the Old Testament is a hermeneutical framework that acknowledges the complex structure of the revelation, and an approach to reading the documents that precede and follow the revelation. The key hermeneutical category for this kind of interpretation is rereading. It captures the ambiguity and concealment of the original writings, but also accounts for the progressive revelation and the attendant growth in understanding of the earlier material. Literary theorist E. K. Brown has said, "There is nothing magical in reading. It is in re-reading that some magic may lie."[8] We are not seeking anything magical, although the category of rereading might open up a relatively sober approach to the fascination with concealment that has animated much mystical interpretation of the Scriptures.

Rereading makes possible an interpretive interplay between the text's parts and its whole. Northrop Frye argues that "the critical operation begins with reading a work straight through, as many times as may be necessary to possess it in totality. At that point the critic can begin to formulate a conceptual unity corresponding to the imaginative unity of his text."[9] Immersive mastery of a text opens up new interpretive possibilities in negotiating the whole-part dialectic, which is one of the main engines in the production of meaning for the reader. The eye of the mind can scan the whole, ranging backward and forward in it. By invoking this spatial metaphor, we are picturing reading as beholding a visually unified object, whose surface our eye can negotiate. This is, of course, not at all what reading a long book is like, either in a codex (where the stacked pages obscure each other), a scroll (where the sentences we have read are rolled up and the sentences we will read are not yet unrolled), or on a computer screen (where digital simulacra of either codex or scroll are presented to us). The verbal-visual trope is an ancient one, with roots in classical rhetoricians like Quintilian, and had already become a commonplace by the Middle Ages. Bonaventure observed that "no one can appreciate the beauty of a poem unless his vision embraces it as a whole."[10]

---

8. E. K. Brown, *Rhythm in the Novel* (Toronto: University of Toronto Press, 1950), 6.

9. Northrup Frye, *The Great Code: The Bible and Literature* (New York: Harcourt Brace Jovanovich, 1981), xii.

10. Bonaventure, *The Breviloquium*, vol. 2 of *The Works of Bonaventure* (Paterson, NJ: St. Anthony Guild Press, 1963), Prologue, 11–12.

Rereading delivers an "awareness of the totality of the text" and allows for "intercommunication" of textual features by correcting against "inherently linear models of reading."[11]

It is interesting that in the field of critical literary theory, rereading is often invoked as a species of reader-response hermeneutics, perhaps because it is focused on the activities of the reader.[12] It can even be made to sound subversive and transgressive, as if in the high-theory war between reader and author, rereading is a matter of taking up arms in anarchic rebellion against the author. Matin Calinescu situates rereading as a counterpractice against the regime of normative first reading, which he investigates as an eighteenth-century innovation. Normative first reading could be a side effect of romanticism, which expects textual love at first sight, or of scientism, which expects self-evident meaning to be transferred at a single reading that does not need to be savored for its literary quality. Calinescu also hypothesizes that printing contributed to the rise of normative first reading. European cultures before printing were not simply oral cultures, but were bookish cultures with few books. Hearing texts over and over meant that before anything new was read for the first time, there had been immersion in rereading of the Bible and some classics. This critical and genea-logical discourse on rereading is still fairly new, and it remains to be seen whether rereading theory will be most at home among edgy comparative literature theorists or among more conservative critics who emphasize the enjoyment of literature. Rereading is, after all, one of the primary pleasures of popular reading. Successful novelists from Jane Austen to J. K. Rowling prove themselves to their fans not by how good their books are for reading but for rereading. Whole new vistas of insight and enjoyment open up to the reader who returns to certain well-structured books, where there is a palpable frisson between intuiting the whole text at once and reclaiming the linear experience of another trip through it.

Scripture, religiously experienced, is obviously another key site of rereading. It is not only an interpretive practice to be embraced by the consumers of the Bible, but because of the cumulative character of the biblical canon, rereading is a crucial element in the production of

---

11. Matin Calinescu, *Rereading* (New Haven, CT: Yale University Press, 1993), 45.

12. A helpful set of essays is found in David Galef, ed., *Second Thoughts: A Focus on Rereading* (Detroit: Wayne State University Press, 1998).

Scripture.[13] Rereading is a mode of the New Testament's use of the Old. R. T. France has pointed out:

> In the argument of Hebrews we see a first-century example of a Christian expositor whose instinct it was to develop his argument by focusing successively on a number of key texts, and in each case not simply to quote it and pass on, but to stay with it, exploring its wider implications, and drawing it into association with other related Old Testament ideas, so as to produce a richer and more satisfying diet of biblical theology than could be provided by a mere collection of proof-texts. Like a dog with a particularly juicy bone, he returns to his chosen text again and again, worrying at it and aiming to get all the goodness out of it for the benefit of his readers.[14]

The New Testament writers follow the lead of Jesus himself in creatively rereading their Scriptures in the light of who he is and what he has done.[15]

Rereading is a mode of scriptural reengagement that allows Trinitarian interpretation to maintain the original meaning of the Old Testament, but also to layer onto it the insights that arise from later developments of its themes. Genesis 1 says that God created the heavens and the earth. A reader who continues through Genesis knows where the story goes from there, and learns a great deal about the character of the God of the first chapter. A rereading of Genesis 1 is enriched by the knowledge that the God of Abraham, Isaac, and Jacob created the heavens and the earth. Or again, a reader who continues through to Deuteronomy learns even more about this character and his ways. A rereading of Genesis 1 is in this case enriched by the knowledge that the God of the exodus created the heavens and the earth. Or again, a reader who continues through to the end of the New Testament learns a great many surprising things about this God, and a rereading of Genesis 1 in

---

13. The best treatment I have seen of rereading in biblical theology is found in Karoline M. Lewis, *Rereading the Shepherd Discourse: Restoring the Integrity of John 9:39–10:21* (New York: Lang, 2008). Lewis is theory heavy, and this book has something of the transgressive attitude of avant-garde literary criticism, but her approach definitely yields results for reading John's gospel in canonical context.

14. R. T. France, "The Writer of Hebrews as a Biblical Expositor," *Tyndale Bulletin* 47.2 (Nov. 1996): 250.

15. Matthew Malcolm, ed., *All That the Prophets Have Declared: The Appropriation of Scripture in the Emergence of Christianity* (Exeter: Paternoster, 2015).

this case is enriched by the knowledge that the God who raised Jesus from the dead created the heavens and the earth. In fact, the Trinitarian rereading of Genesis 1 has to answer several questions: Does the extended sense of the rereading of Genesis 1 include the sense, "In the beginning, the Trinity created the heavens and the earth," or does it rather include, "In the beginning, Jesus created the heavens and the earth," or does it rather include, "In the beginning, God the Father created the heavens and the earth through the Son and the Spirit"? We know it includes, "In the Beginning was the Word, and the Word was with God, and the Word was God." We do not need to sort out all the layers of these questions here. We only need to recognize that rereading preserves the original linear sense while adding the holistic sense, and that much depends on what amount of text counts as the whole.

The modern focus on canon represented by Brevard Childs is helpful in this regard; in a pointed disagreement with critic James Barr, Childs gladly conceded that we must recognize and even emphasize "the role of the Old Testament as a testimony to the time before Christ's coming," but pointed out that Barr "fails to deal adequately with the theological claim of an ontological as well as soteriological unity of the two testaments, which lies at the heart of the New Testament's application of the Old (cf. John 1:1–5; Col 1:15–20; Heb 1:2–3)."[16] Trinitarian theology is canonical rereading of the identity of God, comprehending the total meaning of the text without effacing or replacing the linear meaning.

THE CANONICAL HINGE

We have received much guidance from B. B. Warfield's 1915 essay "The Biblical Doctrine of the Trinity," and now we are ready to draw out its significance for reading the Old Testament. Recall that Warfield said:

We cannot speak of the doctrine of the Trinity as revealed in the New Testament, any more than we can speak of it as revealed in the Old Testament. The Old Testament was written before its revelation; the New Testament after it. The revelation itself was made not in word but in deed. It was made in the incarnation of God the Son, and the outpouring of God the Holy Spirit. The relation of the two

---

16. Brevard S. Childs, *Biblical Theology of the Old and New Testaments: Theological Reflection on the Christian Bible* (Minneapolis: Fortress, 1992), 14.

Testaments to this revelation is in the one case that of preparation for it, and in the other that of product of it. The revelation itself is embodied just in Christ and the Holy Spirit.[17]

Historically speaking, this observation is trivial enough: first comes Jesus, then the Gospels. But two significant corollaries follow from the sequence "event then document." First, the sequence accounts for the oblique way in which the New Testament contains Trinitarian elements. The authors of the New Testament seem to be already in possession of a Trinitarian understanding of God, one they serenely decline to bring to full articulation. The clearest Trinitarian statements in the New Testament do not occur in the context of teachings about God or Christ, but as almost casual allusions or brief digressions in the middle of discourse about other things.

The second corollary is that we should not seek to construct the doctrine of the Trinity from the words of the New Testament alone, where it is not properly revealed so much as presupposed. Instead, we must develop hermeneutical approaches and exegetical skills that let us read the New Testament in the spirit of its own composition: with constant reference back to the revelation in Christ and the Spirit. Our Trinitarian theology should be demonstrated from Scripture, but in a way that recognizes the priority of the actual revelation in events and the dependent character of the inspired texts.

The third corollary is that we should expect the strongest arguments for the doctrine of the Trinity to be found along those seams where the Old Testament's prospective witness and the New Testament's retrospective witness are both present in overlap. That is, the doctrine of the Trinity is best established in an extended thematic study of the way the New Testament uses the Old Testament in its talk of God and salvation. This happy fact is a link between the state of scholarship in the twenty-first century and the second, as we are currently living in a kind of golden age of mature studies of the use of Old Testament by the New Testament.[18] And in the second century with the ancient Jewish canon and the recent documents of the New Testament before him, Irenaeus of

---

17. Warfield, "Biblical Doctrine of the Trinity," 32–33.
18. On top of the wealth of journal articles, see the comprehensive reference work titled *Commentary on the New Testament Use of the Old Testament*, ed. G. K. Beale and D. A. Carson (Grand Rapids: Baker Academic, 2007); and the important survey *Three Views on the New Testament Use of the Old Testament*, ed. Kenneth Berding and Jonathan Lunde (Grand Rapids: Zondervan, 2008).

Lyons wrote a short, classic theological work[19] in which he argued two major points: The Bible is one coherent book in two Testaments, and God is triune. The prophetic and apostolic witnesses, together, determine the shape and certainty of the doctrine of the Trinity.

C. Kavin Rowe has argued that "the two-testament canon read as one book pressures its interpreters to make ontological judgments about the Trinitarian nature of the one God *ad intra* on the basis of its narration of the act and identity of the biblical God *ad extra*."[20] Indeed, he says "it is safe to say that the doctrine of the Trinity would never have arisen on the basis of the Old or New Testaments in isolation."[21] One of the reasons for this is that all the presuppositions that give meaning to the New Testament are articulated in the Old Testament. As G. E. Wright said, "The New Testament is not itself a Bible; it is a small body of literature filled with all sorts of presuppositions which have no meaning to the uninitiated."[22] But Rowe makes the more specific point that the metaphysical heft of the biblical witness resides mostly in the rigorous monotheism of the Old Testament. Without this, the story of Christ and the Spirit would not demand interpretation as things that implicate the very being of God.

If, in fact, the two-Testament canon of Scripture is all one book, then the beginning has to be read in light of the ending. The second half of a sentence has a conclusive interpretive priority over the first half of the same sentence; while the first half has identifying priority over the second half. Likewise the Old Testament has identifying priority over the New, while the New Testament has conclusive interpretive priority over the Old. "The Bible includes within itself a world of anticipation and retrospection, of preparation and completion, whereby various and vital relations are constituted between its several parts."[23]

This Trinitarian hinge is the place for important work on the exegetical basis of Trinitarian theology, and research in this area will be able to locate and identify a host of new demonstrations of the elements of Trinitarian theology. The field is wide and requires the implements of

---

19. Saint Irenaeus of Lyons, *On the Apostolic Preaching* (Crestwood, New York: St. Vladimir's Seminary Press, 1997). The work is from about the year 175.

20. C. Kavin Rowe, "Biblical Pressure and Trinitarian Hermeneutics," *Pro Ecclesia* 11:3 (Summer 2002): 308.

21. Ibid., 299.

22. G. E. Wright, *God Who Acts: Biblical Theology as Recital* (London: SCM, 1952), 29.

23. Thomas Dehany Bernard, *The Progress of Doctrine in the New Testament* (1864; repr., Wenham MA: Gordon College Press, 1972), 3.

professional exegetes for its cultivation, so I name only a few instances here to indicate the sort of work that is possible. C. Kavin Rowe's own treatment of the name *kyrios* (Lord) in the narrative of Luke-Acts is one example of the new approaches proving fruitful in recent years;[24] Richard Bauckham's reading of how Isaiah's theology informs John's gospel is another.[25] The baptismal command of Matthew 28 seems to be a reinterpretation of Daniel 7's vision of the Ancient of Days, the Son of Man, and the heavenly host, blended with the Levitical blessing of Numbers 6 with its threefold occurrence of the revealed name of God followed by the summary, "Thus shall you put my name on the people."[26]

There is great promise here. In fact, it seems to me that creative new ways of demonstrating the doctrine of the Trinity are emerging even more rapidly than the old traditional proofs fell away. This changing of the guard need not be alarming, nor is it a signal that Christian theologians are merely ideologically motivated to find any arguments that serve to prop up their ready-made conclusions, being clever enough to devise new ones as fast as the old wear out. Instead, we, like the more ancient generations of Christians, are under the authority and guidance of the Word of God and are walking along after it, attempting to articulate for our own intellectual cultures and in our own idioms and canons of persuasiveness what we see and understand. We are all catching up with the Bible. Our task in this age is not to cast about looking for ways to replace yesterday's superannuated arguments, but to articulate as faithfully as possible what we find in Scripture.

The doctrine of the Trinity cannot simply be read off of holy history or read in explicit formulation in the words of the Bible. The doctrine of the Trinity is rather a conceptual foregrounding of the entire matrix of economic revelation and must be approached from a place in which all the events of the economy and all the words of Scripture belong together. It is senseless to try to retain the result of the early church's holistic interpretation of Scripture (the doctrine of the Trinity) without cultivating, in a way appropriate for our own time, the interpretative practice that produced that result. The crucial interpretative practice,

24. C. Kavin Rowe, *Early Narrative Christology: The Lord in the Gospel of Luke* (Grand Rapids: Baker Academic, 2009).

25. Richard Bauckham, *Jesus and the God of Israel: God Crucified and Other Studies on the New Testament's Christology of Divine Identity* (Grand Rapids: Eerdmans, 2008).

26. Benedict T. Viviano, O.P., "The Trinity in the Old Testament, from Daniel 7:13–14 to Matthew 28:19," in *Trinity – Kingdom – Church: Essays in Biblical Theology* (Göttingen: Vandenhoeck & Ruprecht, 2001).

both for exegesis and doctrinal theology, is attention to the economy of salvation as a coherent whole. In order to take a sufficiently large view of salvation history, however, theology needs to be instructed that there is such a thing as salvation history, and that in it God is not merely carrying out operations for our benefit, but is actually manifesting himself intentionally. God makes himself known in salvation history: the economy of salvation is the revelation of God's eternal immanent being. This does not go without saying. It did not, in fact, go without saying: God both manifested himself and told us he had done so. The church was clearly informed that in these last days, God had spoken in a Son, and that the name of God into which we are to baptize is the name of the Father, Son, and Holy Spirit. Filled with that knowledge and insight, classic Trinitarianism learned to interpret rightly what had occurred in the sending of Christ and the Spirit and took up the task of reading Scripture for further clarity about the Trinity.

CONVERGENT HYPERFULFILLMENT

The second pattern to be observed is the way lines of thought that seem to emerge from the Old Testament witness along trajectories diverging from each other are, in fact, revealed to have been converging toward each other in God's economy of salvation and revelation. Thus, in the Father's sending of the Son and the Spirit, all God's ways are fulfilled, but they are more than fulfilled—or hyperfulfilled—because they all converge on the events at the Trinitarian hinge of the canon. This convergent hyperfulfillment is most manifest in Jesus, who is both David's son and David's Lord, the root and the branch of Jesse. Taught to look for a messianic son, a suffering servant, a prophet greater than Moses, and the Lord himself, the apostles met them all in one person. Some of this convergent hyperfulfillment can just be asserted on the basis of the personal advent of the Son and Spirit. But for the exegetical case, much depends on demonstrating that, according to the witness of the New Testament, the Lord and the apostles understood the Old Testament in precisely this manner. They drew these conclusions in arguments about David's son being David's Lord (Matt 22:41–46), in their use of layered Old Testament fulfillments, and in numerous other ways. Origen coined the term *autobasileia* (usually translated "absolute kingdom," but literally something like "himself the kingdom") to indicate how Jesus takes over Old Testament categories and, in Henri de Lubac's words, "sublimates and unifies them by making them converge upon himself."[27]

And much depends on showing that even the highest points of the Old Testament witness manifest an awareness of the coming convergence: the fact that Psalm 110 (the text mobilized by Jesus in Matthew 22) is already drawing together priest and king, and that the later chapters of Isaiah envision a servant whose completed work is indistinguishable from the presence of the Lord in person, matters a great deal. Convergence discernible within the Old Testament witness is the ground of convergent hyperfulfillment in the New Testament witness, which alone enables a theological interpretation broad enough to establish the doctrine of the Trinity.

Traditionally, appeals to convergent hyperfulfillment have centered on the christological aspect of the biblical witness. But one of the ways that the categories of classic Trinitarian theology can inform exegetical investigations is by reminding us that the pneumatological aspect is equally significant. In fact, the locus of hyperfulfillment is not simply the coming of the Son, but the coming of the Son and the Spirit together in the fullness of time on the mission of God the Father. The Messiah is the anointed one. If the symbolism of anointing is kept in mind, and the Spirit's role in anointing functions as a live metaphor, then the best term for the point of convergence is that it is *messianic*: The Son who is constituted as Christ by the anointing of the Spirit is the focal point. This reminder is very helpful in keeping the hyperfulfillment argument from converging on such a narrow point (Jesus considered abstractly, in isolation from the Spirit and the Father) that it comes to seem forced and artificial. That sort of artificiality would only open the doctrine up again to the *irrisionem infidelium*, but the solution is to be more comprehensively Trinitarian rather than less so.

It should also be emphasized that all of the interpretive maneuvers we have outlined so far—from negotiating the canonical hinge to tracing the lines of convergent hyperfulfillment—are only possible because of an implicit logic that is eschatological. These moves are only possible in the case of a definitive and unsurpassable self-revelation of God and would lose their persuasiveness and necessity if they were only provisional developments along an ongoing trajectory. The opening passage of the book of Hebrews sketches out the fundamentally eschatological logic that is to be followed. According to Hebrews 1:1–2, the pluriform modes

---

27. Henri de Lubac, "Spiritual Understanding," in *The Theological Interpretation of Scripture: Classic and Contemporary Readings*, ed. Stephen E. Fowl (Cambridge: Blackwell, 1997), 7.

of divine disclosure in the Old Testament are all gathered, fulfilled, and surpassed in the coming of the one who antedates creation itself, yet whose personal identity as the all-inheriting Son of the Father has only been unveiled eschatologically: "Long ago, at many times and in many ways, God spoke to our fathers by the prophets, but in these last days he has spoken to us by his Son, whom he appointed the heir of all things, through whom also he created the world."

All the major authors of the New Testament advance similar claims to the finality of what they have seen in Christ, and that eschatological definitiveness is what makes the Trinitarian interpretive moves not just possible, but urgent and necessary. There are no other hinges in the canon to compare with the one between the covenants; there are no further divine persons to identify retrospectively; and there is only one convergence point of the lines of messianic hyperfulfillment. Ernst Käsemann famously asserted that "apocalyptic is the mother of all Christian theology,"[28] and it is true in the case of the exegetical foundations of the doctrine of the Trinity. Eschatology is the mother of all Trinitarian theology.

NO TO CHRISTOPHANIES

We are about to consider the most fruitful sort of navigating of the canonical hinge for the doctrine of the Trinity, which is prosoponic exegesis. It is a Trinitarian rereading practice with much to commend it, and it delivers a great deal of insight. As we shall see, it is founded on the recognition of the unique character of the actual sendings of the Son and the Holy Spirit, which retrospectively illuminate the Old Testament with Trinitarian light. But the uniqueness of the sendings can also have a negative or critical effect on certain rereading practices, and here I want to identify one of the rereading practices that is less promising.

There is an ancient practice of identifying Old Testament theophanies as manifestations of the second person of the Trinity in particular, that is, as the pre-incarnate Son. Pre-Nicene theologians frequently identified a wide variety of divine appearances in the Old Testament, especially anthropomorphic ones, as the Logos of God becoming accustomed to tabernacling among men. Justin Martyr and even Irenaeus glimpsed in these theophanies a foreshadowing of Christ and declared the appearances to be manifestations of the Logos alone, sent as an intermediary by the

28. Ernst Käsemann, *New Testament Questions of Today* (London: SCM, 1969), 102.

Father. In some cases, while the authors were orthodox, they took their positions based on a kind of naive (by which I mean not quite ontological yet in the years before the Arian crisis) subordinationism according to which the Father was too exalted to appear to creatures but the Son was not. By the fourth century, Arian interpreters understandably claimed this line of reasoning as a support for their Christology. Henry Chadwick even claims Augustine had to revise the interpretative approach to all of these Old Testament passages, because the history of their exegesis had become so closely entangled with the history of subordinationism.[29]

Augustine countered the Arian interpretation by emphasizing that the Son is no less invisible than the Father, and therefore either of them could well have been appearing to the patriarchs. On the other hand, there is no reason it could not also have been "the Father, or the Son, or the Holy Spirit," or "sometimes the Father, sometimes the Son, sometimes the Holy Spirit," or "simply the one and only God, that is the Trinity without any distinction of persons."[30] In part, Augustine is simply appealing to the lack of definiteness on this subject in the Old Testament revelation. Even as a rereader who knows the Trinitarian end of the story and can retrospectively identify persons based on their subsequent clear manifestation, Augustine's judgment is that we do not have clear enough warrant to say what is actually happening in these most mysterious events of the Old Testament. But his more substantive reason for rejecting the idea that these are appearances of the Son (not the Father or the Spirit) has to do with the uniqueness of the visible mission of the Son in the incarnation. If the Father sent the Son repeatedly during the old covenant, it derogates in some way from the uniqueness of the incarnational sending. The question is not so much where the Old Testament Jesus got the body he appeared to the patriarchs in (though that surely calls for some speculation). It is more a matter of the unrepeatable uniqueness of the incarnation of the Son. With Augustine, we might admit that the Son, based on his inner-Trinitarian status as the one who is eternally from the Father and expresses the Father, might be the appropriate messenger of God even in the old covenant. But even

---

29. Henry Chadwick, "The Beginning of Christian Philosophy," in *The Cambridge History of Later Greek and Early Medieval Philosophy*, ed. A. H. Armstrong (Cambridge: Cambridge University Press, 1967), 163. For a detailed analysis of the continuity and discontinuity in this tradition, see Kari Kloos, *Christ, Creation, and the Vision of God: Augustine's Transformation of Early Christian Theophany Interpretation* (Leiden: Brill, 2011).

30. Augustine, *Trinity* 2.3.13, 106.

that admission would only dictate that the special anthropomorphic theophanies of the Old Testament must mean, but not be, the Son. That is, as we saw with the dove and the voice at Christ's baptism, a created manifestation signifying the divine presence is the work of the entire Trinity together rather than one particular person. But it may signify the presence of one particular person of the Trinity. This would be a long way to go for Augustine's kind of analysis. It would place the Son in the old covenant under the form of an economy of signs and intentions,[31] but not in a personal mission parallel to the incarnation.

In modern times these Old Testament manifestations have come to be called christophanies.[32] At the popular level, many conservative Christians have so high a regard for them and such certainty about the identification of the pre-incarnate Christ as the subject of them that they seem to serve as an indicator of a high Christology and a robust Trinitarianism. The underlying idea seems to be that if God is the Trinity now, he must have always have been the Trinity, and therefore his human manifestation must always have been the Son. Even in academic theology, Colin Gunton has accused Augustine of anti-incarnational bias for denying that the Son would encounter the patriarchs in this way.[33] But it seems wise to maintain the uniqueness of the personal visible missions of the Son and the Holy Spirit in the incarnation and Pentecost. This is not to deny that God is active in the Old Testament or in creation at large—in fact, that the Trinity, the entire Trinity, is active and present in appropriate ways. But it is to reject the notion that before or apart from the incarnation, the second person of the Trinity was the subject of visible mission.

RETROSPECTIVE PROSOPONIC IDENTIFICATION

Taking our stand on the ground of the New Testament, looking back through its witness to the events of the incarnation and Pentecost, we are able to ask relevant questions of the Old Testament witness. Having

---

31. This interpretation fits well with the framing provided by Michael Cameron, *Christ Meets Me Everywhere: Augustine's Early Figural Exegesis* (Oxford: Oxford University Press, 2012).

32. Andrew Malone, *Knowing Jesus in the Old Testament? A Fresh Look at Christophanies* (Nottingham: Inter-Varsity Press, 2015), has traced the usage to James A. Borland, *Christ in the Old Testament: Old Testament Appearances of Christ in Human Form* (Chicago: Moody, 1978).

33. It is an ironic charge. See Keith E. Johnson, *Rethinking the Trinity and Religious Pluralism: An Augustinian Assessment* (Downers Grove, IL: IVP Academic, 2011), 112–13.

met Christ and the Spirit, we can look for them in the Old Testament in a way we could not have without having met them in person. This practice is retrospective prosoponic identification. It names a strategy for reading the Old Testament initiated in the New Testament and carried forward by the postapostolic church. Patristics scholar Michael Slusser has described it in similar terms as prosopographic exegesis, a "practice of discerning the speakers or *prosōpa* in reading Scripture."[34] The right question in various complex Old Testament passages is, in general, "Who is talking?" Slusser says that for the church fathers, this inquiry after *prosōpa* was not only "a tool for literary analysis and historical identification, but also and especially one of spiritual perception and theological elaboration." One reason this is important is that this practice is the source of basic Trinitarian vocabulary like the word *person*. It was "the source of the use of the word *persona/prosōpon* in Christian theology."[35]

Prosoponic exegesis is a pervasive feature of the New Testament's use of the Old and is especially pronounced in what we would call Trinitarian contexts. The most striking instance of the prosoponic question being applied as a reading strategy in the New Testament itself is the Ethiopian eunuch asking about Isaiah 53: "About whom, I ask you, does the prophet say this, about himself or about someone else?" (Acts 8:34).

The most advanced, blatant, and densest examples are in Hebrews. But it occurs at every stratum of the New Testament text. Consider, for example, the opening of Mark. Mark opens with "The beginning of the gospel," as written in Isaiah. Not with a genealogy going back to Abraham (as Matthew), not with an author's preface, the conception of John the Baptist, or a genealogy going back to Adam (as Luke), and not with high-flown theological dicta about what happened "in the beginning" (as John). Mark's thirteenth word is a quoted prophetic word. His good news is good news "as written in Isaiah the prophet." That prophetic voice speaks a complex word: it actually seems to be put together from Exodus 23:20; Malachi 3:1; and Isaiah 40:3. Perhaps

---

34. Michael Slusser, "The Exegetical Roots of Trinitarian Theology," *Theological Studies* 49 (1988): 462.

35. Ibid., 463. Stephen O. Presley points out that Slusser's contribution here is that "he calls attention to the dominance of analytical analysis in Trinitarian discussions and reminds us that the very terms of the debates (*prosōpon, hypostasis, ousia,* and *physis*) are derived from the exegesis of Scripture. Thus there is a genetic exegetical discussion underlying the analytical one and the analytical Trinitarian debates should recognize their inherited exegesis" ("Irenaeus and the Exegetical Roots of Trinitarian Theology," in *Irenaeus: Life, Scripture, Legacy,* ed. Paul Foster and Sara Parvis [Minneapolis: Fortress, 2012], 165).

the kernel is Isaiah 40 (thus Mark attributes the whole saying to Isaiah), but the development of this kernel plays on "the way" of the Lord. And to prepare that way, God "apostles his angel" (to cognatize the Greek) before the face of whom?

"I send my messenger before your face." God is speaking, and he sends a messenger to prepare a way for the Lord. What we are hearing at the thirteenth word of Mark is the voice of God the Father speaking to God the Son. In Isaiah, by the inspiration of the Spirit, the Father is telling the Son that he is making a way for him and straightening his path. And when the Son comes into the world, he says to the Father, "A body didst thou prepare for me . . . Lo, I am come (in the roll of the book it is written of me) to do thy will, O God" (as Hebrews 10:5, 7 [ASV] renders Psalm 40:6–8). "The beginning of the gospel of Jesus," for Mark, is the Father describing the economy of salvation to the Son in the prophetic Spirit. Putting it this way may be too explicitly Trinitarian, for characteristically Mark leaves much unsaid. Can we really treat an Old Testament citation as inner-Trinitarian discourse, the Father addressing the Son while we overhear their speaking? Yes, for three reasons.

1. It is written . . . "Behold, I send . . . before your face." God speaks to the Lord. It is simply a matter of tidying up our referents to clarify who "God" is and who "the Lord" is, using Mark's own ideas. "God" is the one who sends Jesus (that is, the Father), and "the Lord" is the one whose coming is prepared by the message of John the Baptist (that is, the Son).

2. Elsewhere in Mark (12:34–37), Jesus interprets an Old Testament passage as conversation between YHWH and the Messiah: he takes Psalm 110 to be David saying that YHWH told David's master, the Messiah, to sit at YHWH's right hand. Other New Testament authors presuppose that certain passages of the Old Testament are to be read as inner-Trinitarian discourse. Hebrews 10 is the boldest, but "prosopological exegesis" is an important mode of interpretation throughout the New Testament, pioneered by Jesus, who provoked the Pharisees with the question about Psalm 110 ("The LORD says to my Lord . . .").

3. Within a few verses, the Father speaks to the Son directly: "You are my beloved Son; with you I am well pleased" (Mark 1:11). Though this time it is a voice from heaven, it is again the words

of the Old Testament.[36] And the Spirit is near at hand when this inner-Trinitarian dialogue is spoken aloud for us to overhear (note: not the third-person "this is my beloved Son," as in Matthew, but the second-person "you are my beloved Son," in agreement with Luke and in line with the second-person address of the Isaiah quotation of verse 2).

We should not lose sight of the retrospective aspect of this reading strategy: only because of the advent of Christ and the Spirit can we seek to go back and identify them. If we immerse ourselves in the Old Testament world itself, without reference to our place in progressive revelation, we would not draw securely Trinitarian conclusions. For instance, the Old Testament is gloriously replete with an array of poetic personifications of God's presence and power. God characteristically uses evocative circumlocutions to describe the way he is personally present and active among his people: Moses asks God for a promise to accompany him, and God responds that he will send his angel, in whom he will put his name. God is present by presence; "the Presence" becomes a way of referring to God. His hand, voice, will, wisdom, glory, arm, breath, law, and so on, are all put forth as his way of being God with us. And sometimes these terms are strikingly personified or hypostasized. To take the Trinitarian step of selecting two of them as actual persons, distinct subsistences eternally abiding within the one divine nature, seems arbitrary and capricious. If we are to promote any of these "figures of speech" to full personhood, why not all of them, leading to a dozen persons in the Godhead?

The answer can only be that we are to approach the Old Testament from this side, asking not "Which of these personifications is somebody?" but "Can Christ and the Spirit, whom we have met at the turning of the ages, be picked out retrospectively from among the many rays of God's old-covenant glory?" And in asking this, we are trying to interpret not simply the events of God's self-revelation, but also the text of his self-revelation. For we are told clearly enough that it is the Word who became flesh. We may also affirm that the wisdom became flesh, or that the arm of the Lord was revealed in Christ, but in each case we are only underlining the same retrospective prosoponic identification.

---

36. See Psalm 2:7; Isaiah 42:1.

The principle obviously needs to be extended to the third person of the Trinity, the Holy Spirit. This pneumatological extension is not simply parallel to the work done with the Son of God, because the Spirit is a different person from the Son, and his difference is registered on both sides of the canonical hinge. In the Old Testament, the range of possible allusions to him, and the relevant semantic domains, are considerably more extensive and indefinite than is the case with the Son. And in the New Testament, the Spirit continues to be revealed in more oblique ways, always with reference to the more direct manifestation of the Son. Nevertheless, the exegetical materials are sufficient for carrying out the pneumatological extension of the process of retrospective prosoponic identification. When this is done at a sufficient level of detail and correlated systematically with the christological investigations, Trinitarian interpretation reaches a kind of conceptual stabilization. Father, Son, and Holy Spirit are discernible in their structured, revelatory, economic relations to each other. This pattern of relation can then be recognized as a free self-communication of God in salvation history.

Prosoponic exegesis has been almost the exclusive property of patristics scholars for decades, and we will see below just how sophisticated their analysis of it has become. No doubt it was prominent for patristics studies because it is an almost unavoidable phenomenon in the writings of the church fathers. But the church fathers did not invent it; they took it from Scripture. They were tutored by the New Testament's use of the Old, which frequently indulges in prosoponic construals. Of course, the New Testament also makes use of a host of other interpretive strategies, most of which are also appropriated and extended by the early church. Irenaeus scholar Stephen Presley points out "literary readings, typological readings, prophecy and fulfillment, verbal connections, organizational functions, illustrative applications, narratival or creedal, prosopological interpretations, and general-to-particular connections" as the tool kit available in the early centuries of Christian theology.[37] But prosoponic exegesis has been overlooked for a long time and is set to make a comeback. In recent years, the good news of prosoponic exegesis is finally making its way across the disciplinary boundary from patristics to biblical studies. The major studies in this field are both by Matthew Bates. He laid the foundation in *The Hermeneutics of Apostolic Proclamation:*

---

37. Stephen O. Presley, *The Intertextual Reception of Genesis 1–3 in Irenaeus of Lyons* (Leiden: Brill, 2015), 4.

The Center of Paul's Method of Scriptural Interpretation[38] and then carried out an ambitious program in *The Birth of the Trinity: Jesus, God, and Spirit in New Testament and Early Christian Interpretation of the Old Testament*.[39] In the former book, Bates restricted his analysis to Paul, explored the classical and Hellenistic background of the interpretive practice, and worked very hard to abide by the rules of historical-grammatical interpretation. This caution will no doubt commend prosoponic interpretation to New Testament scholars; there is much work to be done using these tools. The latter book is more adventuresome, offering "a window into the inner life of God as discerned via person-centered reading of the Old Testament."[40] Bates ranges through the entire New Testament and organizes his material around the life of Christ, including his preexistence and extending to his enthronement at the right hand of God—a topic that cannot be bypassed in prosoponic exegesis because of its foundation in Psalm 110:1, the Old Testament passage most frequently cited by New Testament authors. Bates has also devised a set of categories for working out the complex relations of implied speakers and their temporal locations, which can be quite complex when prophecy and retrospection are taken into account. It is remarkable that prosoponic exegesis, a New Testament phenomenon, had to make its way into biblical studies by way of a long sojourn in patristics.

PROSOPONIC EXEGESIS OF THE PSALMS

The most sophisticated study of prosoponic exegesis to date remains the work of Marie-Josèphe Rondeau,[41] whose two-volume investigation of its use in patristic Psalms commentaries has far-reaching implications. Rondeau's focus on the Psalms gives her a privileged position in several respects: In all of the Old Testament, the Psalms feature the richest mixture of different modes of speech, juxtaposing divine and human, oracular and confessional, with and without discourse markers to signal the changes in speaker. Probably as a result of this, Psalms texts are used with special frequency in the New Testament, sometimes in the

---

38. Matthew Bates, *The Hermeneutics of Apostolic Proclamation: The Center of Paul's Method of Scriptural Interpretation* (Waco, TX: Baylor University Press, 2012).

39. Matthew Bates, *The Birth of the Trinity: Jesus, God, and Spirit in New Testament and Early Christian Interpretation of the Old Testament* (Oxford: Oxford University Press, 2015).

40. Ibid., 7.

41. Marie-Josèphe Rondeau, *Exégèse prosopologique et théologie*, vol. 2 of *Les Commentateurs patristiques du Psautier (IIIe-Ve siècles)* (Rome: Oriental Institute, 1985).

mode of prosoponic exegesis. And for both reasons, the church fathers were especially attracted to the Psalms as the locus of retrospective discernment of the persons of the Trinity.

Rondeau makes the work of Hilary of Poitiers the touchstone of her study. This fourth-century Latin pro-Nicene theologian wrote the great treatise *On the Trinity*, which made abundant use of prosoponic exegesis, but he also wrote a commentary on the Psalms whose opening words are the classic patristic manifesto on prosoponic exegesis:

> The primary condition of knowledge for reading the Psalms is the ability to see as whose mouthpiece we are to regard the psalmist as speaking, and who it is that he addresses. For they are not all of the same uniform character, but of different authorship and different types. For we constantly find that the Person of God the Father is being set before us . . . while in what we might call the majority of Psalms the Person of the Son is introduced . . . [Elsewhere, however], we are to recognize the person of the Prophet by whose lips the Holy Spirit speaks, raising us by the instrumentality of his lips to the knowledge of a spiritual mystery.[42]

Rondeau recognizes in this opening statement something with "the value of an epistemological manifesto" because of the way it insists, "in principle, on the necessity of prosopological method for understanding the Psalter."[43] As "the work of an exegete conscious of his methods," Hilary's introduction "is a piece unique among all the patristic Psalms commentaries that have reached us."[44] It is his hermeneutical self-awareness that makes Hilary's introduction stand out: "Not only does he use the method with remarkable heuristic efficacy, but he takes the opportunity to explain and justify the operation in a way that proves he has a clear awareness of the mechanisms brought into play."[45] And yet, as Rondeau documents in the main body of her book, Hilary is not the inventor of any element of prosoponic exegesis. It is widespread among other pro-Nicene theologians, who picked it up from Irenaeus, Origen, and Tertullian, and has its ultimate foundations in the New Testament's use of the Old.

---

42. St. Hilary of Poitiers, "Homilies on the Psalms: Psalm 1," in vol. 9 of NPNF, 2nd ser., ed. Philip Schaff and Henry Wace (New York: Scribner's Sons, 1899), 236.

43. Rondeau, *Exégèse prosopologique et théologie*, 37.

44. Ibid., 38.

45. Ibid., 74.

It is a truth universally acknowledged that the Psalms are a microcosm of the whole Bible, and a rich storehouse for allegorical and typological readings. But patristic commentaries on the Psalms uniquely elevate prosoponic exegesis to the status of equal player with these other modes of interpretation.[46] Rondeau claims that her study is a contribution that can "bring balance to our view of ancient exegesis,"[47] but in fact her work is more revolutionary than that. Prosoponic exegesis opens up a third avenue of access to Bible interpretation. Typological interpretation, "which makes use of the pair 'promise and fulfillment,' or typological recurrence of the saving acts of God, is based on history, which is surely a fundamental category of Christianity."[48] Building on this, allegorical interpretation is more a purely literary technique, collating textual correspondences for doctrinal or moral ends. But "prosopology . . . is based on the concept of person. This is a category as constitutive for Christianity as is history. Patristic commentaries on the Psalter thus reveal that ancient exegesis has, besides a historical dimension, also an equally legitimate dimension that is 'personalist.'"[49]

The fact that ancient interpreters had at their disposal a method of discerning persons, including divine persons, explains a great deal about the doctrinal presuppositions and results of their interpretive work. The lack of such a method explains much about modern cultures of interpretation. Modern interpreters do, of course, identify speakers, but always within the horizon of historical reconstruction: "who laments; what is the author's intention; is this a first-person articulation of the community's experience; is it a collective 'I,' etc."[50] Prosopology, as Rondeau argues, "identifies the persons who speak according to the

---

46. The only other book with such prosoponic intensity is the Song of Solomon, "the most read and most frequently commented [on] in the medieval cloister" (Jean Leclercq, *The Love of Learning and the Desire for God: A Study of Monastic Culture* [New York: Fordham University Press], 84). Leclercq explores the way monastic Canticles commentaries were meditative and affective; in short, personal, allowing the reader to discern the voice of the beloved speaking directly. One literary feature the Song of Solomon shares with many psalms is the technique of shifting among speakers, with or without discourse markers, calling for similar reading techniques. Rondeau reports Origen's prosoponic approach to the Song of Solomon, of which he says, "This little book, this epithalamium, is a nuptial poem, like a drama" (Rondeau, *Exégèse prosopologique et théologie*, 44).

47. Rondeau, *Exégèse prosopologique et théologie*, 9.

48. Ibid.

49. Ibid. She goes on to describe the purpose of her book: "Besides the study of an unknown exegetical method and its theological fertility, our investigation in patristic commentaries on the Psalter pursues a third track: the word and the concept of person." "Christian revelation deepens and specifies this concept" (11).

50. Ibid., 9.

discourse they hold and thus uncovers a whole set of distinctions and relationships," which she lists:

- between the author and the speaker
- between interlocutors
- between the speaker and the aspect of himself which speaks the word
- between the speaker and the community in whose name he speaks[51]

Such relations are in one way more modest than historical questions, but in another way more expansive. They simply are not pursuing historical answers, but rather are seeking the discernment of persons related by discourse. In its broadest scope, prosoponic exegesis of the Psalms was preoccupied with discerning in any particular psalm "whether David, held in general for the author of the whole collection, speaks on his own behalf or on behalf of another and, in the latter case, on behalf of whom."[52] The person of David thus loomed large over the entire collection and made himself felt in each psalm. How the church fathers got from David to Christ is too familiar a topic to need rehearsing: they read in light of New Testament fulfillment and of Christian doctrine. "Thus prosopology in their hands, is not only an instrument of literary analysis and historical identification, but also and especially an instrument of spiritual perception and theological elaboration."[53]

Among the church fathers, nobody more fully integrated prosoponic exegesis into the doctrine of the Trinity than Hilary of Poitiers. In fact, it is hard to know whether his prosoponic reading strategy with the Psalms gave his treatise on the Trinity its distinctive form, or whether his convictions about the revelation of the Trinity gave him insight into the right way of approaching the Psalms. Whichever direction the current of influence flows, it is Hilary who announced programmatically in his *On the Trinity* that "since we are to discourse of the things of God, let us assume that God has full knowledge of Himself, and bow with humble reverence to His words. For He Whom we can only know through His own utterances is the fitting witness concerning Himself."[54] And

---

51. Ibid.
52. Ibid.
53. Ibid.
54. Hilary of Poitiers, *On the Trinity* 1:18.

that triune self-testimony inevitably took the form of testimony by one divine person about another. In proving the divine sonship of Christ, he announced that it is a doctrine which "we prove by the witness of the Father, by Christ's own assertion," and only then "by the preaching of Apostles, by the faith of believers."[55] Throughout his development of the doctrine of the Trinity, Hilary took frequent recourse to prosoponic exegesis, but the ultimate reason for his doing so was his fundamental commitment to the interpersonal character of the testimony of the persons to each other: "Since no one knoweth the Father save the Son, let our thoughts of the Father be at one with the thoughts of the Son, the only faithful Witness, Who reveals Him to us."[56]

Although her focus is on the church fathers, Rondeau does not miss the fact that "the New Testament puts into the mouth of Christ, explicitly or indirectly, a number of psalm verses."[57] We do not normally think of the church fathers as lacking confidence in their exegetical hypotheses, or as casting about for reassurances that their applications are warranted. But Rondeau notes that they seemed to draw special inspiration from the fact that Jesus prayed the Psalms, and New Testament authors put psalms on his lips at several crucial points: "In light of these indications, the exegete, extrapolating from the isolated verse to the entire poem, imputes to Christ the entire Psalm in question."[58]

REREADING THE PSALMS AS TRINITARIAN PRAISE

The Psalms are indeed a sacred province not only for prosoponic exegesis but for all manner of Trinitarian interpretation. All the necessary components are abundantly present there and are poetically stated in a way that enables them to transcend their original setting. We have already seen how some exegetes in the second and fourth centuries made use of the Psalms as a bearer of Trinitarian theology. An especially artful variation on this usage occurs in the medieval period. As we mentioned in chapter 1, the Carolingian theologian Gerhohus the Great (1093–1169)[59] concluded his commentary on each of the psalms

---

55. Ibid., 1:25.
56. Ibid., 2:6.
57. Rondeau, *Exégèse prosopologique et théologie*, 9.
58. Ibid., 9–10.
59. Also rendered Gerhohus Magnus and Gerhoch of Reichersberg.

with a customized Trinitarian *Gloria Patri* keyed to the vocabulary and themes of each psalm.[60] It is a very sophisticated maneuver. Gerhoch is not finding the Trinity revealed in each psalm, but is making use of the psalm's discrete witness, its distinctive way of speaking, in a canonical celebration of the full counsel of the Bible. Here are examples from five well-known psalms:

1. Psalm 1: Wherefore: Glory be to the Father, Who knoweth the Way of the righteous; glory be to the Son, Who is the Way of the righteous, the Man Who is blessed, and prosperous in whatsoever He doeth; glory be to the Holy Ghost, Who is the Wind that scattereth the ungodly. As it was in the beginning, is now, and ever shall be: world without end. Amen.
2. Psalm 8: ("What is man, that thou art mindful of him?") Wherefore Glory be to the Father, Who hath put all things under the feet of the Son of Man; glory be to the Son, Who, though Son of God, vouchsafed to become Son of Man, and to be made lower than the Angels, and now is crowned with glory and honour as Priest and King; glory be to the Holy Ghost, the Finger of God, by Whom the heavens were made. As it was in the beginning, is now, and ever shall be: world without end. Amen.
3. Psalm 15 ("Who shall abide in thy holy hill?") Wherefore Glory be to the Father, Whose is the holy hill; and to the Son, Who shall abide in it for ever; and to the Holy Ghost, by Whom only we are to reach it. As it was in the beginning, is now, and ever shall be: world without end. Amen.
4. Psalm 19 ("The heavens declare the glory of God") Wherefore Glory be to the Father, from Whom was the going forth of the Sun; and to the Son, Who cometh forth as a Bridegroom out of His chamber; and to the Holy Ghost, the spiritual heat, from which not anything is hid. As it was in the beginning, is now, and ever shall be: world without end. Amen.
5. Psalm 23: And therefore: Glory be to the Father, Who anoints our head with oil; and to the Son, the Shepherd of His people; and to the Holy Ghost, Who provides for us that inebriating

---

60. These can be gathered from J. M. Neale and R. F Littledale, *A Commentary on the Psalms: from Primitive and Mediaeval Writers* (London: Masters, 1869).

chalice which is so excellent. As it was in the beginning, is now, and ever shall be: world without end. Amen.[61]

Gerhoch's Trinitarian psalm doxologies are models of Trinitarian interpretation of the Old Testament. They are rereadings in light of the later developments of the story of salvation told in the canon. They negotiate the canonical hinge expertly, letting the Old Testament maintain its discrete witness rather than ignoring the unrevealedness of the Trinity under the old covenant. The rich vocabulary of the psalms infuses and enriches the Trinitarian theology in such a way that the Old Testament actually influences Trinitarian theology. While they include many fanciful leaps of association, they are fundamentally grounded in Jesus' own appropriation of the Psalms as his personal voice. They point forward to the events of the incarnation and Pentecost, permitting us to distinguish adumbration from revelation. They are uniquely creative, yet grounded in a widespread tradition of Christian use of the psalms; Isaac Watts did robustly christological versions of the psalms in rhyming and metrical English.[62] They set us into the biblical movement of Trinitarian praise, with its vast stretch of reflection on the deep realities antecedent to our salvation: As it was in the beginning, is now, and ever shall be.

---

61. J. M. Neale and R. F. Littledale, *Psalm 1–38*, vol. 1 of *Commentary on the Psalms* (London: Masters, 1869), 95–96, 146–47, 197, 263, 315–16.

62. See Samuel Worcester, *The Psalms, Hymns, and Spiritual Songs of the Rev. Isaac Watts*, new ed. (Boston: Crocker & Brewster, 1859). Watts's psalms can be quite heavy-handed in making David into a Christian, but they are not as daringly Trinitarian as one might hope. Watts entertained some doubts about the clarity of Trinitarian revelation; this hurt his poetry, as well as his ministry.

CHAPTER 9

THESES ON THE REVELATION OF THE TRINITY

1. The revelation of the Trinity is bundled with the revelation of the gospel. God published both at the same time, in the same ways: more obscurely and by way of anticipation under the old covenant, more luminously and by way of fulfillment under the new. The answer to the question, "Was the Trinity made known in the Old Testament?" runs parallel to the question of whether the gospel was. In both cases, Trinity and gospel, we must account for two factors: (1) the consistency of God's entire work of salvation, and (2) the newness in "the revelation of the mystery that was kept secret for long ages" (Rom 16:25), "which was not made known to the sons of men in other generations as it has now been revealed . . ." (Eph 3:5). *Epangel* is not *evangel*, but they are both constitutive of God's one message of salvation.

2. The revelation of the Trinity accompanies salvation. Though it can be stated propositionally and in the form of information, it was not given primarily as information. Rather, this knowledge came along with the carrying out of God's work of salvation. God saves, and further, wants the saved to "understand the things freely given us by God" (1 Cor 2:12). God did not hand down statements regarding the Trinity, but extended his arm to save, an action that by design brought with it knowledge of, and about, the one doing the saving. As B. B. Warfield wrote, "The revelation of the Trinity was incidental to, and the inevitable effect of, the accomplishment of redemption."[1]

3. The revelation of the Trinity is revelation of God's own heart. Theology, broadly considered, is knowledge of God and of all things in God; "all things" are accounted for by a great many doctrines. But the doctrine of the Trinity is theology proper, knowledge of God *in se*. Thus its focus is not on those aspects of the divine nature that are knowable by the things created or of God in relation to things outside of him; those things are spoken of in Scripture substance-wise, according to God's one nature. But the doctrine of the Trinity is a statement about God's interior life, requiring statements relation-wise, internal to the divine being, describing the Father and the Son and the Spirit as they stand toward each other. Prepositions will be decisive here: "That true and absolute and perfect doctrine, which forms our faith, is the confession of God from God and God in God."[2]

4. The revelation of the Trinity must be self-revelation. This knowledge cannot be delegated or delivered by proxy. Hilary of Poitiers again: "Since then we are to discourse of the things of God, let us assume that God has full knowledge of Himself, and bow with humble reverence to His words. For He Whom we can only know through His own utterances is the fitting witness concerning Himself."[3]

5. The revelation of the Trinity came when the Son and the Spirit came in person. "But when the fullness of time had come, God sent forth his Son . . . And because you are sons, God has sent the Spirit of his Son into our hearts, crying 'Abba! Father!'" (Gal 4:4, 6). God did not openly proclaim the existence of his Son and Holy Spirit and then send them; but he sent them. God did not announce the Trinity; rather, the Son of the Father showed up, with their Spirit. "The revelation itself was made not in word but in deed. It was made in the incarnation of God the Son, and the outpouring of God the Holy Spirit."[4]

6. New Testament texts about the Trinity tend to be allusions rather than announcements. The evangelists and apostles write from a background assumption that readers know God the Father because they have met the Son and Holy Spirit. They refer almost offhandedly

---

1. B. B. Warfield, "The Biblical Doctrine of the Trinity," in *Biblical and Theological Studies* (Philadelphia: Presbyterian and Reformed, 1952), 33.
2. Hilary of Poitiers, *On the Trinity* 5:37.
3. Ibid., 1:18.
4. Warfield, "Biblical Doctrine of the Trinity," 33.

to this understanding as something already given, not something to be introduced, put in place, or argued for. There is an obliqueness in nearly every sentence on this doctrine in the New Testament.

7. The revelation of the Trinity required words to accompany it. Since the revelation was made by personal presence rather than by mere verbal announcement, interpreting it is in some ways more like interpreting God's self-revelation through his mighty acts of deliverance than it is like interpreting God's self-revelation through spoken oracles. But not exactly like it, because this particular mighty act of God was the mighty act of sending persons who speak. The Son and the Holy Spirit came preaching and testifying to the truth and reality of their own twofold mission from the Father. Without these words, their personal presences would not have been the eloquent and luminous truth of the knowledge of God. In particular, if the risen Lord had not said, "Baptize in the name of the Father, the Son, and the Holy Spirit," the early church would never have had the confidence to count to three in the doctrine of God. Biblical revelation is always through acts and words having an inner unity (*Dei verbum*), or fact plus meaning (J. G. Machen);[5] in the revelation of the Son, the inner unity of his acts and words is his person.

8. The revelation of the Trinity is the extending of a conversation already happening. When the Father says to the Son, "You are my beloved Son; with you I am well pleased" (Mark 1:11), there is conversation in God. When the Father says to us, "This is my beloved Son, with whom I am well pleased," he adds, "Listen to him" (Matthew 17:5). When we obey and listen to the Son, we find he tells us about his Father. Unlike other doctrines, a leading skill in learning about the Trinity is the skill of overhearing as the Father and Son talk to and about each other in the Spirit. This is especially clear in the New Testament, but if the New Testament is to be believed, it is also characteristic of the Old Testament, where Father and Son were speaking to and about each other in words given by the Spirit to the prophets.

9. The revelation of the Trinity occurs across the two Testaments of the canon. While the New Testament has a strategic priority as the latest moment in the process of progressive revelation, it actually takes both Testaments together to produce the right expectations and interpretive pressure that lead to recognition of the Trinity.

---

5. J. G. Machen, *Christianity and Liberalism*, new ed. (1923; repr. Grand Rapids: Eerdmans, 2009), 25.

In particular, the canonical order is to be observed in the way God's unity is explicated as internally threefold: the Bible is the story of how the one God reveals that divine unity eternally has the form of the unity of Father, Son, and Holy Spirit. Among other things, this is the justification for placing the dogmatic treatise "On the One God" before the full explication of "On the Trinity" (though it will be impossible for Christian exposition to exclude the persons of the Trinity from the treatise "On the One God" completely).

10. The revelation of the Trinity in Scripture is perfect. It's easy to think that the task of theology is to make something useful out of the mess of materials that God gave us in Scripture, or at least to put in logical order what was communicated in historical sequence. Theology can think of itself as synthesizing doctrine from raw materials, so in Trinitarian theology we can get turned around by asking, "Is the Trinity in the Bible?" and meaning, "Can the later synthesis be identified as a legitimate construction from the raw materials given in the Bible?" Something is backward in such a question. In this doctrine especially, it is better to suppose that Scripture speaks from an achieved synthesis and gives partial expression, here and there, to glimpses of that fullness and coherence. To be specific, what we have in Scripture is rightly ordered, with the emphases falling in the right places. One application of this principle is that when a passage of Scripture names the Father and the Son, but then fails to complete the triangle, we should neither pronounce it binitarian nor cram the Holy Spirit into it. In Trinitarian theology, the Holy Spirit in particular has suffered as much from his overzealous promoters as his underzealous neglecters. He is fully God and a distinct person. But triangular symmetry is manifestly not a concern, or emphasis, or prominent motif, of Scripture, and we should not belabor it in every subpoint of our doctrine.

11. Systematic theology's account of the Trinity should serve the revelation of the Trinity in Scripture. Christian theology should be a humble discipline, pointing from itself back to Scripture as much as possible. It may need to invent new terms, make careful distinctions, and construct conceptual schemas to make sense of the evidence; I'm neither justifying theological laziness nor criticizing scholastic predecessors (who tended to obey this rule more than moderns have). But a systematic rendering of the Trinity should be careful not to rocket out of the orbit of the biblical content it is designed to explain. It ought to eventually lead back to good reading of the text. Scott Swain argues that "doctrinal propositions apart from the exegetical arguments that they summarize are at best ambiguous,"[6] and this is especially true in Trinitarian theology, where the dynamics of the arguments can be so conceptually seductive as to alienate theological affections from Holy Scripture. Because of what the inspired text is—the words of the Father and the Son speaking in the Spirit—readers may actually come into contact with the triune God in them. The systematic theology of the Trinity ought to help open that possibility, not occlude it.

---

6. Scott R. Swain, *The God of the Gospel: Robert Jenson's Trinitarian Theology* (Downers Grove, IL: IVP Academic, 2013), 121.

SUBJECT INDEX

SCRIPTURE INDEX

AUTHOR INDEX

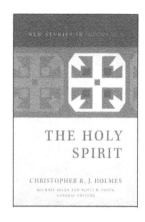